Contents

List of figures

List of tables

List of contributors

Fabrizio Balassone, Bank of Italy, Rome, Italy

Peter Bernholz, Centre of Economics and Business (WWZ), University of Basel, Switzerland

Charles B. Blankart, Humboldt University, Berlin, Germany

Geoffrey Brennan, RSSS, Australian National University, Canberra, Australia

Giuseppe Eusepi, University of Rome 'La Sapienza', Italy

Daniele Franco, Bank of Italy, Rome, Italy

Sergio Ginebri, University of Molise, Campobasso, Italy

Bernard Grofman, University of California, Irvine, USA

Barbara Krug, Erasmus University of Rotterdam, The Netherlands

Luciano Marcello Milone, University of Rome 'La Sapienza', Italy

Dennis C. Mueller, University of Vienna, Austria

Marcella Mulino, University of L'Aquila, Italy

Pier Carlo Padoan, International Monetary Fund, Washington, DC, USA

Martin Paldam, Aarhus University, Denmark

Christoph A. Schaltegger, Swiss Federal Tax Administration, Bern, Switzerland

Friedrich Schneider, Johannes Kepler University of Linz, Austria

Rolf Strauch, European Central Bank, Frankfurt a.M., Germany

Gordon Tullock, George Mason University, Arlington, VA, USA

Giuseppe Vitaletti, University of Macerata, Italy

Acknowledgements

This book has its origin in the ECSPC/CIDEI first conference held on 17–19 May 2001, under the auspices of the Italian Economic Association (SIE).

The European Center for the Study of Public Choice (ECSPC), based at the University of Rome 'La Sapienza', is an institution that since its inception in 1999 has been eager to face European constitutional/institutional issues.

The idea of having a publication with selected papers emerged quite naturally out of a conference that brought together academics and officials actively engaged in the institutions around which the conference was organized. It is the breadth of the subjects relevant to the European institutions that is the justification of this volume.

The conference was made possible through funding generously provided to ECSPC by the Italian National Research Council (CNR), the University of Rome 'La Sapienza', the Bank of Italy, CREDIOP, the Province of Rome, the Representation in Italy of the European Commission.

Our thanks are due to Philip Jones, Lars P. Feld and Alan Hamlin for kindly and swiftly serving as outside referees.

A very special note of appreciation is due to Maria Delle Grotti for her conscientious work in every stage of the editing process of this volume.

Dymphna Evans, Publisher at Edward Elgar, efficiently provided us with her editorial advice and support. Matthew Pitman, Editor and Karen McCarthy, Senior Desk Editor, were unfailingly helpful in checking out the manuscript and in tracking down those bits that suffered convoluted prose. We are grateful for this help.

Giuseppe Eusepi
University of Rome 'La Sapienza'
Friedrich Schneider
Johannes Kepler University of Linz

Introduction

Giuseppe Eusepi and Friedrich Schneider

The essays collected in this volume address a host of issues related to the much-studied EU's fiscal and monetary institutions. The works date from 2001, a time when interacting breakthroughs in fiscal and monetary matters were under way that made possible the introduction of the euro in 2002.

What used to be called the EMS (European Monetary System) at the end of the 1970s is reckoned to have begun the process of institutional reforms which was gathering pace by the end of 1980s and which took off in the 1990s with the Maastricht Treaty (1992) and the Amsterdam Treaty (1997), with its Stability and Growth Pact.

Of this institutional productivity the present volume attempts to present a representative selection. And even those who are well informed can benefit from a clear account of aspects and solutions they may have taken for granted. Had the conference concerned itself only with a pure retrospective on fiscal and monetary institutions, the need for a volume might have seemed less pressing. The essays collected in this volume offer instead a perspective on a wide variety of current fiscal and monetary issues. These issues are discussed in nine chapters, each of which is made up of a presentation followed by one comment, in some cases two, except for Chapter 4. The comments are provocative and help readers to unearth subtleties and nuances underlying the various contributions.

The analysis of the *status quo* regarding institutions that have evolved in a two-decade span or more has inevitably led the authors to use an evolutionary approach. Yet, although this approach, a Hayekian evolutionary position as such is not to be found in their analyses. Despite the obvious differences in style and contents of the various contributions, the theme that is voiced throughout the volume is the need for a fiscal constitution. No appeal could be more appropriate now that a constitutional convention is working.

The first part of the volume, 'The underside of EU fiscal institutions: budget, deficit, debt and regulation', is made up of four chapters and deals with various fiscal issues. In the opening chapter, Fabrizio Balassone and Daniele Franco elucidate to what extent EMU's (European Monetary Union's) past achievements have made headway in the field of public finance. To this end, they review the literature on budgetary rules from its very beginning to the years immediately before the Treaty of Maastricht. They consider a host of issues. In particular they deal with the arguments brought forward to justify EMU fiscal rules and identify the newness of the issue faced by the EU as a multinational structure suffering from lack of a federal organization. According to the authors, moral hazard sprang from the highly decentralized setting of fiscal policy in EMU and is responsible for having induced the rejection of both the dual budget approach and the distinction between ordinary and extraordinary finance. Such a scenario was a big push towards the adoption of a detailed multilateral surveillance procedure as well as predetermined limits for the annual deficit with the aim of achieving a balanced budget over the cycle.

In Chapter 2, Peter Bernholz attempts to shed light on the financial situation of the member states of the European Union. The improvement of the deficit and debt situation, maintains the author, has been positively influenced by the conditions of the Maastricht Treaty and the Stability Pact, as well as by the favourable phase of the business cycle. However, this is not a smooth process. Most of the countries that are candidates for membership still perform well below those criteria. And he suggests that in order not to endanger the fiscal situation of the EU, they should be admitted only after fulfilling those requirements. The central budget of the EU, on the other hand, already provides for additional expenses linked to the transition period after membership has been granted. Furthermore, the author addresses the potential impact of the ageing of the population on the fiscal stability of the Union due to the old age pension systems of the member states. He therefore urges more radical reforms.

Giuseppe Eusepi tackles the question of a federal solution for the EU in Chapter 3. Within this framework the author analyses the two contrasting views of tax harmonization and tax competition, which he denotes as the orthodox approach and the constitutional approach respectively. In his view the first approach conceives of government as a maximizer of social welfare, the second as a revenue maximizer. Eusepi takes a theoretical position that exposes how the so-called tax harmonization among EU member states is in reality a cover-up for an EU welfare state, which is almost impossible to cope with at an individual member-state level. He invites readers to question the misleading assumption behind the harmonization procedure seen as a tool to prevent externalities. In his view, even accepting the paradigm of a benevolent omniscient government, with harmonization the EU is cutting its coat according to the cloth of a supranational welfare state. He then argues that a fiscal constitution would, through fiscal competition, shrink government size and would lead to a fiscal equilibrium with consequent economic growth.

A chapter by Geoffrey Brennan concludes the first part. He emphasizes that regulation represents one possible 'policy technology', to be contrasted with budgetary operations in a number of ways. He directs attention to the significance of public revenue constraints on the operation of governments and the way in which regulation might be seen to finesse those revenue constraints. The implications of the 'power to regulate' for public activity in an era of increasing globalization are explored. In particular, he confronts the standard or public economics approach with the public choice approach. On the first front, he notes that regulations do not induce excess burdens between taxed and untaxed activities that are features of budgetary policy. Thus, the superiority of budgetary policy over regulations, which standard public economics assumes, cannot be accepted. From the public choice viewpoint, regulation, at least in some cases, allows the exploitation of less organized and numerous groups, such as consumers and taxpayers. Moreover, regulation may be a way for the government to avoid the various disciplines that the budgetary process imposes. Hence, from the public choice perspective the picture emerging from the regulation/budgetary alternative is more complex and equivocal. Incentives to regulate arise from the escalating difficulties in raising revenues.

Part II, 'Becoming EURO: internal stability and international crises', examines the role that the EMU, based on the euro, can play. This is done from the perspective of both the EU's member states – by analysing the vicissitudes that have urged its construction – and from the wider world perspective characterized by the Asian financial crisis.

Pier Carlo Padoan in Chapter 5 highlights how early critics of EMU pointed to economic and institutional drawbacks of the project. The scenario they depicted was that the euro would not meet the requirements of an optimum currency area and would be plagued by the institutional disequilibrium between a supranational and an unaccountable central bank on the one side and national governments on the other. If proved true, both aspects would inevitably lead to the failure of the EMU project. The author, by using an evolutionary perspective, melds these two issues and argues that the evolution of the economic structure of EMU is pursuing a vigorous policy on many different fronts, working towards an efficient and viable European economic and institutional model.

Drawing upon 'endogenous currency areas', Padoan argues that monetary integration will enhance transformations in the integrating economies, thus making them eligible for the adoption of a single currency. Some evidence is provided by referring to the literature on the optimum currency area such as cyclical convergence, regional convergence, specialization and labour markets. He imparts a firm understanding of the evolution of these aspects under different monetary regimes and degrees of convergence in

Europe. He then seeks to point out, through the concept of policy spillover, that the centralization of monetary policy in Europe leads to changes in other policy areas, such as cooperation between the single monetary policy and national budget policies, budget cooperation in EU-12 and convergence towards a 'stable budget regime'. He foresees further development in convergence in other policy areas, such as tax policy and labour market policy. He also explores the great impact of macroeconomic and structural integration on economic policy regimes in Europe over the past decades and in turn on the endogeneity of the EMU currency area.

The problem of how best to approach the new situation that has arisen after the creation of the EMU and the Asian crisis is the focus of Schneider's Chapter 6. In the new scenario, he speculates on the prospects of a more powerful and effective international monetary organization. To address this new challenge, the new institution will need to be genuinely independent of its major donors so as to be prepared to act efficiently when called to assist countries in financial trouble. A related issue involves the role that this institution should play in controlling monetary policy and in providing instruments to intervene in countries' fiscal policies.

A provoking chapter by Gordon Tullock ends Part II. He addresses the important question of whether the euro is bound to fail or to survive. Tullock inadvertently teaches us to be cautious whenever the task of foreseeing 'future history' is undertaken. However, any forecasting error by a scholar can be more easily justified than any wrong evaluation of past history. It is from past history, the history of the Federal Reserve Bank – on which the ECB (European Central Bank) was modelled – that Tullock draws in trying to find answers to his question. He explores the background of the Federal Reserve Bank, which did very little (though European countries' central banks did even less) to cure the Great Depression and to stop inflation after World Wars I and II.

Moving from this premise, Tullock considers a host of questions. For example, he wonders whether the ECB would possess sufficient power to keep the euro stable if inflationary tensions were to occur due to a full-employment fiscal policy. His answer is in the negative. This is particularly worrisome since such a scenario is likely to loom on the horizon. Even though it is no longer at its height, the resilient Keynesian theory would reinvigorate and find governments' support. Should this happen, 'No amount of monetary discipline can compensate for fiscal folly', as Grofman writes in his comment quoting his colleague A Waffle.

Finally, Part III, 'Two issues at work: voting and contracting', is made up of two chapters that are tightly linked to the preceding parts. Specifically, Blankart and Mueller argue that many, if not most, parliamentary democracies are characterized by a parliament that is elected to represent the opinions of the population and a government that is elected by the parliament to execute a particular political programme. They believe that the combined application of the two procedures is necessarily imperfect and deviates more from voters' preferences than if only one of the procedures is applied. Explicit in the authors' discussion is the assumption linking unaccountable governments, voter alienation, strategic voting and governmental instability to this institutional mix. Blankart and Mueller's solution relies on a structure able to eliminate many of the imperfections through the introduction of two logically consistent models of parliamentary democracy: either a 'pure form of representative democracy' (PRD), where collective opinions are formed in the parliament, or a 'pure two-party form of representative democracy' (TPD), where the government programme is chosen by the voters.

In the concluding chapter, Martin Paldam, by using an Edgeworth box, examines a contract between a small country like Denmark and a large organization like the EU. To this end, he divides the population of the country into two groups: people and élite linked by a contract bearing two explicit parameters: an exchange of sovereignty and a net transfer. The author points out that in a small country the power people would obtain by entering the organization is infinitesimal, while the élite would perceive a net power gain. Despite the methodological difficulties, Paldam is able to draw convincing and provocative conclusions from his model.

It is customary among academics to conclude by underlining that there is still much work to be done. No conclusion would be more appropriate in our case. In fact, the chapters included in this volume do not depict only the fiscal and monetary *status quo*, but look into these issues and speculate on their prospects for the future. In particular, the EU must rethink the need for a fiscal constitution. This point is becoming of crucial importance with the enlargement of the EU and the opening up to other ten countries which will have the right to vote in 2004. The overall effect will be an increasing redistribution resulting in a crisis of the EU budget. This scenario would involve more regulation, as Brennan argues. While the creation of the ECB and the introduction of the euro are unquestionably one of the most successful steps in recent years, the works under way of the European Convention make us think that a fiscal constitution is unlikely to be included in the upcoming European constitution. The consequence will be that probable and perhaps deeper crises could be on the EU's doorstep.

PART I

The underside of EU fiscal institutions: budget, deficit, debt and regulation

1. EMU fiscal rules: new answers to old questions?

Fabrizio Balassone and Daniele Franco*

1. INTRODUCTION

Fiscal sustainability is a central tenet of European Monetary Union (EMU); it is a precondition for financial and monetary stability. Budgetary flexibility is needed for stabilization policy; it has become more important in EMU as member states can no longer rely on a monetary policy tailored to national needs or to exchange rate adjustments. EMU fiscal rules have been designed with the goal of ensuring that national policies keep a sound fiscal stance while allowing sufficient margins for budgetary flexibility in bad times.[1]

The Stability and Growth Pact commits EMU member states to a medium-term objective of a budgetary position close to balance or in surplus. The main rationale for such a target is that its attainment will allow member states to deal with normal cyclical fluctuations while keeping the government deficit within the value of 3 per cent of GDP set in the Treaty of Maastricht.[2] Compliance with this threshold, and with the 60 per cent ceiling for the debt to GDP ratio, will prevent the public finances of EMU member states from taking unsustainable paths.

In this chapter we try to assess to what extent the issue facing the founders of EMU was a new one in the field of public finance and to what extent the solution chosen can be regarded as innovative. To this end, we review the literature on budgetary rules from its very beginning to the years immediately before the Treaty of Maastricht (section 2). The review is largely based on quotations drawn from economists and policy makers. On the basis of this review, in section 3 we argue that the bulk of EMU fiscal regulation does not qualify as innovative; however, the interaction between the multinational nature of EMU and the lack of a federal political authority (a truly innovative feature) shaped the solution chosen. The highly decentralized setting of fiscal policy in EMU gave prominence to moral hazard issues, and EMU fiscal rules, while drawing heavily on ideas that are central to the long-lasting debate on fiscal rules, are innovative in the way in which different approaches are blended and complemented by innovative and pragmatic choices.

2. THE BALANCED BUDGET RULE AND ITS AMENDMENTS

Mankind has always displayed a certain degree of awareness of the potential negative effects of excessive borrowing. Exhortation to sound fiscal behaviour can be found as early as in the Bible: 'And thou shalt lend unto many nations, but thou shalt not borrow' (Deuteronomy 15:6).

Several centuries later, as Hansen (1941, p. 110) reminds us:

> Scholastic theologicians, like Thomas Aquinas, were bitterly opposed to loans . . . Political philosophers of the early modern period continued to regard the prior accumulation of treasures as superior to borrowing . . . [For] Jean Bodin . . . emergencies should be met by accumulated hoards, and only war provided justification for extraordinary levies or loans. Thomas Hobbes was more realistic . . . [allowing] the monarch [to resort] occasionally even to the public credit . . . [but] Adam Smith reverted to the older tradition . . . Hume likewise wrote . . . [that] to mortgage the public revenues . . . [is] a practice that appears ruinous.

Burkhead (1954) notes that there is a common body of doctrine that may be characterized as the classical view of debt and deficits that goes from Smith to Mill. These writers recognized that there are productive uses to which borrowed resources may be put; however, they feared that unproductive use was more likely, and strongly opposed deficit finance when giving policy advice. They noted that interest payments would pose a burden on future taxpayers, but their main concern was the loss of wealth borne when the deficit was incurred in the first place.

Smith opposed the unbalanced budget on the ground that government borrowing would deprive society of resources which could be invested more productively. He also noted that beyond a certain threshold debt inevitably leads to national bankruptcy.

Say (1853, p. 483) argued that the possibility of borrowing allows governments

> to conceive gigantic projects that lead sometimes to disgrace, sometimes to glory, but always to a state of financial exhaustion; to make war themselves and stir up others to do the like; to subsidize every mercenary agent and deal in the blood and the consciences of mankind; making capital which should be the fruit of industry and virtue, the prize of ambition, pride, and wickedness.

Ricardo (in Sraffa, 1952–73, vol. iv, p. 197) refers to debt as 'one of the most terrible scourges which was ever invented to afflict a nation', as 'a system which tends to make us less thrifty, to blind us to our real situation'. He feared that the citizen initially 'deludes himself with the belief, that he is as rich as before' and then, faced with the taxes levied to pay for the debt, is tempted 'to remove himself and his capital to another country, where he will be exempted from such burthens' (ibid., pp. 247–8).

In short, for a long time the only budgetary rule was that of a balanced budget. This rule was probably based on an analogy between government and family finance drawn when the budget of the state was the budget of a monarch and separate from the finances of his subjects. The precept was therefore to avoid living beyond one's means. Premchand (1983, p. 4) quotes Adam Smith: 'what is prudence in the conduct of every private family, can scarcely be folly in that of a great kingdom', or, as Dickens's Mr Micawber puts it in *David Copperfield*, 'if a man had twenty pounds a year for his income, and spent nineteen pound nineteen shillings and sixpence, he would be happy, but . . . if he spent twenty pounds one he would be miserable'.

In the second part of the nineteenth century, the precept of the balanced budget still found a widespread endorsement. Ursula Hicks notes that 'Gladstonian budgeting is inextricably bound up with the theory of the ever-balanced (or even over-balanced) budget' (Hicks, 1953, p. 25) and quotes the following statement by Lowe, a disciple of Gladstone: 'I would define a Chancellor of the Exchequer as an animal who ought to have a surplus; if under extraordinary conditions he has not a surplus he fails to fulfil the very end and object of his being' (ibid.).[3]

Deficit and debt drew less attention from economists. For instance, as Burkhead (1954) notes, Marshall's *Principles* devotes no attention to these issues. Moreover, Puviani (1903) devotes most of his analysis of fiscal illusion to public expenditure and revenue. While he notes that politicians may prefer borrowing to extraordinary levies because citizens underestimate future interest burdens, this argument remains relatively unimportant in his analysis of the methods employed by governments to influence citizens' perception of fiscal policy.

The consensus on the balanced budget is witnessed by Pigou (1929, p. 233):

> in normal times the main part of a government's revenue is required to meet regular expenditure that recurs year after year. There can be no question that in a well-ordered State all such expenditure will be provided for out of taxation, and not by borrowing. To meet it by borrowing . . . would involve an ever-growing government debt and a corresponding ever-growing obligation of interest. . . . The national credit would suffer heavy damage; . . . This thesis is universally accepted.

Even after the Keynesian revolution the virtue of a balanced budget continued to be praised. Truman's 1951 *Economic Report of the President* stated that 'we should make it the first principle of economic and fiscal policy in these times to maintain a balanced budget, and to finance the cost of national defence on a "pay-as-we-go" basis'.

As Schumacher (1944, p. 86) noted, the precepts of sound public finance were grounded in the opinion that the economy is self-equilibrating:[4]

> The logical corollary of orthodox economics is orthodox finance. If it is believed that all factors of production are normally and inevitably utilised by private business, it follows that the State can obtain the use of such factors only by preventing private business from using them. . . . From this it follows that the first principle of 'sound' public finance is that the budget should be balanced.

Almost seventy years later than Pigou, Buchanan (1997, p. 119) echoes his words:

> the first century and one-half of our national political history did, indeed, embody a norm of budget balance. This rule was not written in the constitution document, as such, but rather it was part of an accepted set of attitudes about how government should, and must, carry on its fiscal affairs.

However, even in family finance borrowing is not necessarily evil. Even classical advocates of the balanced budget were aware of the necessity of allowing borrowing in certain circumstances and of its usefulness in others. Therefore economists have had a hard job in trying to specify under what circumstances exceptions to the balanced budget rule were to be allowed, caught between the Scylla of missed opportunities as a consequence of the constraint and the Charybdis of waste and instability caused by its removal.

The need for exceptions as well as the need for tight rules to deal with them was clearly recognized by Pigou (1929, p. 39). He deemed it to be plain that when

> non-remunerative government expenditures *on a wholly abnormal scale* have to be undertaken, as in combating the consequences of an earthquake or to meet an imminent threat of war . . . to collect what is required, and required at a very short notice in these conditions, through the machinery of taxation is politically and administratively impracticable. [Italics added].

He also argued that concerning 'government expenditure devoted to producing capital equipment . . . *the fruits of which will subsequently be sold to purchasers for fees* . . . it is generally agreed that the required funds ought to be raised by loans. . . . Upon this matter . . . there is no room for controversy' (ibid., p. 36, italics added). Finally, he notes that 'since changes in taxation always involve disturbance, to keep the rates of taxation as nearly as possible constant from year to year . . . it may be desirable . . . to arrange a budget so that good and bad years make up for one another, *a deficit in one balancing a surplus in another*' (ibid., p. 35; italics added).

2.1 Ordinary vs Extraordinary Finance

One first exception was thus found in the distinction between ordinary and extraordinary finance: the former dealt with recurrent expenditures, to be financed by recurrent revenues so as to avoid the depletion of non-renewable assets; the latter dealt with one-off outlays to be backed also by borrowed funds. And the rationale for this exception was found by way of analogy to family finance. De Viti de Marco (1953) points out that 'if an individual has to face an expense which he reckons to exceed his annual income . . . he will either have to sell his assets or raise a loan' (p. 390, our translation) and applies the same line of reasoning to public finances.[5]

De Viti de Marco is very much aware of classification problems, as the extraordinariness of an outlay is a matter for subjective assessment both at the individual and at the collective level: 'this subjective element does not allow to define a rigorous and objective rule that draws the line . . . between ordinary and extraordinary finance' (ibid., our translation). Margins for moral hazard and opportunistic behaviour arise as 'the distinction between "ordinary" and "extraordinary" receipts and expenditure is admittedly not clear-cut, depending ultimately on the judgement of the classifying authority as to whether the receipts and expenditure in question are to continue indefinitely in the future' (United Nations, 1951, p. 61).

While extreme cases were easily identified (on the one hand, interest outlays and salaries; on the other, the cost of a war), in some cases it is not straightforward to see what is ordinary and what is not. 'It is impossible to define *ex ante* what is an extraordinary outlay. Building a school may be an extraordinary effort for a small town, an ordinary one for a big city' (Einaudi, 1948, p. 318; our translation). Ultimately, as stated by Sir F. Phillips, writing in 1936 (quoted in Middleton, 1985, p. 82),

> there is no great technical difficulty in producing for a series of years budgets which are balanced at the end of the year to the nearest penny . . . Perhaps half a dozen financial writers in the country would understand from the published accounts what was happening, but I doubt if any one of the half dozen is capable of making the position clear to the public.

National experiences did not differ much. 'In the case of France, the extraordinary budget was proverbially the dumping place for all expenditures which could not be balanced by tax receipts' (Hansen, 1941, p. 199). In 1945 Keynes notes in a memorandum for the National Debt Enquiry (21 June 1945, in Moggridge and Robinson, 1971–89, vol. xxvii, pp. 406–7) that in the UK

> the present criterion leads to meaningless anomalies. A new G.P.O. is charged 'below', a new Somerset House 'above'. A Capital contribution to school buildings is 'above' in the Exchequer Accounts and is paid for out of Revenues, and is 'below' in the Local Authority Accounts and is paid for out of loans. The cost of a road is 'above', of a railway 'below'. And so on.[6]

In Canada, although not always realized even by Canadians, a budgetary distinction between ordinary and capital expenditures has been made ever since the confederation in 1867. The official reports show surpluses in 50 of the 66 years following 1867; but if the accounting were made on the US basis, surpluses would appear in only 15 of the 66 years (Hansen, 1941, p. 199).[7]

2.2 The Double Budget

The double budget is a refinement of the ordinary/extraordinary distinction that reduces the degree of arbitrariness of the decision concerning which expenditures can be deficit-financed. The budget is split into a current and a capital account. While the former must be balanced or in surplus, the latter can run a deficit (the so-called 'golden rule') and thus allows to spread the cost of durables over all the financial years in which they will be in use rather than charging it entirely to one year. It can be a powerful instrument in overcoming liquidity constraints and fostering economic development structurally.

Arguments along these lines can be found earlier than the dual budget debate *per se*. The productive character of a large part of public outlays was noted by German scholars in the second part of the nineteenth century. They also argued that government can borrow to finance undertakings that are expected to improve the income of future generations (Cohn, 1895). Bastable (1927, pp. 670–71) argues that

> non-economic (i.e. is non-remunerative) expenditure is primarily to be met out of income, and, unless it can be so dealt with, ought not to be incurred . . . [and] . . . that borrowing should hardly ever be adopted except for strictly economic expenditure, and then only when the extension of the State domain is clearly advisable.

The usefulness of a dual budget has been long debated.[8] It is still an unsettled issue, which has been tackled in different ways in different countries and at different times. Sweden introduced the dual budget in 1937 and suppressed it in 1980.

First of all, the distinction between current and capital items retains a certain degree of ambiguity which can be used opportunistically. 'The classification procedures which are to be followed in separating "current" and "capital" transactions are among the most controversial and difficult questions in budgetary procedure, especially in view of the frequent abuses of so-called "capital budgets" in hiding deficits which otherwise would have become apparent' (United Nations, 1951, p. 11).

According to Lindbeck (1968), this distinction 'facilitated tactical political manoeuvres and hampered the fiscal policy debate for many years [in Sweden] by focusing it on complicated bookkeeping issues understood by very few and of very little economic relevance' (p. 34).

In principle, one can distinguish between, first, durable goods producing a direct revenue; second, durable goods producing an indirect revenue as, respectively, investments by publicly owned enterprises and public infrastructures that reduce the costs borne by private producers and/or consumers; and, third, durable goods with pure consumption functions. It may be argued that the last should be excluded from the capital account as they do not affect growth and thus do not imply a future financial benefit for the public sector; therefore they worsen the sector's net worth.

In practice, however, the divide between the second and the third category is very unclear. In the case of infrastructures, for example, there is the issue of the treatment of expenditures determined by the attempt to reduce the impact on the environment. If the overall costs increase, should these expenditures be considered as producing an indirect revenue or as pure consumption? If for this reason we include in the capital account all durables, we end up creating a distortion in allocation based only on duration, rather than on contribution to growth, thus 'the analogy with private accounting may be conductive to an irrational preference for capital expenditures over current expenditures' (Goode and Birnbaum, 1955, p. 1).[9]

Clearly there are current expenditures, such as those increasing human capital, that can make a relevant contribution to growth as 'indirect revenue need not come through a durable good' (Steve, 1972, p. 164; our translation). If one is not careful about the expenditures to be included in the capital section, the dual budget may result 'in a preference for expenditures on physical assets rather than greater spending for intangibles such as health or education' (Colm and Wagner, 1963, p. 125). Thus 'the need for a return, either in the limited financial sense or in the broader context of the social return, is a view that needs to be applied over a wider spectrum of public expenditures and not confined to capital budget only' (Premchand, 1983, p. 296).

However, the inclusion in the capital account (which can be financed through debt) of all expenditures contributing to human capital would imply high levels of deficits and pose serious problems of classification.[10] One should also take into account that a part of expenditures replaces existing capital.

Furthermore, the possibility to borrow, without strict limits, in order to finance investments can lower the attention paid when evaluating the costs and benefits of each project. In a way, with the double budget the analogy between government and private finance moves from the household to the business sector, where the distinction between current and capital budget is customary. But the analogy between public sector accounts and those of private enterprises overlooks the absence of mechanisms that would penalize the public body investing in low-revenue projects.

2.3 Stabilization Policy

Another attempt at justifying deviations from the balanced budget rule came from Keynesian theory, where the budget plays a crucial role in cushioning the effects of cyclical downswings in the economy compensating for insufficient private demand. Therefore a balanced budget was no longer to be achieved in each financial year but to be attained over the whole length of the economic cycle.

On 5 April 1933, Keynes wrote in *The Times*: 'The next budget should be divided into two parts, one of which shall include those items of expenditure which it would be proper to treat as loan-expenditure in the present circumstances.' Later he sharpens the distinction between the government's own current expenditure and a capital budget to provide for sufficient national investment. On 15 May 1942 he writes in 'Budgetary Policy' (in Moggridge and Robinson, 1971–89, vol. xxvii, pp. 277–8):

> I should aim at having a surplus on the ordinary budget, which would be transferred to the Capital Budget, thus gradually replacing dead-weight debt by productive or semi-productive debt . . . I should not aim at attempting to compensate cyclical fluctuations by means of the ordinary budget, I should leave this duty to the capital budget.

Fiscal policy in Sweden and in the USA moved along these lines.[11] In 1937 Sweden reformed its budget rules and abandoned the annual balancing. In Lindbeck's account, the Swedish reform was based on the idea that

> in normal times the capital budget should be financed by loans whereas the current budget should be financed by taxes. In boom periods the current budget should, however, be overbalanced, hence part of the capital budget would be

financed by taxes; in recession the current budget should be underbalanced, hence partly financed by loans. (Lindbeck, 1968, p. 33)

Hansen (1941, p. 219) explains how in the USA

President Roosevelt . . . divided federal expenditures into 'ordinary' and 'extraordinary'. The former relate to the 'operating expenditure for the normal and continuing functions of government' . . . [and] . . . should be met out of current revenues' . . . He expressed the hope that in times of prosperity current revenues would so far exceed ordinary expenditures as to produce 'a surplus that can be applied against the public debt' . . . The extraordinary expenditures, which are concerned with loans, capital expenditure and relief of need, he deemed to be sufficiently flexible in character as to permit their contraction and expansion as a partial offset for the rise and fall in the national income.

However, the idea of balancing the government accounts over the course of the business cycle had an exceptionally brief life span. Blinder and Solow (1974) point out that while it 'had considerable appeal . . . in the immediate post-Keynesian years, when the balanced budget was [still] influential, it is almost never discussed nowadays' (p. 37). It was the turn of functional finance to take the lead.

Functional finance rejects completely the traditional doctrines of 'sound finance' and the principle of trying to balance the budget over the solar year or any other arbitrary period . . . government fiscal policy . . . shall all be undertaken with an eye only to the results of these actions on the economy. (Lerner, 1943, p. 41)

Hansen noted that 'if one adopts wholeheartedly the principle that government financial operations should be regarded exclusively as instruments of economic and public policy, the concept of a balanced budget, however defined, can play no role in the determination of that policy' (1941, p. 188).

The way in which these ideas were first met is exemplified in the following passage by Chamberlain, Chancellor of the Exchequer, in 1933 (quoted in Sabine, 1970, p. 15):

If I were to pretend I could lay out a programme under which what I borrowed this year would be met by a surplus at the end of three years, everyone would soon perceive that I was only resorting to the rather transparent device of making an unbalanced budget look respectable.

It was also pointed out that

the requirement of a balanced budget was and still is the simplest and clearest rule to impose 'fiscal discipline' and to hold government functions and

> expenditure to a minimum . . . Even an avowedly counter cyclical policy is believed to give rise to an upward trend in expenditures that might not otherwise occur. The expenditures undertaken to counteract a depression are unlikely to be discounted in the succeeding boom. If the boom is countered at all, the measures taken will be credit restriction or increased taxation. (Smithies, 1960)

The obstacles posed by politics to a symmetric and timely reaction of the budget to cyclical developments were stressed. Agreement over the appropriate budgetary items to use may take too long; it may prove difficult to reduce expenditures once they have been increased. Drees (1955) and Steve (1972) provide early discussions of the relevance of the balance of powers between the parliament and the government and of the relationship between the government and its parliamentary majority: budgetary rules cannot be evaluated *per se* but need to be set in the overall institutional context.

Among the remedies suggested to the political problem described, an enhanced reliance on automatic stabilizers and the so-called formula flexibility were suggested. The latter consisted in the introduction of a predetermined relationship between tax rates (or benefits levels) and the level of economic activity.[13]

But support in favour of functional finance was strong.

> Even if stability in the budget has something to recommend it, stability in the economy is surely better . . . Who makes the rule? Who decides when to abide to it and when to countermand it? Furthermore, within the framework of a political democracy, the case for taking stabilization policy out of the hands of politicians is an uneasy one: into whose hands shall it be placed? . . . No budgetary rule can be provided with a solid intellectual foundation. This will hardly be new to economists. The best that can be said for rules is that some of them may be better than incompetently managed discretionary policy . . . (Blinder and Solow, 1974, pp. 43 and 45)

This view was broadly accepted in some public finance textbooks.[14]

Along the same lines, though less aggressively, Steve (1972) notes that 'budgetary policy cannot be reduced to simple rules, it should take into account the overall effects of the budget on private demand components and national income' (p. 170; our translation).[15]

The stagflation in the 1970s; the difficulties concerning the estimate of the actual impact of budget changes on the economy; the risks of fine-tuning given the lags between the decision to change the budget and its implementation; the development of theoretical models questioning the possibility for the government to influence the level of government activity all contributed to a decline of interest in the theory of functional finance.

Advocates of the balanced budget regained the fore.

> The balanced-budget principle played a crucial role in holding the pre-keynesian fiscal constitution together, and constraining the otherwise inherent biases of that system to over-expenditure and deficit finance. Once the balanced-budget had been bowled over by the Keynesian revolution, those biases were unleashed. (Buchanan et al., 1978, p. 47)[16]

Politicians praised again the virtues of balanced budgets:

> At one time, it was regarded as the hallmark of good government to maintain a balanced budget; to ensure that, in time of peace, Government spending was fully financed by revenues from taxation, with no need for Government borrowing. Over the years, this simple and beneficent rule was increasingly disregarded . . . And I have balanced the budget. (Nigel Lawson, Budget Statement, 1988)

The recent policy debate has largely recognized that in normal circumstances automatic stabilizers ought to be allowed to operate freely.[17] On the contrary, discretionary fiscal action is generally considered problematic in view of irreversibility and timing problems and of the uncertainty about its effects.[18]

3. EMU FISCAL RULES: NEW ANSWERS TO OLD QUESTIONS?

European Monetary Union represents a new historical development. For the first time a number of sovereign countries adopt a common currency while retaining independent fiscal policies. The need for fiscal rules complementing monetary union has been at the core of the debate on EMU since the early 1990s.[19]

Some arguments were put forward against the introduction of fiscal rules at the European level. It was noted that fiscal rules may have costs in terms of stabilization policies and may hamper the achievement of allocative and distributive objectives. It was also noted that excessively stringent rules may be counterproductive. If the Pact leads to an unduly tight fiscal stance in one or more countries, pressure may mount on the European Central Bank (ECB) to deliver a monetary offsetting (Canzoneri and Diba, 2001). Otherwise, the credibility of the Pact may be endangered.[20]

However, the prevailing view in the policy debate was clearly in favour of the introduction of formal rules. It was argued that procedural or fiscal rules are necessary because the factors that in recent decades have determined fiscal profligacy in several countries have not disappeared. Moreover, the multinational dimension of EMU is likely to increase the need for such rules.

Stark (2001, p. 79) describes the genesis and the rationale of the Stability and Growth Pact;[21] he stresses how in Europe, up to the early 1990s, lax fiscal policy

> occurred although it is indisputable that unsound fiscal policy practices have adverse effects on price stability, growth and employment: large deficits and large public debt place constraints on the ability of a country . . . to act during different stages of the business cycle . . .; the State's absorption of resources which would otherwise have found their way into private investments results in higher long term interest rates . . . a stifling government debt ratio impair(s) the overall efficiency of an economy and create(s) risks to price stability . . .; these problems are especially pronounced in monetary union since . . . the policy of a single country might have adverse consequences for all the other participating countries.

These arguments combine the two main strands of opinion about the budgetary balance: the one stressing the importance of stabilization policies and budgetary flexibility and the other maintaining that unbalanced budgets imply distortions in the allocation of resources (see Buti et al., 1998).

It was also pointed out that, without strong rules, the legal independence of the ECB may turn out to be an empty shell because of pressure by high-debt countries for *ex ante* bailout (refraining from raising interest rates in conditions of inflationary tensions) or *ex post* bailout (debt relief through unanticipated inflation). EMU can induce unilateral fiscal expansions since governments may feel less inclined to preserve fiscal rectitude, as individually they face a less steep interest rate schedule in a monetary union than under flexible exchange rates.

The debate on fiscal rules in EMU was grounded on the wider debate that took place in the 1990s on the role of fiscal institutions and procedures in shaping budgetary outcomes (see Kopits and Symansky, 1998). While certain political configurations, such as weak coalition governments, have been recognized as conducive to budgetary misbehaviour or to hampering attempts to redress the budgetary situation,[22] inadequate budgetary institutions and procedures may also contribute to a lack of fiscal discipline.[23]

In this context, institutional reforms in the fiscal domain have been discussed and introduced in several countries. As noted by Beetsma (2001), these reforms come in two main categories: (a) the introduction of procedural rules conducive to responsible fiscal behaviour; and (b) the introduction of a fiscal rule, that is, a permanent constraint on domestic fiscal policy in terms of an indicator of the overall fiscal performance (budget balance, borrowing, debt, reserves) of central and/or local government.

In national experiences, both types of measures have proved to be effective tools in containing political biases in fiscal policy making and in achieving and sustaining fiscal discipline. In a multinational context, the adoption of harmonized tight budgetary procedures may lead to fundamental problems from the point of view of national sovereignty (Beetsma, 2001). Moreover, institutional reforms are more difficult to monitor centrally, compared to numerical targets. The latter are also simpler to evaluate and easier to grasp by public opinion and policy makers. In the end a clear consensus emerged about the introduction of common numerical rules and an elaborated multilateral surveillance mechanism (see Buti and Sapir, 1998 and Stark, 2001).

The fiscal framework of EMU was developed gradually. The Treaty of Maastricht in 1992 set the fiscal criteria to be met for joining Monetary Union. The Stability and Growth Pact (SGP), adopted by the European Council in Amsterdam in June 1997, developed these criteria with a view to permanently restraining deficit and debt levels while allowing room for fiscal stabilization. The Pact also strengthened the monitoring procedures complementing the quantitative rules.

3.1 A Description[24]

As we stated in the introduction, EMU fiscal rules have been designed with the goal of ensuring that national policies keep a sound fiscal stance while allowing sufficient margins for budgetary flexibility in bad times.

The Treaty of Maastricht stated that budget deficits cannot be larger than 3 per cent of GDP unless (a) under exceptional circumstances, such as deep recessions, (b) they remain close to 3 per cent, (c) the excess only lasts for a limited period of time.[25] If the deficit exceeds the 3 per cent limit when the above three conditions are not met, the deficit is deemed 'excessive' and it sets off a procedure intended to force corrective measures by the deviating country. If such measures are not taken, the Treaty foresees monetary sanctions which increase as situations of excessive deficit persist.[26]

The Stability and Growth Pact specified what is meant by 'exceptional' and 'limited period' in the clauses allowing a deficit greater than 3 per cent of GDP not to be considered 'excessive'. A recession is considered exceptional if real GDP diminishes by 2 per cent. Milder recession (where the reduction in real GDP is of at least 0.75 per cent) may also be considered exceptional if, for example, it is abrupt. The excess above 3 per cent must be reabsorbed as soon as the 'exceptional circumstances' allowing it are over.

The Pact also specified that each country should aim for a medium-term objective of a budgetary position 'close to balance or in surplus'. According to the guidelines provided by the European Council,[27] the choice of the medium-term target should take into account both the budgetary risks of recessions and those linked to fluctuations of other economic factors (for example, interest rates). Countries with debt ratios above 60 per cent of GDP should also take into account the need to reduce such ratios, at a satisfactory pace, towards the threshold. Moreover, an increase in the debt ratio during recessions should be avoided.[28] Finally, other risk factors, such as the effects of demographic trends, ought to be taken into account.[29]

According to the European Council, compliance with the Pact should be assessed in relation to the cyclical position of the economy. In practice, EMU fiscal rules require that each member state choose a budgetary target in cyclically adjusted terms and let automatic stabilizers or discretionary action operate symmetrically around it. The lower this budget balance with respect to the 3 per cent threshold, the wider the margins for countercyclical policy without running the risk of an excessive deficit.

Each member state must submit its budgetary targets officially in multi-year budgetary documents (Stability Programmes); these documents are updated annually and are subject to a review by the European Commission aimed at assessing their consistency with EMU fiscal rules.

Overall, the approach taken by the EU can be characterized as less flexible than the solutions adopted in some federally structured countries (see Balassone and Franco, 1999):

(a) the rules are defined on the basis of established numerical parameters;
(b) *ex post* compliance with the parameters is required each year; overshoots must be rapidly dealt with;
(c) margins of flexibility are envisaged only in connection with exceptional cyclical events (established *ex ante* as a decline in GDP) or in any case events beyond the governments' control;
(d) no special provision is made for investment expenditure,[30]
(e) monitoring procedures are envisaged, whereby peer pressure is strengthened by the European Council's power to make formal representations to governments of the need to adopt corrective measures during the year and by the application of pre-established monetary sanctions.

3.2 New Answers to Old Questions?

With European Monetary Union, for the first time the need for fiscal rules arises in a multinational context. The review in the previous section shows how the arrangements adopted are deeply embedded in the long-lasting debate on budgetary rules. The novel features of EMU guided the choice between alternative solutions and required the introduction of some innovations.

The need to reconcile fiscal soundness and budgetary flexibility led to a combination of different approaches:

(a) setting a predetermined upper bound for the deficit is a new pragmatic solution;[31]
(b) balancing the budget over the cycle is a precept derived from the Keynesian approach. In 1951 a report by the United Nations, commenting the 1937 Swedish reform, points out that 'while counter-cyclical budgeting introduced an element of flexibility in the fiscal policy of Government, the concept of "financial soundness" has been retained' (UN, 1951, p. 69);
(c) prudence when fixing the average target to be achieved over the cycle ('close to balance or in surplus') has a classical flavour. In 1927, Bastable argued that 'the safest rule for practice is that which lays down the expedience of estimating for a moderate surplus, by which the possibility of a deficit will be reduced to a minimum' (Bastable, 1927, p. 611).

The stress on fiscal soundness motivates the rejection of a dual budget approach and of any distinction between ordinary and extraordinary finance. However, pragmatism called for the allowance of margins for exceptional circumstances; this rests on the idea that 'in some circumstances, indeed, a balanced budget is a pedantic luxury, which a community, hard pressed by sudden and exceptional misfortune, can ill afford' (Dalton, et al., 1934, p. 12).

A broadly balanced budget, like that required by the SGP, may negatively affect the public investment level; this effect can be especially relevant during the transition to the low debt levels consistent with the chosen structural balance. The double burden determined by this transition can be assimilated to that arising from the transition from a pay-as-you-go to a funded pension system. However, besides the criticism of the double budget system examined in the previous sections, in the context of EMU the golden rule would be an obstacle to deficit and debt reduction. In particular, given the ratio of public investment as a percentage of GDP, the long-run equilibrium level of government debt could be very high, especially in an environment of low inflation. This could imply that the debt ratio would rise in low-debt countries, while in high-debt countries there would be a very slow pace of debt reabsorption. The golden rule would also meet with practical difficulties, such as the evaluation of amortization, and would make the multilateral surveillance process more complex, by providing leeway for opportunistic behaviour. Governments would have an incentive to classify current expenditure as capital spending (see Balassone and Franco, 2000b).

The asymmetry in EMU between the monetary regime, with the single currency and a single monetary authority, and the political landscape, lacking an authority of federal rank, gave prominence to moral hazard issues. This is probably at the root of the rejection of both the dual budget and the distinction between ordinary and extraordinary finance. It motivated the adoption of a detailed multilateral surveillance procedure and the introduction of a predetermined limit for the annual deficit in a framework that envisages the targeting of a balanced budget over the cycle.[32]

EMU may be termed a 'radical federation', where in the absence of fiscal rules member states enjoy absolute autonomy in matters of public expenditure and taxation and recourse to debt. In this context, the stability of monetary and financial conditions represents a public good to which all local governments contribute by maintaining sustainable budget positions. There is an incentive for each local government to exploit the benefits accruing from the discipline of others without itself complying with the rules. This creates a double cost for the other entities: the free-rider's excessive indebtedness can put pressure on interest rates to rise; it can also result in bankruptcies requiring bail-outs.[33]

The need for monitoring was felt also in earlier days. For instance, Durrell (1917) argues that 'the public and the Parliament should be satisfied that . . . there is some authority which . . . will give timely warning if that expenditure or those obligations are either outrunning the revenue provided for the year or engaging the nation too deeply in the future' (p. 242). However the monitoring procedure adopted for EMU is novel with respect to its scale, complexity and tightness.

Until now the chosen mix of approaches has been successful in securing a reduction in budget deficits and debt across EMU member states. It remains to be seen whether it will also be successful in maintaining fiscal discipline once instituted. Unfavourable economic developments will put EMU's fiscal constitution to the test and the issue of legitimacy of rules in a democracy pointed out by Blinder and Solow may come to the fore again.

Fiscal rules can be successfully implemented over a long period of time only if public opinion considers them a valuable contribution to policy making. In the words of Bastable (1927, p. 761):

> it but remains to again lay emphasis on the fact that good finance cannot be attained without intelligent care on the part of the citizens. The rules of budgetary legislation are serviceable in keeping administration within limits; but prudent expenditure, productive and equitable taxation, and due equilibrium between income and outlay will only be found where responsibility is enforced by the public opinion of an active and enlightened community.

NOTES

* Research Department, Banca d'Italia. The views expressed in this chapter are those of the authors and do not represent those of the Banca d'Italia. The authors wish to thank Professor Sergio Steve for his comments and suggestions.

1. The economic policy framework of EMU is extensively examined in Buti and Sapir (1998) and in Brunila et al. (2001). The theory of fiscal sustainability and its links with EMU fiscal rules are reviewed in Balassone and Franco (2000a); see also the papers in Banca d'Italia (2000). On the flexibility allowed by EMU fiscal rules see Buti et al. (1997) and Balassone and Monacelli (2000).
2. The actual definition of this medium-term objective requires several factors to be taken into account; see section 3.1.
3. Hicks relates this view to the objective of reducing the debt and taxation, to the prevailing favourable economic conditions and also to some difficulties in managing the budget. She notes that the growth of administrative expertise in budgeting contributed to the development of a different approach in the 1930s.
4. Schumacher, while reporting these views, did not share them.
5. De Viti de Marco goes on to justify deficit finance as a less painful alternative to extraordinary taxation, which may penalize liquidity constrained taxpayers.
6. On the UK experience, Clarke (1998, p. 64) also notes that

   > in the best Gladstonian tradition. . . . On the expenditure side, what mattered was expenditure above the famous 'line' in the Exchequer accounts, dating from the Sinking Fund Act of 1875, broadly . . . distinguishing a revenue account from a capital account – but by no means unambiguously . . . Only an old Treasury hand could be expected to know the difference within this hybrid accounting framework . . . therefore, the simple moral imperative of balancing the budget was in practice wrapped in the esoteric conventions of the public accounts

7. In Italy, in the late nineteenth century and the early twentieth century, revenues and expenditures related to the construction of railways were included in a special balance sheet and separated from other ordinary and extraordinary items. Revenues were represented by the proceeds of the sale of bonds, expenditures by the outlays for investment projects (see Nitti, 1903). *De facto*, an item-specific golden rule was implemented.
8. See the accounts in Premchand (1983) and Poterba (1995). For a recent discussion in the context of EMU, see Balassone and Franco (2000b).
9. For a discussion along these lines see also Steve (1972, pp. 163–5). Steve also notes that drawing the line between durable goods with direct and indirect revenue would pose similar problems.
10. Bastable (1927) had already acknowledged the usefulness of non-remunerative expenditures such as those on education, improved housing and the like; however, he also pointed out that there is a 'difficulty of application. The results of expenditure of the kind are hard to trace or measure, and any statement respecting them must rest in a great degree of conjecture' (pp. 621–2).
11. These developments reflected common problems but were to a large extent unrelated. On the relationship between Swedish fiscal policy and Keynesian theories see Lundberg (1996). He recalls that, in 1929, Lindahl considered the use of fiscal policies to affect the level and composition of demand and that Myrdal was asked to write an appendix to the government budget proposal of January 1933 on the issue of the feasibility of active fiscal policies.
12. Middleton (1985) reviews the debate on budgetary policy in the UK in the 1930s. In 1933 the Treasury stressed the risks related to unbalanced budgets:

   > Would not the ordinary taxpayer and the business man very soon begin to have a feeling of uneasiness and apprehension? After all people will realise that the bill must

> be paid if not this year next year or the year after. Uncertainty and apprehension about the future would very quickly cancel out any immediate psychological benefit which the reduction of taxation by unbalancing the Budget would promote. (1985, p. 88)

13. Biehl, in summarizing several papers on fiscal policy issues, notes that

> It is strange to see that, e.g., the old-fashioned concept of the simple budget balance rule is still widely used in many countries and that . . . the full employment budget concept, the structural margin of fiscal impact concept, and the concept of the cyclically adjusted neutral budget . . . are only known to a small circle of specialists. (1973, p. 6)

14. See, for instance, Johansen (1965), in which the use of budgetary items for stabilization policy is unquestioned, the focus of the analysis being on the choice of the most appropriate instruments.
15. Steve stresses that the budget balance cannot be considered in isolation: the level and composition of public revenue and expenditure are extremely important.
16. Keynes's own views about active fiscal policy were rather prudent. He stressed the need to control inflation and retain appropriate market incentives. In evaluating the UK budget in 1940, he noted

> The importance of a war budget is not because it will 'finance' the war. The goods ordered by the supply department will be financed anyway. Its importance is *social*: to prevent the social evils of inflation now and later; to do this in a way which satisfies the popular sense of social justice; whilst maintaining adequate incentives to work and economy. ('Notes on the Budget', 21 September 1940, in Moggridge and Robinson (eds), 1971–89, vol. XXII, p. 218)

17. The issue is extensively discussed in OECD (1999). OECD notes that 'in the future governments should guard against the asymmetric use of automatic stabilizers, although this obviously does not preclude all discretionary action, particularly for structural reasons' (p. 145).
18. See European Commission (2001), Kilpatrick (2001), Taylor (2000) and Wren-Lewis (2000).
19. For a review of the justifications put forward for the Pact and for an analysis of its potential macroeconomic implications see European Commission, Buti and Sapir (1998), Artis and Winkler (1997) and Eichengreen and Wyplosz (1998).
20. It was also noted that the multiplicity of fiscal authorities does not provide strong arguments in favour of permanent constraints on the deficit as it may actually dilute the pressure on the central bank. According to Canzoneri and Diba (2001), a more relevant reason to have fiscal rules is to underpin the 'functional', as opposed to the 'legal', independence of the central bank. Without a credible deficit criterion ensuring government fiscal solvency, the central bank would not be able to keep control of the price level.
21. See also Costello (2001).
22. See, for instance, Roubini and Sachs (1989), Alesina and Drazen (1991), Alt and Lowry (1994), Alesina and Perotti (1995) and Balassone and Giordano (2001).
23. See, for instance, von Hagen and Harden (1994) and the essays in Strauch and von Hagen (2000).
24. A more detailed description of the rules is provided in Buti and Sapir (1998) and in Cabral (2001).
25. The three conditions make the 3 per cent threshold extremely binding (see Buti et al., 1997).
26. See Cabral (2001) for a description.
27. Council Resolution on the Stabilty and Growth Pact, 17 June 1997; Council Regulation

n. 1466/97, 7 July 1997; Council Declaration, 1 May 1998; Opinion of the Monetary Committee, 12 October 1998 as approved by the Council.

28. Art. 104C of the Treaty says that when the ratio is above 60 per cent of GDP it must 'diminish sufficiently' and approach 60 per cent 'at a satisfactory pace'. If the ratio increases, the excessive deficit procedure begins. It should be noted that, while the Treaty allows exceptions to the 3 per cent deficit criterion, it does not for the criterion concerning the debt ratio. See Balassone and Monacelli (2000).
29. The choice of the medium-term fiscal target is examined in Artis and Buti (2001), Dalsgaard and de Serres (2001) and Barrel and Dury (2001).
30. No distinction is made in the Treaty between current and capital expenditure for the purposes of determining the deficit. The volume of capital expenditure is included only among the relevant factors to be borne in mind when deciding whether there is excessive debt.
31. The deficit ceiling, although arbitrary, is reminiscent of the results obtained by Domar (1944) in the analysis of fiscal sustainability assuming a constant deficit. Perhaps conscious of the partial equilibrium nature of Domar's results, the introduction of a debt ceiling as well avoids convergence at high levels of debt. See Balassone and Franco (2000a).
32. EMU fiscal rules are targeted at national governments while many EMU member states have a federal or highly decentralized structure. A free-riding problem can re-emerge at national level. This problem is analysed in Balassone and Franco (1999).
33. The risks clearly increase if member states are asymmetric in some relevant respect (for instance, accumulated public debt). These considerations are likely to have motivated the inclusion of a 'rule' concerning not only deficits but also debt.

REFERENCES

Alesina, A. and A. Drazen (1991), 'Why are Stabilizations Delayed?', *American Economic Review*, **82**, 1170–88.

Alesina, A. and R. Perotti (1995), 'The Political Economy of Budget Deficits', *IMF Staff Papers*, **42**, 1–31.

Alt, J.E. and R.C. Lowry (1994), 'Divided Government and Budget Deficits: Evidence from the States', *American Political Science Review*, **88**, 811–28.

Artis, M.J. and M. Buti (2001), 'Setting medium-term fiscal targets in EMU', in Brunila et al. (2001).

Artis, M.J. and B. Winkler (1997), 'The Stability Pact: Safeguarding the Credibility of the European Central Bank', CEPR Discussion Paper, No. 1688, August.

Balassone, F. and D. Franco (1999), 'Fiscal Federalism and the Stability and Growth Pact: A Difficult Union', *Journal of Public Finance and Public Choice*, **XVII**, (2–3), 137–66.

Balassone, F. and D. Franco (2000a), *Assessing Fiscal Sustainability: A Review of Methods with a View to EMU*, Rome: Banca d'Italia.

Balassone, F. and D. Franco (2000b), 'Public Investment, the Stability Pact and the Golden Rule', *Fiscal Studies*, **21** (2), 207–29.

Balassone, F. and R. Giordano (2001), 'Budget Deficits and Coalition Governments', *Public Choice*, **106**, 327–49.

Balassone, F. and D. Monacelli (2000), 'EMU Fiscal Rules: Is There a Gap?', Temi di discussione, No. 375, Rome: Banca d'Italia.

Banca d'Italia (2000), *Fiscal Sustainability*, Proceedings of the Banca d'Italia Workshop on Public Finance held in Perugia, 20–22 January, 2000, Rome.

Barrel, R. and K. Dury (2001), 'Will the SGP ever be breached?', in Brunila et al. (2001).

Bastable, C.F. (1927), *Public Finance*, London: Macmillan.

Beetsma, R. (2001), 'Does EMU need a stability pact?', in Brunila et al. (2001).

Biehl, D. (1973), 'Introduction of Round Table discussion', in H. Giersch, *Fiscal Policy and Demand Management*, Tübingen: J.C.B. Mohr.

Blinder, A. and R.M. Solow (1974), *The Economics of Public Finance*, Washington, DC: The Brookings Institution.

Brunila, A., M. Buti and D. Franco (eds) (2001), *The Stability and Growth Pact – The Fiscal Architecture of EMU*, Basingstoke: Palgrave.

Buchanan, J.M. (1997), 'The Balanced Budget Amendment: Clarifying the Arguments', *Public Choice*, **90**, 117–38.

Buchanan, J.M., R.E. Wagner and J. Burton (1978), 'The Consequences of Mr. Keynes', Hobart Paper 78, Institute of Economic Affairs, London.

Burkhead, J. (1954), 'The Balanced Budget', *Quarterly Journal of Economics*, **LXVIII**, (May), 191–216.

Buti, M., D. Franco and H. Ongena (1997), 'Budgetary Policies During Recessions – Retrospective Application of the Stability and Growth Pact to the Post-War Period', *Recherches Economiques de Louvain*, **63** (4), 321–66.

Buti, M., D. Franco and H. Ongena (1998), 'Fiscal Discipline and Flexibility in EMU: The Implementation of the Stability and Growth Pact', *Oxford Review of Economic Policy*, **14** (3), 81–97.

Buti, M. and A. Sapir (1998), *Economic Policy in EMU – A Study by the European Commission Services*, Oxford: Clarendon Press.

Cabral, A.J. (2001), 'Main aspects of the working of the stability and growth pact', in Brunila et al. (2001).

Canzoneri, M.B. and B.T. Diba (2001), 'The stability and growth pact: a delicate balance or an albatross?', in Brunila et al. (2001).

Clarke, P. (1998), 'Keynes, Buchanan and the balanced budget doctrine', in J. Maloney (1998), *Debt and Deficits*, Cheltenham, UK and Northampton, USA: Edward Elgar.

Cohn, G. (1895), *The Science of Finance*, Chicago: University of Chicago Press.

Colm, G. and P. Wagner (1963), 'Some Observations on the Budget Concept', *Review of Economic Studies*, **45**, 122–6.

Costello, D. (2001), 'The SGP: how did we get there?', in Brunila et al. (2001).

Dalsgaard, T. and A. de Serres (2001), 'Estimating prudent budgetary margins', in Brunila et al. (2001).

Dalton, H., T. Brinley, J.N. Reednam, T.J. Hughes and W.J. Leaning (1934), *Unbalanced Budgets – A Study of the Financial Crisis in Fifteen Countries*, London: George Routledge and Sons.

De Viti de Marco, A. (1953), *Principi di Economia Finanziaria*, Torino: Einaudi.

Domar, E.D. (1944), 'The Burden of the Debt and the National Income', *American Economic Review*, December, 798–827.

Drees, W. Jr (1955), *On the Level of Government Expenditure in the Netherlands after the War*, Leiden: H.E. Stenfert Kroese.

Durrell, A.J.V. (1917), *The Principle and Practice of the System of Control over Parliamentary Grants*, London: Gieves Publishing House.

Einaudi, L. (1948), *Princìpi di Scienza della Finanza*, Torino: Boringhieri.

Eichengreen, B. and C. Wyplosz (1998), 'Stability Pact: More Than a Minor Nuisance?', *Economic Policy*, April, 67–104.

European Commission (2001), *Public Finances in EMU – 2001*, Brussels.

Goode, R. and E.A. Birnbaum (1955), *Government Capital Budgets*, Washington, DC: International Monetary Fund.

Hansen, A.A. (1941), *Fiscal Policy and Business Cycles*, New York: Norton & Co.

Hicks, U.K. (1953), 'The Budget as an Instrument of Policy, 1837–1953', *The Three Banks Review*, 16–34.

Johansen, L. (1965), *Public Economics*, Amsterdam: North-Holland.

Kilpatrick, A. (2001), 'Transparent Frameworks, Fiscal Rules and Policy-making under Uncertainty', in Banca d'Italia (2001), *Fiscal Rules*, Proceedings of the Banca d'Italia Workshop on Public Finance held in Perugia, 1–3 February, 2001, Rome.

Kopits, G. and S. Symansky (1998), 'Fiscal Policy Rules', IMF Occasional Paper, No. 162.

Lerner, A.P. (1943), 'Functional Finance and the Federal Debt', *Social Research*, **10**, 38–51.

Lindbeck, A. (1968), 'Theories and Problems in Swedish Economic Policy in the Post-War Period', *American Economic Review*, June Supplement, 1–80.

Lundberg, E.F. (1996), *The Development of Swedish and Keynesian Macroeconomic Theory and its Impact on Economic Policy*, Raffaele Mattioli Foundation, Cambridge: Cambridge University Press.

Middleton, R. (1985), *Towards the Managed Economy: Keynes, the Treasury and the Fiscal Policy Debate of the 1930s*, London: Methuen.

Moggridge, D. and A. Robinson (eds) (1971–89), *The Collected Writings of John Maynard Keynes*, London: Royal Economic Society.

Nitti, F.S. (1903), *Princìpi di Scienza delle Finanze*, Napoli: Luigi Pierro.

OECD (1999), *Economic Outlook*, No. 66, Paris.

Pigou, A.C. (1929), *A Study in Public Finance*, 2nd rev. edn, London: Macmillan.

Poterba, J.M. (1995), 'Capital Budgets, Borrowing Rules and State Capital Spending', *Journal of Public Economics*, **56**, 165–87.

Premchand, A. (1983), *Government Budgeting and Expenditure Controls: Theory and Practice*, Washington, DC: International Monetary Fund.

Puviani, A. [1903] (1973), *Teoria dell'Illusione Fiscale*, Milano: F. Volpi, ISEDI.

Roubini, N. and J.D. Sachs (1989), 'Political and Economic Determinants of Budget Deficits in the Industrial Democracies', *European Economic Review*, **33**, 903–38.

Sabine, B.E.V. (1970), *British Budgets in Peace and War. 1932–45*, London: Allen and Unwin.

Say J.B. (1853), *A Treatise on Political Economy*, translation from the 4th French edn, Philadelphia: Lippincott, Grambo & Co.

Schumacher, E.F. (1944), 'Public finance – its relation to full employment', in F.A. Burchardt (ed.), *The Economics of Full Employment*, Oxford: Basil Blackwell.

Smithies, A. (1960), 'The Balanced Budget', *American Economic Reviews*, **L** (2), 301–9.

Sraffa, P. (ed.) (1952–73), *The Works and Correspondence of David Ricardo*, Cambridge: Cambridge University Press.

Stark, J. (2001), 'Where did the pact come from? Genesis of a pact', in Brunila et al. (2001).

Steve, S. (1972), *Lezioni di Scienza delle Finanze*, Padova: Cedam.

Strauch, R. and J. von Hagen (eds) (2000), *Institutions, Politics and Fiscal Policy*, Dordrecht: Kluwer.

Taylor, J.B. (2000), 'Reassessing Discretionary Fiscal Policy', *Journal of Economic Perspectives*, **14** (3), 21–36.

United Nations (1951), *Budgetary Structure and Classification of Government Accounts*, New York: UN.

von Hagen, J. and I. Harden (1994), 'National Budget Processes and Fiscal Performance', *European Economy Reports and Studies*, No. 3, pp. 311–418.

Wren-Lewis, S. (2000), 'The Limits to Discretionary Fiscal Stabilization Policy', *Oxford Review of Economic Policy*, **16** (4), 92–105.

COMMENT

Rolf Strauch

Public finances need to be balanced in the long run over an infinite horizon as an inevitable restriction of the intertemporal budget constraint. However, it is less clear to what extent this restriction is binding for finite horizons. The important question raised by the authors is therefore whether public accounts should be balanced in the short or medium term. The authors try to answer this question by a historical review of sources reaching from biblical verses to proposals from modern times of a cyclically adjusted budgetary balance. The answer we get from these historical sources is 'Yes, budgets should be balanced', because it is economically sensible and normatively good. The first main message from the study is therefore that the European fiscal framework continues an important line of budgetary and economic reasoning stretching through history. In light of the current criticism levelled against the European fiscal framework, those supporting and implementing the surveillance procedures may find this confirming.

The authors then provide a nice overview of different budgetary systems and concepts which have been used in history to capture the different functions of public finances. First, there was a distinction between ordinary and extraordinary financing needs leading then to the double budget, separating more clearly between capital and current spending funds. Second, the notion of a cyclical component of the budget or a medium-term budget balance in the course of the business cycle became more prominent in the 1930s, although it was dismissed by many academics during the following decades.

What remains as a baseline of this review, then, is that the specific regulations of the Stability and Growth Pact are in fact not as new and innovative as policy makers and academics may believe. This is again a useful finding because it puts the current worries about the implementation and credibility of the European fiscal framework into perspective. More importantly, it offers the opportunity to learn from history. If the founders of EMU had taken a look back at history, they would have noticed that making operational the concepts they employ has already been a lasting problem in the past, and that the current debate is not likely to vanish or be easily resolved, if at all.

The authors then go on to argue that the current European fiscal framework has, however, one new element, which is the highly decentralized setting of the monetary union, with one supranational monetary authority and independent national fiscal authorities. Due to this constellation, giving prominence to moral hazard issues, a detailed multilateral surveillance procedure was created. It is above all these procedural requirements, in the multilateral setting, which the authors consider the truly innovative element of the European fiscal framework.

It is certainly right that the political structure of EMU, with a centralized monetary policy and explicitly decentralized fiscal policy, is unique to industrialized economies at the current stage of history. But this does not fully hold for earlier times and it is surprising that Balassone and Franco are somewhat historically short-sighted in this regard. There have been different forms of multilateral monetary unions among Latin and Scandinavian countries in the nineteenth century.[1] The main reason why the authors missed this aspect is possibly their perspective, which largely takes national fiscal arrangements as the relevant point of comparison. However, this only allows for a partial assessment of the institutional foundations of EMU in two respects.

The specific question posed by the founders of EMU was: what fiscal foundations do we need for the functioning of a monetary union and a stable currency? Or in short ('Waigelian' terms): how do we get a hard currency? Setting fiscal constraints to make the euro a hard currency was presumably needed to sell the idea of a monetary union to the Germans. The context in which these fiscal institutions have to be seen is thus not that of other fiscal rules. For the current context the main project was the creation of a stable currency, based on an independent central bank, a no-bailout clause and a fiscal restraint. Instead of going through the literature on fiscal rules, the authors should have analysed the literature on the economic foundations of monetary stability and the institutional basis set to ensure the 'soundness of the currency'. As a consequence, they completely fail to see whether a fiscal rule as an integral part of the institutional setting underpinning monetary stability presents an institutional innovation for the creation of common currency areas and monetary unions. The virtue of central bank independence has not been generally accepted, even in academia, until the 1980s or 1990s, and it is mostly considered sufficient to engineer a central bank as an autonomous decision maker which is not allowed to bail out the government. Therefore one might suspect that the European fiscal framework may indeed present a remarkable innovation.

Second, the authors do not fully explore the multinational nature of the European fiscal framework. Their main concern is the existence of a moral hazard problem in this context, requiring clear rules and stronger surveillance mechanisms than can often been seen at the national level. However, national government systems may provide different checks and balances which do not exist in the international arena. From a political economy perspective, one would expect that heads of states might strive to seize as little sovereignty as possible. The moral hazard problem discussed by the authors is indeed not fully solved. Possibly the unwillingness to commit to a more stringent fiscal framework restricting themselves rather than economic insight. Even more importantly, governments assigned themselves a decisive role in the implementation of the surveillance procedure which ultimately rests on the decisions taken by the ECOFIN Council. The role of the Council implies that 'sinners' would have to impose sanctions on themselves. This is, however, unlikely to happen, particularly if several countries experience excessive deficits at the same time. Many observers have questioned the virtue of this arrangement for the credibility of the European fiscal framework from the very beginning. By now, the weakness of the system has even been clearly recognized by the European Commission.[2]

Overall, the contribution by Balassone and Franco is not only a very useful but also an enjoyable read for those of us who are usually bugged by columns of budgetary figures and difficult equations in their everyday professional life. It fruitfully explores the 'history of thought' on a specific aspect of public budgeting. However, it fails to fully capture the institutional and economic context of a monetary union as the historical point of comparison for the innovative elements of the European fiscal framework.

NOTES

1. See Michael Bordo and Lars Jonung (2000), *Lessons for EMU from the History of Monetary Unions*, London: IEA.
2. See European Commission Communication on 'Strengthening the Co-ordination of Budgetary Policies', issued on 27 November 2003.

2. Indebtedness and deficits of the nations of the European Union

Peter Bernholz

1. INTRODUCTION

The subject of this chapter is relatively simple. First it examines the facts concerning the development and the present state of the deficits and debts of the member states. Second, we have to ask ourselves under what conditions this situation can be maintained, in the sense that indebtedness as a percentage of GDP does not increase in the future. Related to this topic, we must ask whether the conditions of the European Stability Pact are sufficient for this purpose. Third, related to this is the question of what problems may turn up as a result of the age structure of the population and the old age pension systems. A final problem may be the costs of the enlargement of the Union.

2. THE DEVELOPMENT OF DEBTS AND DEFICITS

The development of the debts and deficits of the member states as percentages of GDP during recent years is shown in Figures 2.1 and 2.2. On the whole, developments seem to be positive for the period from 1998 to 2000. Indeed, before the downturn of economic activity beginning in 2001 deficits decreased in all countries. In this sense, the Maastricht Conditions and the Stability Pact may have had a positive influence.

But first, the public debts of France, Germany and Austria stagnated, and that of Greece even increased slightly. Second, the Belgian, Italian and Greek debts as a percentage of GDP are still much higher than the strict application of the Maastricht criteria would have required. Third, if we take the better growth performance during in 1998–2000 into account (Figure 2.3), the development of debts and deficits seems to be much less satisfactory. As a consequence, the European Central Bank (ECB) has already warned that efforts to stabilize the fiscal situation must be strengthened. Whether this will and can be done as the economy cools seems to be doubtful for some countries.

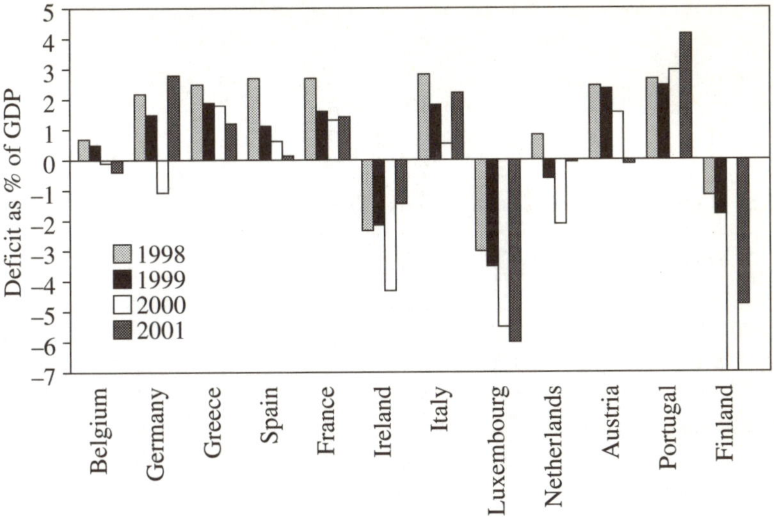

Source: ECB, *Monthly Report* (Monatsberichte), February 2003.

Figure 2.1 Deficits of member countries of the euro area, 1998–2001

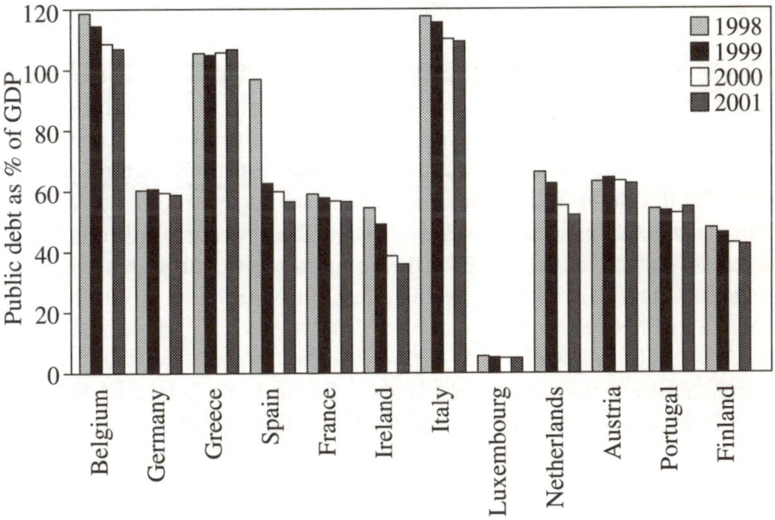

Source: See Figure 2.1.

Figure 2.2 Development of public debts of countries of the euro area, 1998–2001

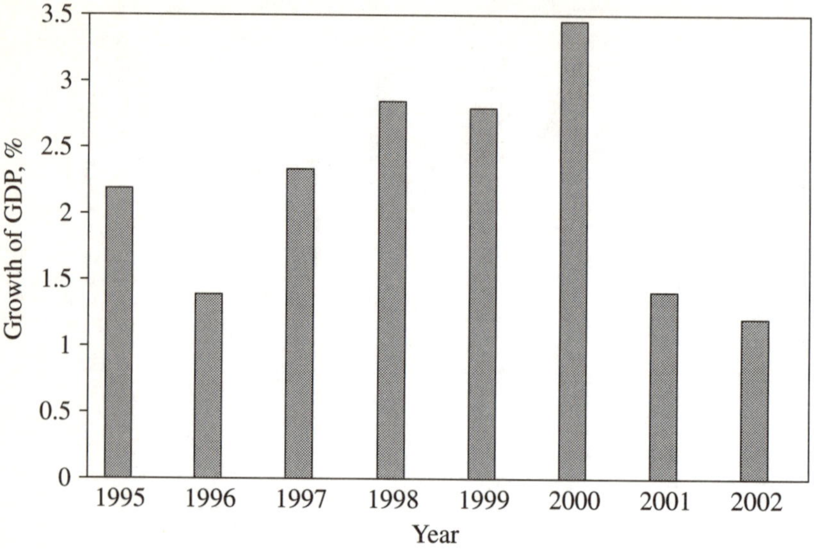

Note: The figure for 2002 is the average of the first three quarters only.

Source: ECB, *Monthly Report* (Monatsberichte), March 2001 and February 2003.

Figure 2.3 Growth rates of GDP of the euro area, 1995–2002

Finally, other important questions remain. What will be the consequences for national finances of the development of the budget of the European Union itself, given the expansion of membership planned for the years to come? And what will be the consequences of the ageing population on the implied public debts and deficits of the member states? Before turning to these questions, however, let us look at the economic conditions which must be fulfilled to prevent a further increase of public debts as a percentage of GDP.

3. ECONOMIC CONDITIONS FOR PREVENTING FURTHER GROWTH OF PUBLIC DEBT

3.1 Symbols

We introduce the following symbols:

$S(t)$ Total debt of general government, end of period t;
$Y(t)$ GDP during period t;

w	Growth rate of GDP;
$D(t)$	Total annual deficit of government and public sector during period t;
$DP(t)$	Primary deficit of government and public sector during period t;
$DS(t)$	Secondary deficit of government and public sector during period t;
r	Interest rate;
t	Time (year).

3.2 Assumptions

Public debt as a share of GDP does not increase:

$$S(t)/Y(t) \leq S(t-1)/Y(t-1) \tag{2.1}$$

Growth of GDP:

$$Y(t) = (1+w)\,Y(t-1) \tag{2.2}$$

Definition of change of debt:

$$S(t) = S(t-1) + D(t) \tag{2.3}$$

Relationship of types of deficits:

$$D(t) = DP(t) + DS(t) \tag{2.4}$$

Definition of secondary deficit:

$$DS(t) = rS(t-1) \tag{2.5}$$

3.3 Derivation of Results

It follows from (2.1)–(2.2) that:

$$S(t)/[(1+w)\,Y(t-1)] \leq S(t-1)/Y(t-1),$$
$$S(t) \leq (1+w)S(t-1).$$

By inserting (2.3) we get:

$$S(t-1) + D(t) \leq (1+w)S(t-1),$$
$$D(t) \leq wS(t-1). \tag{2.6}$$

From (2.4) and (2.5) we derive:

$$rS(t-1) = D(t) - DP(t),$$
$$S(t-1) = [D(t) - DP(t)]/r.$$

Inserting this expression into (2.6), we have:

$$D(t) \leq (w/r)[D(t) - DP(t)],$$
$$DP(t) \leq (1 - r/w)D(t),$$
$$DP(t) \leq [(w-r)/w]D(t). \tag{2.7}$$

Inequalities (2.6) and (2.7) must be fulfilled to prevent an ever-increasing deficit, eventually leading to bankruptcy of the state, which is either into open bankruptcy or into a hidden one in the form of inflation.

3.4 A Numerical Example

In the following example we set the public debt at $0.6 = 60$ per cent of GDP, in accordance with the (with possible exceptions) Maastricht admission criteria. Also, let us assume $w = 2.5$ per cent and $r = 4$ per cent. We redefine $S(t-1) = S$, $D(t) = D$ and $DP(t) = DP$. Then, by using inequalities (2.6) and (2.7) we can calculate the results shown in Figure 2.4.

It follows that, with a national debt of 60 per cent, only a total deficit of 1.5 per cent and a primary surplus of 0.9 per cent is admissible or required, respectively, to prevent a further deterioration of the debt situation, provided that the real interest rate is 4 per cent and the growth rate of GDP 2.5 per cent.

For a debt of 120 per cent of GDP the figure for the total deficit is 3 per cent and the necessary surplus of the primary deficit is 1.8 per cent.

4. ENLARGEMENT OF THE EU AND POSSIBLE BUDGETARY DANGERS

The financial situation of the member states of the EU may also envisage future burdens if the accession of new members puts such a strain on the expenditures of the Union that an increase of the contributions or a decrease of subsidies to them should materialize. As a consequence, let us first look at the budgetary situation of the EU and its provisions for facing these challenges (Table 2.1). Second, a short analysis of the budget of the candidates for membership is called for.

As can be seen from the table, the financial situation of the EU does not

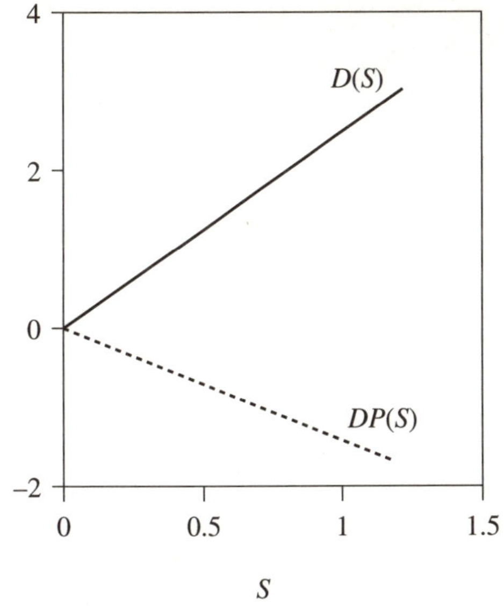

$r := 0.04 \ w := 0.025$

$S := 0, 02 \ldots 1.2$

$D(S) := w \cdot S \cdot 100$

$$DP(S) := (w - r) \cdot \frac{D(S)}{w}$$

DP(*S*)	*D*(*S*)
0	0
0.5	–0.3
1	–0.6
1.5	–0.9
2	–1.2
2.5	–1.5
3	–1.8

Notes:
S = Government debt as share of GDP;
D and *DP* = Total and primary deficit as share of GDP.

Figure 2.4 Total and primary deficits keeping debt constant as share of GDP (in % of GDP)

seem to lead to any significant problems for the member states. As the European Commission's Agenda 2000 (1997) expressed it: 'There are various indications that it should be possible to cover the development . . . to be financed from the Community budget over the period 2000–2006 without raising the resources ceiling from its level of 1.27 per cent of GNP.'

In fact, room has already been made in the budgetary planning for payments to the candidates for membership, and there is still a certain reserve, since the threshold for total expenditures given by the limit of 1.27 per cent of the GNP of the Union has not been reached. On the other hand, the budget calculations for 2001 may easily be surpassed by additional expenses in the agricultural sector caused by mad cow disease and other problems. More hazardous than such factors may be the budgetary situation of the candidates for membership. If their budgetary situation is not sound, this may lead to pressures to get more financial support from the Union or to weaken monetary policies of the ECB. We now examine the respective figures for the countries considered for membership (Tables 2.2 and 2.3, Figure 2.5).

Table 2.1 Budget of the EU with forecast to 2006 (million euro)

	Current prices			2001 prices			
	2000	2001	2002	2003	2004	2005	2006
Expenditures							
Agriculture	41730	44530	45674	45538	44488	43624	43344
Structural and Cohesion Funds	32678	32720	32106	31503	30758	30758	30343
Internal policies	6031	6272	6386	6500	6614	6729	6853
External action	4627	4735	4745	4756	4776	4776	4787
Administration	4638	4776	4880	4984	5088	5197	5296
Reserves	906	916	666	416	416	416	416
Pre-accession aid	3174	3240	3240	3240	3240	3240	3240
Total expenditures	93792	97189	97697	96937	95380	94740	94279
Ceiling, accession payments			4306	6979	9247	11899	14792
Total expenditures w. ceiling			102003	103916	104627	106639	109071
In % of GNP own resource	1.12	1.11	1.17	1.18	1.14	1.12	1.12
Ceiling, % of GNP	1.27	1.27	1.27	1.27	1.27	1.27	1.27
Revenues							
Agricultural and sugar levies	2038.4	1967.7					
Customs duties	11665.3	12291.7					
VAT	34048.6	33467.2					
Fourth resource	37805.1	43245.5					
Miscell. and surplus prev. year	3883.2	1597.3					
Total revenues	89440.6	92569.4					
Deficit	4351.4	4619.6					

Source: European Commission, General Budget of the European Union for the Financial Year 2001. Brussels/Luxembourg, January 2001.

Table 2.2 Deficits of candidates for EU membership as percentage of GDP

	1997	1998	1999	2000	2001
Cyprus	5.3	5.5	4.02	2.9	
Czech Rep.	4.7	5.3	6.3	3.3	2.8
Estonia	−2.5	0.06	0.16	−0.16	−2.6
Hungary	7.2	8.3	5.2	3	5.2
Latvia	−0.7	−0.15	3.8	2.7	1.4
Lithuania	1.9	0.4	7.05	1.3	0.36
Malta	9.8	5.6			
Poland	2.8	2.3	2.0	3.1	5.5
Romania	3.9	−1.7	−2.0		
Slovak Rep.	5.5	4.7	6.4	5.9	6.2
Slovenia	1.5	0.6	0.8	0.96	1.1
Turkey	8.5	8.4	13.0	11.4	19.6

Sources: For Czech Republic, Hungary, Poland and Slovak Republic: OECD, *Economic Outlook*, Vol. 2002/2, No. 72, December.
For other countries: IMF, *International Financial Statistics*, Monthly Reports.

Table 2.3 Gross foreign debt of the whole economy (in % of GDP)

	1995	1996	1997	1998	1999
Cyprus	60.4	64.3	96.3	128.0	155.4
Czech Rep.	24.6	24.2	24.5	23.2	24.0
Estonia	9.39	10.69	25.18	29.0	23.0
Hungary	65.3	60.6	52.9	53.9	55.9
Latvia	12.3	10.2	10.6	15.6	21.2
Lithuania	12.29	14.25	15.04	17.7	25.5
Malta	60.9	71.2	93.6	201.2	214.1
Poland	30.47	27.38	26.35	29.17	33.65
Romania	16.7	22.9	26.1	19.7	23.7
Slovak Rep.	19.6	22.57	32.61	36.78	38.86
Slovenia	10.98	19.08	19.06	20.31	28.46
Turkey	37.85	37.01	37.96	37.46	50.47

Note: Most figures for 1999 are estimated.

Source: Eurostat.

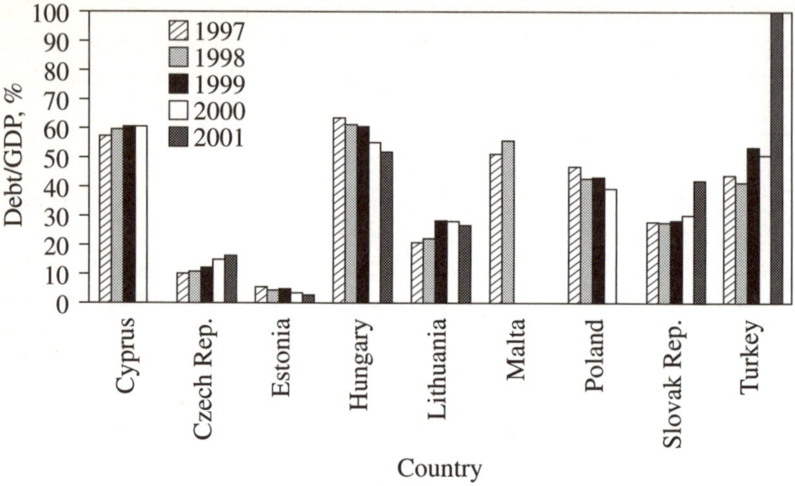

Note: Data for Latvia. Romania and Slovenia were not available.
Source: IMF, *International Financial Statistics*, Monthly Reports.

Figure 2.5 Debts of candidates for EU membership, 1997–2001

The incomplete figures, which for some countries do not even include 2000, show significant differences between the candidates. Besides government debt as a percentage of GDP, which has not been available for all countries (Figure 2.5), total foreign indebtedness of the candidates for membership has been included. The foreign debts of Cyprus and Malta as a percentage of GDP were very high indeed, in 1999 (Table 2.3); none of the other countries reaches 60 per cent. The picture is different for government debt (Figure 2.5). Here only the government debt of Turkey was much higher than 60 per cent and that of Cyprus slightly higher than 60 per cent of GDP in 2001. The deficit situation of the countries striving for EU membership is worse (Table 2.2), since four countries were still beyond the Maastricht criterion of 3 per cent in 2000. The worst deficits were experienced by Turkey, with 11.4 per cent of GDP in 2000 and 19.6 per cent in 2001, a country which experienced a financial and monetary crisis and suffered from a high rate of inflation (54.4 per cent in 2001) for years. Recently, the situation has improved. The Hungarian and Polish deficits have increased to 5.2 and 5.5 per cent of GDP in 2001.

It follows that there is cause for concern, and that there is good reason not to grant admission to several candidates before adequate reforms have been completed. I quote again the European Commission: 'Although efforts have been made in most candidate countries to stabilize general government balances in the reporting period, the sustainability of public finances remains a cause of concern in almost all candidate countries, albeit to different degrees.'

5. PENSIONS AND AGEING OF THE POPULATION

A greater threat for financial stability may arise from the ageing of the population in the member states of the EU, together with the characteristics of obligatory pension systems usually administered by the state. As the share of retired persons in the population rises and the share of younger working people falls, severe problems are faced, especially by pay-as-you-go pension systems. The benefits to the retired and the obligatory contributions or taxes of the still active population, as given by the age structure of the population, usually imply an implicit debt of the government. This is so because presently valid contributions or taxes will not be sufficient to cover presently promised benefits, given the ageing of the population.

The questions arising from this problem have been taken up by so-called 'generational accounting'. In this approach, starting from certain assumptions, the implicit debt is calculated and added to the explicit public debt. Using these figures, it is possible to determine the increase of taxes and (or) reduction of benefits necessary to prevent a further increase of the total public debt (compare section 3). The results for the explicit, implicit and total debts of EU member countries are presented in Figure 2.6. The standard assumptions which have been made in the respective studies are a discount rate of 5 per cent and a real growth rate of 1.5 per cent. Moreover, 'The demographic forecasts are based on data from national authorities and range over 200 years. Thereafter the effects of fiscal policy, due to discounting, are negligible' (European Commission, 1999, No. 6, p. 2). Space constraints preclude further description of the methodology used in this approach here. The interested reader may turn for details to the study (ibid.) which has been done by several authors. For our purposes it is sufficient to consider the consequences for the fiscal situation of member states.

Interestingly, total debts are much lower than explicit debts for Ireland, and, more surprisingly, for Belgium. For all other countries total debts are much higher than explicit debts, with the exception of Italy. The situation is worst for Finland, Austria and Sweden, where total debt reaches levels of 253.2, 192.5 and 236.5 per cent of GDP respectively.

Figure 2.7 gives the tax increases in percentage of GDP necessary to maintain the present level of benefits and expenditures. The rise in taxes would have to take place at once. Other solutions to the problem would be

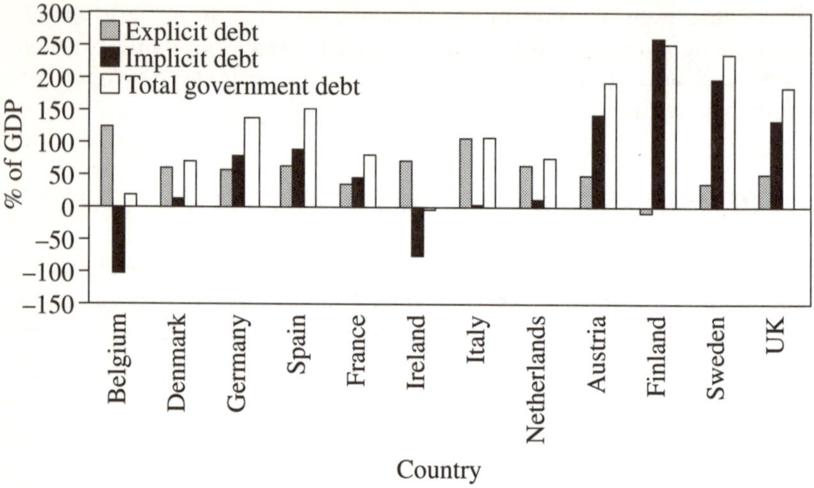

Source: European Commission (1999).

Figure 2.6 Explicit, implicit and total government debt of EU countries, 1995, according to generational accounting

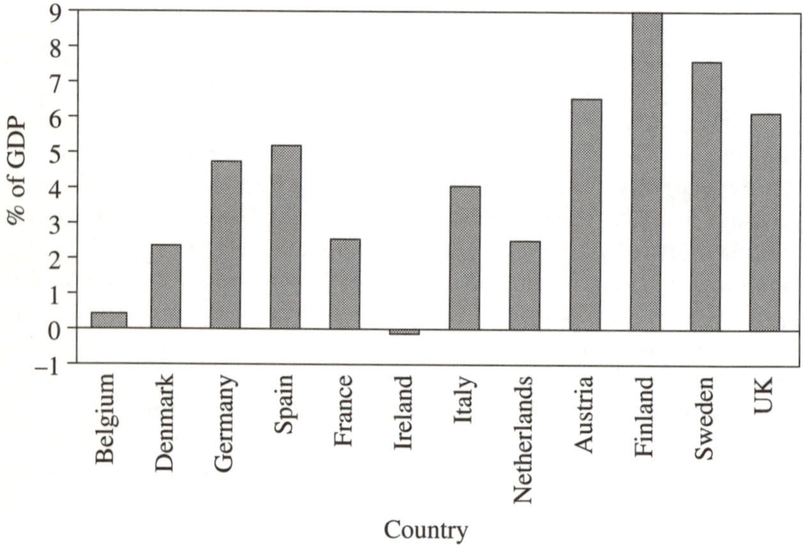

Source: See Figure 2.6.

Figure 2.7 Necessary increase of all taxes with unchanged benefits a corresponding decrease of old age benefits, or a mixture of both, or finally, a much higher immigration of people of working age. In any case, the future fiscal situation of most member states looks rather dismal if we take the problems of an ageing population into account.

6. INCREASING GOVERNMENT EXPENDITURES AND DEFICITS

Two laws or empirical regularities are well known to political economists: Wagner's law (or, rather, Umpfenbach's law) of an increasing share of government expenditures in GDP, and the law (as yet unattributed) of a rising share of expenditures of the central government in total government expenditures in federal states. What are the reasons for this latter regularity? One may be the fact that the agents of the central government, such as parliament or constitutional court, enjoy the right to determine the jurisdictional boundaries with the member states of the federation. Another may be that central government promises to the financially poorer members of the federation a system of redistribution administered by itself, and possibly soon combined with conditions determined by it. Specialists in this field may be able to add other, perhaps more decisive, reasons for the growth of central government.

The EU is not yet a federal state. But since it already has a central administration, let us examine whether it has been influenced by this law. An answer to this question is relevant here, since a relative extension of the share of revenues going to the centre is apt to erode the tax basis of member states.

In Figure 2.8 the development of appropriations for payments of the EU is shown, together with the ceiling as set by the agreements of member states. As can be seen, both figures have increased during the period from 1993 to 1999. To show that the relative share of the centre in total government expenditures has also risen, we have to compare this increase with the change of expenditures of the national governments. Now, the expenditures of the EU have fallen from 49.7 per cent in 1993 to 45.9 per cent in 1999, and for the euro area from 49.8 per cent in 1993 to 44.7 per cent in 1999 (Figure 2.9).

This means that the share of the EU in total government expenditures has risen. So even in this loose confederation this law or regularity can be observed. Let us now turn to Wagner's law, and ask whether it has been valid for the member states of the EU during recent years. What are the reasons for this phenomenon, which has been observed for decades?

In a democracy parties compete to gain and maintain government power.

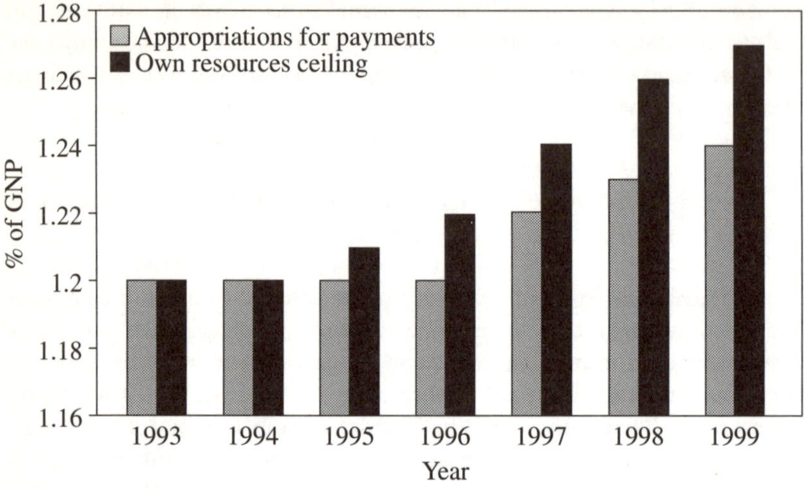

Source: European Commission, General Budget of the European Union for the Financial Year 2001, Brussels/Luxembourg, January 2001.

Figure 2.8 Growth of EU expenditures as share of GNP

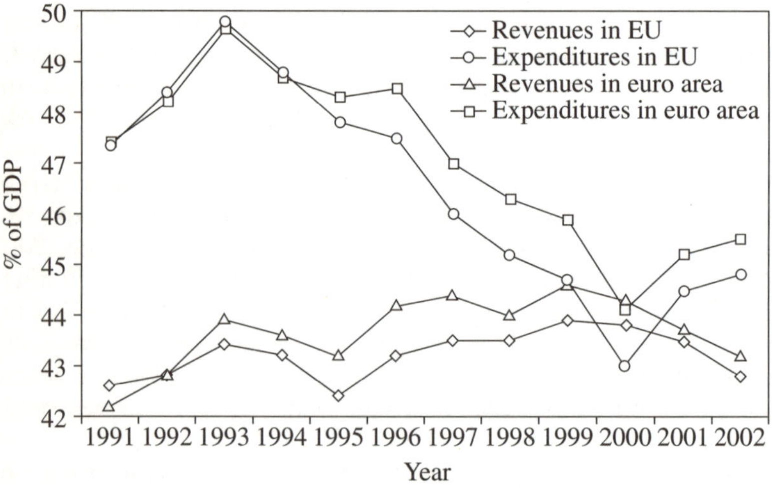

Note: Estimates for 2002.
Source: OECD, *Economic Outlook*, Vol. 2002/2, No. 72, December.

Figure 2.9 Development of revenues and expenditures in the EU and the euro area

As a consequence the party or parties in power have to try to gain as many votes as possible in the next election to secure at least a majority in parliament. However, voters are rationally uninformed about matters which are not relevant to them.

The negligible chance that their individual vote could make a difference to the outcome of the election does not warrant more than very little effort and expense to inform themselves about party platforms and their possible consequences. Consequently, they are only well informed about what is important to them, usually their and their relatives' job security, their wages and incomes, and the availability of not too expensive housing. They are thus usually ignorant about fiscal and monetary policies and their future consequences. Moreover, these matters are complex and not easily understood without specific education. On top of this, the positive, though usually short-lived consequences of an expansionary fiscal or monetary policy, namely an upturn of the economy and a decrease of unemployment, follow more quickly than their negative consequences in the form of public deficits and higher prices. As a consequence, because of the complexity of the problems and of their rational ignorance, voters will judge the performance of the government mostly by the results of former policies and even by events not caused by government measures.

The fiscal and monetary policies preferred by the party or parties in power, given this rational ignorance of voters, are the following. The government usually has to concentrate the benefits of its actions on small segments of the population, so that they are felt, whereas the costs have to be spread widely so that they are not felt. This is especially easy in a growing economy where, even with an increasing share of public revenues in GDP, disposable incomes of individuals are still growing. Additionally, expenditures can be increased without burdening anybody through higher taxes by taking refuge in borrowing. It is true that the government must pay interest on a rising debt, but this lies in the future, after the next elections. Also, additional expenditures spent at the right time before elections will stimulate the economy and reduce unemployment, leading to better re-election chances. This gives rise to the so-called political business cycle, much discussed in public choice theory (Frey, 1978). But with the passage of time interest payments on a higher and higher debt consume a rising share of government revenues and lead to higher interest rates in the markets, crowding out worthwhile investments. Finally market participants may even believe the government to be an insecure debtor and demand a risk premium on interest. Given these relationships, it is tempting for the ruling party (parties) to finance part of the public deficit by creating money, that is by taking refuge in borrowing from the central bank. This prevents, at least for some time, higher short-term interest rates and allows the positive effects just mentioned. Inflation follows only with a time-lag after the election, can be fought immediately afterwards, and has the appealing side-effect of reducing the real public debt.

But these disinflationary measures have negative effects on economic activity and employment, and thus they have to be abolished in time to allow a new stimulation of the economy before the next election. As a consequence there exists an inflationary bias of democratic governments in peacetime. Also, it should be obvious from the above arguments that the forces for inflationary deficit-financing are strengthened if economic growth is slow or lacking, because in such circumstances any increase of the tax burden will reduce disposable per capita income.

Our last arguments point to the relationship of growing public expenditures as a share in GDP to the development of public deficits and debts. Moreover, they explain why the Maastricht criteria and the Stability Pact were thought to be important by governments and central banks of the member states of the EU to secure the stability of the new common currency, the Euro. All these measures were obviously deemed necessary to bind the hands of government with the purpose of preventing the working of Wagner's law, increasing deficits and debts, and finally the resulting pressure on the ECB to finance the deficits and to reduce the debt by creating money.

We are already convinced that this policy has had a certain success in reducing deficits and debts of the member states as a share of GDP. On the other hand, as shown in Figure 2.8, this has not been the case for the expenditures of the EU. To complete the picture, we look at the development of expenditures and revenues of the member states taken together (Figure 2.9).

It is interesting to observe that the Maastricht criteria and those of the Stability Pact were seemingly successful before the downturn of economic activity began in 2001, probably in combination with international systems competition ('globalization'), in reducing the share of expenditures in GDP. But this has not been the case concerning revenues (before the recession reduced them after 2000), probably at least partly as a result of efforts to meet the deficit conditions. How far these successes have been helped by the upswing in the business cycle until 1999 and will persist over whole cycles, remains to be seen. Also, the slightly rising revenues may point to the difficulty of preventing the working of Wagner's law in the long run. But the development could also prove dangerous to maintaining or reducing debts and deficits.

It seems that a rise of expenditures (at least given present magnitudes) leads to lower growth rates of GDP (Bernholz, 1986, 1990; Peden and Bradley, 1989; Tanzi and Schuknecht, 1997; Weede, 1986), which would have negative effects on the development of revenues.

It thus seems advisable to maintain competition in the tax and social security systems of member states. A harmonization, which is a cartelization of these systems, would remove the competition, limiting the tendency of governments to raise taxes and obligatory contributions.

REFERENCES

Bernholz, Peter (1986), 'Growth of Government, Economic Growth and Individual Freedom', *Journal of Institutional and Theoretical Economics* (*Zeitschrift für die gesamte Staatswissenschaft*), **142**, 661–83.

Bernholz, Peter (1990), 'The Completion of the Internal Market: Opportunities and Dangers Seen from an Institutional Perspective', in *The Macroeconomics of 1992*, CEPS Paper No. 42, Brussels.

European Commission (1997), 'Enlarging the EU. For a Stronger and Wider Union', *Agenda 2000*, Vol. 1, Strasbourg: Communication of the Commission, 1st July.

European Commission (1999), 'European Economy: Generational Accounting in Europe', No. 6.

Frey, Bruno S. (1978), 'Politico-Economic Models and Cycles', *Journal of Public Economics*, **9**, 203–20.

Peden, Edgar A. and Michael D. Bradley (1989), 'Government Size, Productivity and Economic Growth. The Post-War Experience', *Public Choice*, **61**, 229–45.

Tanzi, Vito and Ludger Schuknecht (1997), 'Reforming Government: An Overview of Recent Experience', *European Journal of Political Economy*, **13** (3), 395–417.

Weede, Erich (1986), 'Catch-up, Distributional Coalitions and Governments as Determinants of Economic Growth or Decline in Industrialized Societies', *British Journal of Sociology*, **37**, 194–220.

COMMENT

Geoffrey Brennan

In this chapter, Peter Bernholz has given us a useful summary statement of the situation in the various nations within the EU with respect to their deficits and their public indebtedness. He provides not only the statistics for accumulated public debt, but also attempts to estimate the implicit debt involved in the future tax liabilities embodied in quasi-contractual social security benefit obligations. As he shows, the inclusion of these implicit debt calculations can make a very significant difference to the overall debt position of various countries. As his Figure 2.6 indicates, some countries with rather low 'explicit' debt – Finland and Sweden, most notably – have very large total debt positions. The most conspicuous case is that of Finland, whose explicit debt is negligible but whose calculated implicit debt is so large that its aggregate measured debt (implicit plus explicit) is the largest of all the EU countries, measuring something around two and a half times annual GDP. On the other hand, Belgium, which has a very high explicit debt – around 140 per cent of annual GDP – has a total debt position that is quite modest, presumably because its old age pension scheme is in actuarial surplus.

It is well known that implicit debt calculations are rather sensitive to various critical assumptions – and in particular, to assumptions about retirement ages and about female participation in the workforce. Nevertheless, if, under most plausible assumptions, the implicit debt is 250 per cent of annual GDP, then there are presumably worst-case scenarios that would place it at considerably more than that. Bernholz does not rehearse the details of the methods by which implicit debt levels are actually calculated. That is not his purpose. Nor does it bear much on the general thrust of the argument. For even if alternative calculation methods served to suggest that the implicit debt could actually be much lower, the general thrust of the argument would still hold – namely, that overall debt levels are highly influenced by implicit debt calculations and that the implicit debt needs to be included in any measure of overall indebtedness.

That said, the broader question is why the overall debt and deficit position of various countries should be an object of concern in the EU context. The Maastricht Conditions certainly indicate that there was concern – over both current deficit levels and aggregate public debt. And the presence of these conditions raises three issues. First, is it really the case that these parameters ought to be an object of concern? Second if they are an object of concern, to whom should they be such an object? I have in mind specifically whether they should concern the EU overall, or the individual member countries. And third, if they are a proper object of concern, what grounds do we have for thinking that the EU will be a means by which the relevant problems can be solved?

I raise these issues more as puzzles than in any spirit of critique of the Bernholz chapter. Bernholz himself gives us two reasons why the level of debt might be an object of legitimate concern. One is that having a high level of debt encourages governments to undertake inflationary policies. Because borrowers' liabilities are typically denominated in nominal terms, the real value of those liabilities is reduced when inflation occurs. So when governments are in substantial debt, it pays them to inflate. There may of course be political and/or other constraints on their capacity to pursue inflationary policies; but *ceteris paribus* higher indebtedness creates an incentive for governments to have higher inflation rates than they might otherwise have, and this is presumptively a 'bad thing'.

Or at least so the argument goes. But if inflation is presumptively a bad thing, it is worth pursuing the question as to how far the presumption carries us. Take the implicit debt case. Suppose that demographic factors mean that the quasi-contractual agreements entered into during the periods when the terms of the social security system were established turn out to be terms that the country cannot really afford. What precisely is meant by 'really afford' here is worth some elaboration. In the limit, of course, there is the possibility that the pension commitments actually exceed the maximum amount of revenue that the government can extract under any plausible formal tax arrangements. In this case, the government would literally go bankrupt if pensioners insisted on the full value of their claims. Of course, it is doubtful whether pensioners would so insist: the bankruptcy of their pension fund is not an outcome that any of them is likely to want. So some modification of claims seems likely.

But when claims are made about the non-viability of public pension schemes, something less drastic than public bankruptcy is usually at stake. What is meant is that the capacity of governments to spend on other objects of current priority will be diminished to the point where extremely hard choices will have to be made. In this case, too, the likelihood that the quasi-contractual commitments embodied in current pension 'entitlements' will be regarded as inviolate is highly unlikely. The truth is that previous governments have entered into arrangements that turn out to have been somewhat reckless. Those arrangements involve a promised redistribution from future generations to the generation working when the pension provisions were introduced. That redistribution is not justified on equity grounds. And its efficiency consequences have turned out to be pretty disastrous. The only barrier to wholesale rewriting of the pension contracts is their quasi-contractual nature. And this is a special problem when the pension recipients make up a significant part of the voting community – and conceivably a majority.

In this setting, it is not clear that a little inflation may not be a good idea. Or at least, that is so if the pension entitlements are specified in nominal terms. If that were so, then inflation would amount to a more or less proportional tax on the pension entitlements of current pension recipients. And if the time path of inflation were appropriately managed, then reasonable equity could be achieved between different generations of pension recipients and the dangers of galloping inflation possibly minimized. One may not like inflation. It may have other incidental redistributive and efficiency consequences. And there is always the possibility that inflation might get out of hand. But if earlier governments have made excessive commitments – possibly totally reckless ones – then inflation may not be the worst of the possible responses.

Or at least all this is so if inflation actually solves the problem. But in many pension schemes, the entitlements are themselves determined by retirement salary and are subsequently indexed by reference to the CPI or equivalent. In that case, there is very little scope for inflation to 'solve the problem'. In that event, however, there is no reason to think that implicit debt threatens inflation. Implicit debt does indeed represent a problem; but that problem is not that it encourages inflationary tendencies.

In that sense, implicit debt and explicit debt are unlike. For explicit debt *can* be eroded by inflation, and does represent an anxiety if one sees inflation as a major evil. In this spirit, countries like Belgium, which have large explicit debt but very modest (and perhaps negative) implicit debt, remain an inflationary anxiety. In short, a distinction between implicit and explicit debt needs to be retained, because the threats they pose involve different likely policy responses. If one were to hold the (slightly unfashionable) view that a little low-level inflation, if it can be kept within reasonable bounds, is not the worst of all possible evils, then implicit debt seems to represent a more major concern than explicit debt.

The question remains, however, whether that concern is mostly one for the country concerned. If any member of the EU were to get into major fiscal difficulties, this would doubtless have implications for the other member countries. The question is whether the presence of the EU makes governments that face significant long-term fiscal problems more or less likely to do something about those problems. Perhaps the anxiety is that each government will look to others to bail it out. But I am not entirely convinced. The threat of a kind of fiscal management takeover by the EU seems likely to make countries more attentive to their long-term fiscal problems, not less.

There seems no doubt that the primary losers from any collapse of the fiscal system of any member country will be the claimants on that fisc, and specifically social welfare and pension recipients. The central arena for the handling of long-term fiscal problems will therefore be the domestic politics of the member country. What seems conceivable, however, is that threats of discipline from 'higher up' within the EU may be an important domestic political instrument in enabling member countries to deal with what might otherwise be much more intractable political problems. That indeed seems to be the hope.

Whether that hope is well grounded, however, seems to depend on a number of assumptions about the workings of politics at both member-country and EU levels – assumptions that deserve to be disinterred. To put the point at its most generous, it is not entirely obvious that formation of the EU will do much in itself to solve the emerging fiscal problems of member countries.

3. Tax harmonization–tax competition once again: who gives the EU orchestra the A?

Giuseppe Eusepi*

1. INTRODUCTION

The introduction of a European fiscal constitution into the more general EU institutional design has spawned speculations on its potential impact. This chapter captures these speculations at the crossroads between fiscal harmonization and fiscal competition and addresses the impact of these two different approaches on the type of EU that will emerge. Therein lies the complex question of whether the EU will be reproducing the welfare states of the member countries on a larger scale, or rather the EU prefigured by the theorists of fiscal constitutionalism. With fiscal harmonization the EU is apt to face an ever-increasing fisc and a market in retreat. Conversely, fiscal competition is likely to lead eventually to an EU with a fisc in retreat and an ever-increasing market. Much of the extant discussion on this issue hopelessly muddles the two alternatives, so it is important to seek grounding in the schools of thought to which they belong: the tax harmonization approach is firmly fixed in the welfare economics philosophy, while the tax competition approach reflects the constitutional political economy philosophy. The former approach – henceforth orthodox approach (OA) – leads to fiscal centralization, the latter – henceforth constitutional approach (CA) – leads to fiscal competition and to the related efficiency and efficacy in production. Despite their opposite outcomes, the two approaches might be deemed to have a common origin in the Tiebout–Olson model. The reason why the two approaches reach opposite conclusions is due, among other things, to the different role assigned to externalities. Except for the case of dimensionally optimal jurisdictions, the OA approach is based on a presupposition that competitive interjurisdictional relationships give rise to permanent and increasing externalities. Although CA also argues that tax competition among jurisdictions may generate temporary externalities, it emphasizes that they tend to disappear in the long run. To CA, in fact, competition is a self-learning procedure and for that reason long-lasting externalities are a sign of too little competition rather than too much.

There were strong grounds for thinking that the contrasts between the two visions could be smoothed by testing empirically the two hypotheses. This would of necessity require that international institutions be comparable, but this is utterly impossible unless institutions are considered as homogeneous or models able to capture those differences are elaborated. And one of the reasons why contrasts between the two visions have not been solved can be attributed precisely to the fact that current models fail to capture those differences. Current models overlook too many details, which could prove to be of importance, due to the limits that mathematical tools impose. It is no wonder, then, that empirical works have not provided evidence that fiscal competition reduces governments' rents, as CA maintains.

There is yet another factor adding ambiguity to the problem. This has to do with the despot component of the benevolent despot paradigm. To some, the battle against the model of the benevolent dictator has been won; my theoretical scheme could thus be accused of being a caricature of the current debate just because most of the discussion here is devoted to this topic.

Deprecating CA's approach has become a widespread exercise, as the literature concerning the impact of fiscal constraints on governments' efficiency testifies. Akai and Sakata (2002) are among the few who provide evidence for a positive correlation between fiscal decentralization and economic growth. Conversely, Edwards and Keen (1996) have developed the argument that governments may reduce expenditures benefiting citizens without altering governments' rents. Although the authors engage in a sophisticated analysis with painstaking accuracy, it is a shame that they fail to see that governments' rents remain unaffected by expenditure cuts precisely because centralization reduces competition. This criticism is warranted on the basis of the Leviathan-type logic.[1] According to this view, tax centralization, under the guise of supporting local expenditures autonomy, in fact impedes the working of competition among the various levels of governments. As a result, fiscal autonomy is strongly limited by the transfer mechanism through which central governments cover a relevant fraction of the expenditures decided autonomously by local governments. The present decisional congestion in the EU depends on the lack of a formal constitution allowing for a separation between rules to be followed in constitutional decisions from those to be followed in ordinary political decisions.[2] The solution of this inconsistency would require:

1. The relinquishment of the unanimity principle on fiscal decisions, which would prompt member states to give up a share of competencies in favour of an EU government, which is a federal solution rather than a confederal one;
2. An appropriate or procedurally oriented fiscal constitution and not an outcome-oriented one (as is the case of the Maastricht Treaty, whose constraints can be easily circumvented just through tax harmonization).

2. A NEW TYPE OF POLITY

The EU is a unique political construction. It is not the federal solution adopted by the American colonies, with which they put a stop to their subjugation by England; nor does it in any way resemble the creation of nation-states with which some European countries solved their conflicts in the eighteenth and nineteenth centuries; nor finally is it like the so-called Soviet federal solution, whose peculiarity was the absence of democracy rather than federalism.

What nowadays is known as the EU was born as a superstate, perhaps with the United States of Europe in mind as a final institutional setting. Though the EU is highly developed in multiple areas, including currency, laws and justice, the EU is now no longer a superstate, nor yet a federal union. Unquestionably, some institutions and some procedures are fraught with incoherence compared with some standard paradigms, but one should not forget that the EU is a new kind of organization: instead of being a simple union among states that give rise to a nation, it is a union among states that were nations already and which are developing into an ever-increasing supranational organization.

The most contentiously debated subject within this union of nation-states is whether this union should have a new constitution, and above all a fiscal constitution. While there is a quasi-general consensus on having a new constitution, the idea of having a fiscal constitution finds widespread resistance.

In what follows I shall concentrate almost exclusively on the fiscal harmonization/fiscal constitution argument. The supporters of the OA approach argue that a fiscal constitution limiting the governments of the member states as well as the government of the Union would be detrimental or useless at the most, since to limit government action is equivalent to precluding the achievement of Pareto-superior welfare positions. It is on this claim that OA has chosen the fiscal harmonization option,[3] which is identified as one of the key challenges facing the EU. Constitutional political economists, who have espoused Wicksell's principles instead of Pigou's, have reacted against OA's mainstream by demonstrating that the logic of the so-called fiscal harmonization is coherent only if one accepts the benevolent despot paradigm[4].

But even in this formulation, a feasibility problem still remains and would involve effectiveness and efficiency problems. One of the primary propositions of OA is based on the ability-to-pay principle which, by espousing the Pigouvian principle, separates the two sides of the fiscal account[5]. This separation reveals its full inconsistency as soon as a realistic component is introduced into the scheme of a perfectly benevolent government. In this respect, CA insists, the benevolent despot paradigm is the Achilles' heel of OA.

3. THE GOVERNMENT AS A BENEVOLENT AGENT

To start with, let us leave aside the despot component of the benevolent despot paradigm and, following OA, conceive of government as a perfect maximizer of social welfare, behaving, also from the citizens' point of view, in an effective and efficient way thanks to an electoral system that works reasonably well and which keeps the government perfectly informed. Assume that the governments of the 15 member states that make up the EU fall within this scheme and that, as prescribed by the existing rules, they contribute to the EU budget on the basis of the country/EU's GNP[6]. In these conditions, it is clear that the governments of all member states would accomplish their fiscal duty towards the EU government and that all citizens would have their welfare maximized.

Let us now add a little realism to this, and assume that member countries apply different tax rates due to differences among them in terms of both economic growth and public/private mix[7]. It is OA's contention that if tax rates were harmonized there would be additional gains in terms of EU's welfare. This is not in the least true for CA. OA should specify how these advantages from adopting harmonization are achievable in a context where all governments of member states behave in a benevolent way.

Yet absurd as OA's construction is, let us accept by assumption that an increase in welfare is feasible through harmonization. Inasmuch as all 15 governments, though applying different tax rates, are perfectly benevolent and fully informed as well, how would the negotiation among governments leading to tax rate harmonization work? The relevant assumptions require that governments not only know citizens' demands perfectly, but are also interested in satisfying them in order to win re-election. In a nutshell, differences in tax rates are contingent upon the diversity in the demand mix public goods/market goods which different governments have to cope with. So interpreted, differences in tax rates might be viewed as resulting from differences in demands and the various benevolent governments simply respond in a way that is both effective and efficient. But if one admits, following OA, that additional advantages can be ensured by fiscal harmonization, only those governments that by pure chance applied a tax rate which is now adopted by all governments to harmonize could claim to be well informed and benevolent. It is patently clear that a conclusion of this sort is ultimately unrealistic. Yet, because of the existence of more options to reach a harmonized tax, it is likely, though not necessary, that the harmonized tax rate is the one used by the government that applies the highest tax rate (marginal government of the system). If so, CA argues, this solution bears with it a political cost in terms of loss of votes in all countries but the marginal one.

In sum, the more the individual government of a member country charged low rates before, the more it loses voting support now with harmonization. What seems important here is that none of the governments would lose tax base (no externality) due to harmonization: all effects coming from maximization would remain within the individual countries and would consist in an increase in fiscal economy towards market economy. The increase in fiscal economy is higher as soon as we move from marginal to inframarginal governments; the government that loses consensus most is of course the one that charged the lowest tax rates before harmonization. It is glaringly apparent that fiscal harmonization has an impact diametrically opposed to that which competition has on the market.

To clarify the analysis I shall develop a simplified example with two blocks of countries characterized by free movement of goods and factors of production, and taxation based on the origin principle, with governments operating within the institutional restraints of Maastricht.

Let us denote:

A all inframarginal countries;
B the marginal country;
a the tax rate applied in A;
b the tax rate applied in B, with $b > a$, where a and b represent the indirect taxation, in particular VAT;
X good produced by and exchanged between A and B.

The Orthodox or Tax Harmonization Approach

Let the governments of countries A and B begin to bargain in order to reach the harmonization of tax rates. Of course, each government is entitled either to refuse or to accept the terms of a negotiation according to its maximizing utility function, which can be expressed by:

$$U = u[G(t); t; \pm T],$$

where $G(t)$ is the public expenditure covered through taxation,

t is the tax rate decided by each government, $t = \{a, b\}$,

T are the transfers to compensate externalities involved in the bargaining process. Their being positive or negative depends on whether the government is a receiver or a payer.

$$\frac{\partial U}{\partial G} > 0$$

$$\frac{\partial U}{\partial t} < 0$$

$$\frac{\partial U}{\partial G}\frac{\partial G}{\partial t} + \frac{\partial U}{\partial t} = 0$$

$$\frac{\partial U}{\partial(-T)} < 0$$

$$\frac{\partial U}{\partial(+T)} > 0$$

On this ground country *A*'s government accepts to raise its tax rate since the resulting increase in yields is associated with an increase in government expenditures without any transfer to country *B*'s government. Country *B*'s government, in turn, accepts to keep its tax rates unchanged since *A*'s exports are lower, while *B*'s yields will certainly not decrease. Figure 3.1 illustrates this reasoning graphically.

With tax harmonization we shall have:

- consumers in country *B* who bought goods from country *A* now suffer an increase in the price of those goods caused by the harmonization of tax rates so their surplus is reduced;
- consumers in country *B* who bought the goods produced inside their country suffer a reduction in prices, because now domestic production increases;
- producers in *B* suffer *A*'s competition less due to fiscal differentials so their surplus increases;

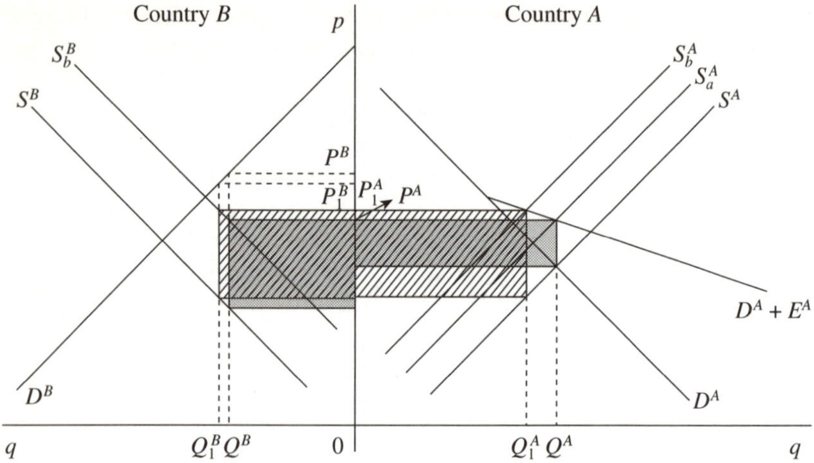

Yield of the governments before harmonization
Yield of the governments after harmonization
E Exports of country *A* to country *B*

Figure 3.1 The impact of tax harmonization on a two-country scheme

- country *B*'s government enjoys larger tax revenues due to an increase in domestic production;
- country *A*'s consumers suffer a higher price of all goods as a consequence of the increased taxation;
- Producers in *A* suffer a reduction of the surplus caused by the joint effect of the increased tax rate and the reduction in exports;
- country *A*'s government enjoys a higher yield from taxation.

Fiscal harmonization is not only incompatible with the voting motive of the CA approach, but, more important here, it also exposes the striking inconsistencies within OA – or at least the feasibility problems that OA faces.

In a supranational context, we face *different* voting systems that are supposedly optimal but nevertheless give rise to different tax rates that necessarily have to be harmonized. As I have indicated, the political process that is at stake with tax harmonization makes one think that the decisive government will be the dearest or marginal one. Furthermore, like CA, OA would not accept that the tax rate of inframarginal governments of member states should be decided by voters/government of the marginal country. Yet, once the harmonization solution has been adopted, it is quite likely that this will happen. On this logic it is the marginal government, not the median one, that is decisive precisely because all inframarginal governments are inclined to maximize their revenues on condition that they haven't to transfer revenues to the marginal government (a transfer that presumably would take place if the harmonized tax rate were that of the median government and not that of the marginal one). VAT harmonization that forbids rates 'not lower than' instead of forbidding rates 'not higher than' is supportive of the realism of this argumentation. Table 3.1 reports trends of VAT during the 1960s–2000s.

Table 3.1 The evolution of VAT rates applicable in the member states

Member state	Reduced rate	Standard rate	Increased rate	Parking rate
Belgium				
01/01/1971	6	18	25	14
01/01/1978	6	16	25	–
01/12/1980	6	16	25 | 25+5	–
01/07/1981	6	17	25 | 25+5	–
01/09/1981	6	17	25 | 25+8	–
01/03/1982	1 | 6	17	25 | 25+8	–
01/01/1983	1 | 6	19	25 | 25+8	17
01/04/1992	1 | 6 |12	19.5	–	–
01/01/1994	1 | 6 |12	20.5	–	12
01/01/1996	1 | 6 |12	21	–	12
01/01/2000	6	21	–	12
Denmark				
03/07/1967	–	10	–	–
01/04/1968	–	12.5	–	–
29/06/1970	–	15	–	–
29/09/1975	9.25	15	–	–
01/03/1976	–	15	–	–
03/10/1977	–	18	–	–
01/10/1978	–	20.25	–	–
30/06/1980	–	22	–	–
01/01/1992	–	25	–	–
Germany				
01/01/1968	5	10	–	–
01/07/1968	5.5	11	–	–
01/01/1978	6	12	–	–
01/07/1979	6	13	–	–

Table 3.1 (*continued*)

Member state	Reduced rate	Standard rate	Increased rate	Parking rate
01/07/1983	7	14	–	–
01/01/1993	7	15	–	–
01/04/1998	7	16	–	–
Greece				
01/01/1987	3 | 6	18	36	–
01/01/1988	3 | 6	16	36	–
28/04/1990	4 | 8	18	36	–
08/08/1992	4 | 8	18	–	–
Spain				
01/01/1986	6	12	33	–
01/01/1992	6	13	28	–
01/08/1992	6	15	28	–
01/01/1993	3 | 6	15	–	–
01/01/1995	4 | 7	16	–	–
France				
01/01/1968[a]	6	16.66	20	13
01/12/1968[a]	7	19	25	15
01/01/1970	7.5	23	33.33	17.6
01/01/1973	7	20	33.33	17.6
01/01/1977	7	17.6	33.33	–
01/07/1982[b]	4 | 5.5 | 7	18.6	33.33	–
01/01/1986	4 | 5.5 | 7	18.6	33.33	–
01/07/1986	2.1 | 4 | 5.5 | 7 | 13	18.6	33.33	–
17/09/1987	2.1 | 4 | 5.5 | 7 | 13	18.6	33.33	28
01/12/1988	2.1 | 4 | 5.5 | 7 | 13	18.6	28	–
01/01/1989	2.1 | 5.5 | 13	18.6	28	–
08/09/1989	2.1 | 5.5 | 13	18.6	25 | 28	–
01/01/1990	2.1 | 5.5 | 13	18.6	25	–
13/09/1990	2.1 | 5.5 | 13	18.6	22	–
29/07/1991	2.1 | 5.5	18.6	22	–
01/01/1993	2.1 | 5.5	18.6	–	–
01/08/1995	2.1 | 5.5	20.6	–	–
01/04/2000	2.1 | 5.5	19.6	–	–

[a] Up to 1/1/1970, the VAT rates were applicable to a price inclusive of VAT itself. As from 1/1/1970, the VAT rates apply to prices net of tax.
[b] 4% rate 1/7/1982 to 1/1/1986 was provisional.

Ireland				
01/11/1972	1 | 5.26	16.37	30.26	11.1
03/09/1973	1 | 6.75	19.5	36.75	11.1
01/03/1976	10	20	35 | 40	–
01/03/1979	1 | 10	20	–	–
01/05/1980	1 | 10	25	–	–
01/09/1981	1.5 | 15	25	–	28
01/05/1982	1.8 | 18	30	–	–
01/03/1983	2.3 | 5 | 18	35	–	–
01/05/1983	2 | 5 | 18	23 | 35	–	–
01/07/1983	2 | 5 | 8 | 18	23 | 35	–	–
01/05/1984	2.2 | 10	23 | 35	–	–
01/03/1985	2.4 | 10	23	–	–
01/03/1986	1.7 | 10	25	–	–
01/05/1987	1.4 | 5 | 10	25	–	–
01/03/1988	2 | 5 | 10	25	–	–
01/03/1989	2.3 | 10	25	–	–
01/03/1990	2.3 | 10 | 12.5	23	–	–
01/03/1991	2.7 | 10 | 12.5	21	–	–
01/03/1992	2.5 | 12.5	21	–	16
01/03/1993	2.8 | 12.5	21	–	12.5
01/01/1996	3.3 | 12.5	21	–	12.5
01/03/1997	3.6 | 12.5	21	–	12.5
01/03/1998	4 | 12.5	21	–	12.5
01/03/1999	1.2 | 12.5	21	–	12.5
01/03/2000	4.3 | 12.5	21	–	12.5
01/01/2001	4.3 | 12.5	20	–	12.5
01/03/2002	4.3 | 12.5	21	–	12.5
Italy				
01/01/1973	6	12	18	–
01/01/1975	6	12	30	18
18/03/1976	6	12	30	18
10/05/1976	6 | 9	12	30	18
23/12/1976	1 | 3 | 6 | 9	12	30	18
08/02/1977	1 | 3 | 6 | 9 | 12	14	35	18
03/07/1980	2 | 8	15	35	18
01/11/1980	1 | 2 | 3 | 6 | 9 | 12	14	35	15 | 18
01/01/1981	2 | 8	15	35	18
05/08/1982	2 | 8 | 10 | 15	18	38	20
19/04/1984	2 | 8 | 10 | 15	18	30 | 38	20
20/12/1984	2 | 9	18	30	–
01/08/1988	2 | 9	19	38	–
01/01/1989	4 | 9	19	38	–
13/05/1991	4 | 9 | 12	19	38	–
01/01/1993	4 | 9	19	–	12

Table 3.1 (continued)

Member state	Reduced rate	Standard rate	Increased rate	Parking rate
01/01/1994	4 | 9	19	–	13
24/02/1995	4 | 10	19	–	16
01/10/1997	4 | 10	20	–	–
Luxembourg				
01/01/1970	4	8	–	–
01/01/1971	2 | 5	10	–	–
01/07/1983	3 | 6	12	–	–
01/01/1992	3 | 6	15	–	–
01/10/1992	3 | 6	15	–	12
Netherlands				
01/01/1969	4	12	–	–
01/01/1971	4	14	–	–
01/01/1973	4	16	–	–
01/01/1976	4	18	–	–
01/01/1984	5	19	–	–
01/10/1986	6	20	–	–
01/01/1989	6	18.5	–	–
01/10/1992	6	17.5	–	–
01/01/2001	6	19	–	–
Austria				
01/01/1973	8	16	–	–
01/01/1976	8	18	–	–
01/01/1978	8	18	–	30
01/01/1981	13 | 8	18	–	30
01/01/1984	10	20	–	32
01/01/1992	10	20	–	–
01/01/1995	12 | 10	20	–	–
Portugal				
01/01/1986	8	16	30	–
01/02/1988	8	17	30	–
24/03/1992[a]	5	16	30	–
01/01/1995	5	17	–	–
01/07/1996	5 | 12	17	–	–
Finland				
01/06/1994	12 | 5	22	–	–
01/01/1995	17 | 12 | 6	22	–	–
01/01/1998	17 | 8	11	–	–

[a] On 24 March 1992 Portugal abolished the zero rate. All goods and services previously zero-rated are now taxed at 5%.

Sweden				
01/01/1969	6.38 | 2.04	11.11	–	–
01/01/1971	9.89 | 3.09	17.65	–	–
01/06/1977	11.43 | 3.54	20.63	–	–
08/09/1980	12.87 | 3.95	23.46	–	–
16/11/1981	11.88 | 3.67	21.51	–	–
01/01/1983	12.87 | 3.95	23.46	–	–
01/07/1990	13.64 | 4.17	23.46	–	25
01/01/1992	18	25	–	–
01/01/1993	18	25	–	–
01/07/1993	21 | 12	25	–	–
01/01/1996	6 | 12	25	–	–
United Kingdom				
01/04/1973	–	10	–	–
29/07/1974	–	8	–	–
18/11/1974	–	8	25	–
12/04/1976	–	8	12.5	–
18/06/1979	–	15	–	–
01/04/1991	–	17.5	–	–
01/04/1994	–	17.5	–	8
01/01/1995	8	17.5	–	–
01/09/1997	5	17.5	–	–

Source: 'Vat rates applied in the member states of the European Community', DOC/2908/2002 European Commission Directorate – General Taxation and Customs Union.

One finding is evident. With the exception of Finland, VAT has registered an increasing trend in all member countries. That my thesis rings true is supported by the fact that it is perfectly in line with the unanimity rule adopted in fiscal decisions. The choice of the median government, in fact, would assume a simple majority rule[8].

So far the analysis has focused almost exclusively on the tax side to which harmonization appeals, so let us now introduce the expenditure side in the European setting of the post-Maastricht Treaty where governments' fiscal behaviours are subdued to a sort of constitutional constraint in quantitative terms. Challenges still abound for Maastricht into the next years. To speak of an outcome-oriented constitutionalization that claims consistency with fiscal harmonization is like trying to nail five pounds of Jell-O to the wall with a 16-penny nail. And in fact, it is patently clear that the 3 per cent deficit/GNP requirement can be satisfied either by reducing expenditures *pro tanto* or by increasing tax rates *pro tanto*[9]. Of course, the two alternatives are not neutral for the EU governments. On the CA view, to cut expenditures in order to accomplish the 3 per cent requirement might not involve a shortage of public goods, as OA predicts, but simply a reduction in those political rents which bureaucracy misappropriates, thus channelling the resources available to market uses.

Conversely, the tax-rate increase option, on which harmonization is calibrated, involves the substitution of public expenditure for market solutions. Just because the two options are not neutral, governments will mostly operate through the tax side option, as already seen. As CA acknowledges, harmonization has nothing else to call on. The Maastricht imperative is that deficit spending must not exceed 3 per cent, but no limit to fully financed public expenditure is ever mentioned.

4. THE GOVERNMENT AS REVENUE MAXIMIZER AND THE FISCAL CONSTITUTION

Although *prima facie* there may appear to be contradictions between the assertions in the preceding section and the contents of this section, one should regard harmonization as a politico-bureaucratic prescription that works as an antidote to the exit option. Harmonization encourages the adoption of higher marginal rates and it is exactly these that impede reactions or the exit option as a way to remove tax bases from excessively burdensome governments.

Let us imagine that jurisdiction *A* reduces its tax rate on all goods and services, including those that are exported to jurisdiction *B*, thus competing with both producers and *B*'s government. Jurisdiction *A* can be considered equally well as either one of or even all inframarginal jurisdictions of the EU. In what sense does jurisdiction *A* harm jurisdiction *B* (the marginal one), as OA would contend? To be clearer, is it possible that the externality *A* gives rise to can be at the same time negative and positive for all the agents in *B*? The answer is no, unless jurisdiction *B* is viewed as a monolithic block. But since *B* is made up of agents with divergent interests, such as those among producers, consumers and the government, the external effects are certainly positive for *B*'s consumers; negative for *B*'s producers and, only on certain conditions, for *B*'s government. Again, to clarify the analysis let us go back to the two-block countries example.

The Constitutional Approach

Assuming that *B* reduces its tax rate from *b* to *a*, we may assume that a graphic representation looks as in Figure 3.2.

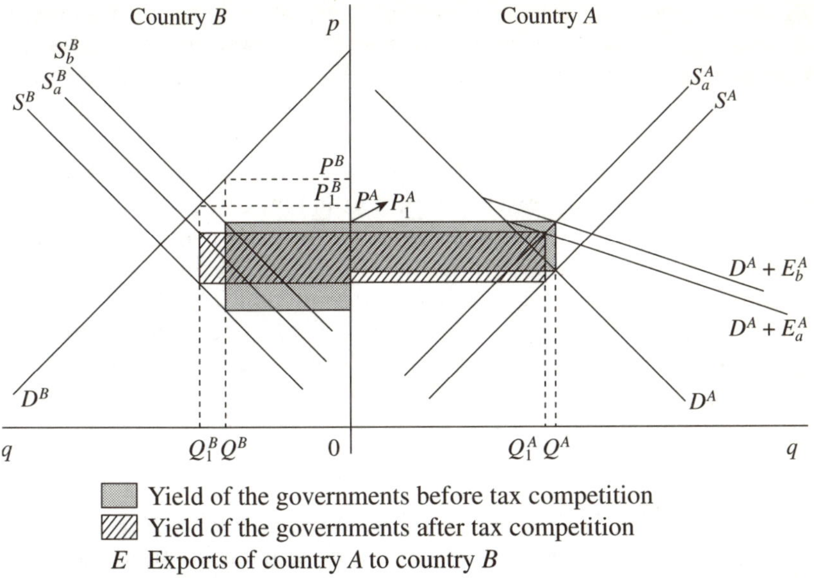

Figure 3.2 The impact of tax competition on a two-country scheme

With the introduction of tax competition we would have:

- consumers in country *B* enjoy a higher surplus because, as a consequence of a tax rate reduction, all prices go down;
- producers in country *B* increase their surplus because *B*'s imports fall;
- *B*'s tax yields decrease, though the loss is partly offset by an increase in the quantity of the goods produced internally;
- consumers in country *A* pay a lower price and so have a larger surplus;
- producers in *A* suffer a reduction in their exports;
- government has fewer resources because of the decrease in taxable domestic goods.

Hence the externality concept turns out to be somewhat ambivalent. As my example shows, to OA, externalities are either positive or negative according to whether the evaluating agents are the consumers, the producers, or *B*'s government. Of course, in a fiscal harmonization perspective, neither *A*'s nor *B*'s governments are entitled to reduce their tax rates. The obligation that *A* has to harmonize gives rise to externalities that are negative for

B's consumers (purchasers of the products exported by *A*), but would also damage *A*'s consumers, who could have paid a lower tax rate and hence lower prices. Fiscal harmonization, by impeding a government from lowering its tax rates, harms potential consumers who might have purchased goods from countries that *ceteris paribus* have more efficient governments.

Thus baldly summarized, fiscal harmonization or centralization seems to be advantageous for all governments: it would prevent governments from competing with each other over tax bases and would permit them to behave inefficiently. There is yet another factor pushing CA against harmonization. This has to do with the despot component omitted in the OA scheme which gives rise to adverse selection, and is a fitting demonstration of Gresham's law applied to governments: 'bad government drives out good'.

5. IMPLICATIONS

With the preceding reasoning in mind, let us see the implications in the EU context. Let us imagine that an agreement on fiscal harmonization has already been reached. This involves all governments using the same tax rate and possibly, also, the same procedure to calculate tax bases and even the same collection costs. Under these admittedly restrictive conditions, the OA pundits maintain that there wouldn't be distortions or externalities attributable to the fisc. According to CA, this is so because OA remains silent over the level of public expenditures and over the comparative burden of bureaucracies. If these two components are introduced into the analysis, CA points out, there must be serious doubts that harmonization represents a preferred position for EU citizens, who will certainly pay equal tax rates, but will not enjoy the same level of public goods. Such an arrangement leads to departures from the ideal model of maximization resulting in different tax prices or equal prices for services that differ in quantity and/or quality.

Clearly, the limits or margins implied in the OA approach are irretrievably spurious and hence completely different in nature compared to the limits in the CA approach. To clarify this requires that attention be paid to the despot component of the 'harmonizing' benevolent despot. Conceiving of a fully benevolent government as somebody who has to be constrained is unreasonable because one should incorporate the despot component within the OA logic. But under this condition tax harmonization would result in a decision made up of intergovernmental collusive relationships.[10] We may conclude, then, that harmonization is calibrated on the despot component rather than the benevolent one. The biggest obstacle to the understanding of what is involved in harmonization is that of oversimplification. That governments should be limited, and why the *quis custodiet* problem applies (see Brennan and Hamlin, 2000), is an obvious problem when viewed in CA terms, but it becomes even an extravagant one when viewed within the logic of the fully benevolent government advocated by OA, which is inclined to refer to the issues posed by harmonization as if they constituted only gains in welfare. According to this interpretation governments should fix the same tax rate via political negotiations among EU governments. The OA enthusiasts are overoptimistic about EU governments' ability to jockey the different countries into cooperating with each other to obtain efficient results. This solution would design an organization in which governments that are more efficient are not allowed to compete with the less efficient ones.

And, in fact, the fixing of the same tax rate via political negotiations among EU governments not only does not ensure that the results obtained are efficient, but rather ensures that those governments that are more efficient are unable to compete with the less efficient ones. This cannot be helped, for there is no way of forcing harmonization to fit in with the logic of limits and consequently with the fiscal constitution logic. The kinds of questions that CA regards as central to the EU taxation are those about the best way to limit fiscal decisions and not about the optimal tax rate to be fixed.

The federal standpoint, towards which the EU seems to be oriented, involves not only a divided political loyalty, but also a divided fiscal loyalty, which is incompatible with the harmonization approach. If there is to be a constitution for the EU (and with the entry of other countries the need for it becomes all the greater), then it has to be a fiscal constitution. This would eliminate the myth of citizenship rights viewed as corresponding to an equal level of public goods and services. If this myth remains, a solution to the problems that presently block decisions is unlikely to be found.

In section 3 it was argued that underlying the tax harmonization philosophy was the hypothesis of the state as a Leviathan, and the watershed between OA and CA is precisely here. In a tax harmonization context, political decisions are tailored according to politico-bureaucratic or supply-led incentives, which are much more pervasive than the signals coming from citizens' demand. The result is an upward alignment of the tax rate that involves a large portion of public economy compared to market economy.

Some commentators (for example Blankart and Neumann, 1999) have recommended replacing the current contribution mechanism from member countries with a direct EU tax. They argue that this would eliminate the necessity for the current veto power, without any risk to member states, provided that the EU's direct tax be subject to unanimity. A related issue concerns the role that constitutional binds could play in ensuring the proper institutional structure underlying a fiscal system made up of competing governments. Against tax competition persistent and even increasing ideological barriers are still at work owing to the interest that national governments and their oversized bureaucracies have in keeping their exclusive taxing power as long as they can. CA, with its emphasis on the demand side, is more interested in signals coming from citizens than in those coming from politicians and bureaucrats. Once all governments are bound by a fiscal constitution, CA maintains, the most efficient government will have to supply public goods at the lowest tax price. The most efficient government is that which ensures a given standard of services by charging the lowest tax prices. In contrast, OA criticizes CA's failure to consider the equity issue, which seems an ill-addressed charge. In fact, CA sets out to separate the role of guarantee or equity – understood as fiscal rights and obligations fixed by the constitution – from the provision of public goods and services that belongs to the government, whose distinctive element is the tax price the government requires. Since CA ascribes evaluation to citizens rather than to governments and bureaucrats, the right mix of equity and efficiency is apt to be optimized. In this sense, competition is a disciplining, not a destructive, institution for governments[11]. Truth to tell, a destructive effect would take place if governments were to compete by resorting to dumping, in the same manner as private enterprises sometimes do with the aim of impeding new firms from entering a certain market. Given the balanced budget provision, this would hardly happen because tax dumping would involve a budget deficit. Thus, tax competition may yield a downward alignment of tax rates through subsequent adjustments and not via bureaucratic decisions, whereas with harmonization the alignment would occur upward. The two alignments are radically different and mimic the logic of price in a competing market *vis-à-vis* the monopoly price. On this point the watershed between CA and OA is less dramatic: neither of them maintains that a price resulting from competition is unjust; it is simply a price that cannot be fixed *ex ante* by the government to its advantage. Yet harmonization has gone in the opposite direction, concerning itself more with relationships among governments than with those between government and citizens. By offering a supply-side solution it overlooks citizens' demands in favour of the interests of both bureaucracy and politicians. This entails an enlargement of government economy compared to market economy. CA would contend that harmonization classifies as unjust in that it is a monopoly price. By embodying in the harmonization device extravagant justice claims, OA has found a way to give appearance of benevolent to a government that is a monopolist. A pure benevolent government cannot be unjust by definition.

If we extend the exchange logic to the relationship between governments and governed, as CA does, the tax price will emerge on a quasi-contractual basis. The government must not have the power to determine the rate unilaterally,[12] much as in contracts a single party is prevented from determining the conditions that regulate the relationships between the two parties. The quasi-contractual or competitive procedure puts together the two sides of the fiscal account through a simultaneous single act consisting of an expenditure proposal and the related covering instrument. CA views this Wicksellian-like arrangement, at least *lato sensu*, as fostering contractual capabilities.

Another lingering concern behind tax harmonization involves the principles of taxation. Tax harmonization is the result of a unilateral decision taken by governments that compute tax rates on the citizens' ability-to-pay principle. One striking shortfall of this pattern is that it is completely divorced from the expenditure side since public expenditure is not perceived as a 'countervalue'. Conversely, tax competition is based on the benefit principle, so that tax prices can be viewed as an exchange between taxpayers and government[13].

Thus far, I have primarily focused on goods exchange. For completeness, I shall briefly focus on the taxation of capital income. Let us suppose an EU fiscal constitution providing limitations to governments that can tax according to their own best judgement yet with an eye toward the ballot box in order to be re-elected in the next election, say in two years[14], and let us see what happens to jurisdictions *A* and *B* in the preceding example. Differently from above, let us consider taxation of capital incomes that are more sensitive than goods to fiscal differentials. If *A*'s government decides to lower taxation on capital income that before was harmonized (see CEPR, 1993), surely a certain amount of capital would flow to jurisdiction *A* from jurisdiction *B*, with *B*'s government losing tax base. To compensate the shortage in revenues, *B*'s government must increase taxation over less mobile goods, namely domestically consumed ones. Such a scenario, according to OA, would increase distortions in *B*, which would not have occurred within the harmonization paradigm. To OA, thus, introducing competition is equivalent to creating externalities. CA counter-argues that the increase in distortions in jurisdiction *B* is instead a result of the decision taken by the government to keep public expenditure unaffected.

6. CONCLUSIONS

This chapter has attempted to demonstrate the sorts of contribution which a fiscal constitution can make to the particularly troubled area of taxation.

It has focused on the questions which are posed by harmonization while indicating the appeal that tax competition has.

Whoever attempts to introduce an alternative to existing institutions has necessarily to take up a clear-cut position, if he hopes to say anything to the point. Lest my exposition be thought at odds with my avowed intentions, let me summarize the contrasts between OA and CA as follows:

1. Would tax rate harmonization cancel fiscal discriminations (externalities), as OA argues, or would it rather introduce them, as CA counterargues?
2. If tax harmonization really corrected externalities, as OA contends, why shouldn't public expenditures and regulations also be harmonized, so that there would be fiscal neutrality for the citizen quite independently of the member country he decides to live in?
3. Why should the best solution for the taxpayer be the one that makes all governments neutral to him? And more generally, why shouldn't a citizen build human attachments with persons and things in the place where he lives and decides to stay on even in the presence of likely small tax differentials?[15] And finally,
4. For what reason should a government that follows the harmonization logic behave in a more efficient and effective way compared to another that has to choose within constitutional constraints?

NOTES

* My thanks to Alessandra Cepparulo for her assistance with data collection and for providing advice on figures.

1. See Brennan and Buchanan (1980); Feld and Kirchgässner (2001). For a survey see Kirchgässner (2002).
2. See Buchanan and Tullock (1962) and de Jasay (1996).
3. A systematic treatment of the orthodox position that goes back to Pigou can be found in Dahlby (1996).
4. A classical book on this point is still Brennan and Buchanan (1980).
5. For this reason all the margins, which, according to the welfare economists should be equalized, are spurious; consequently the corrective intervention by the government would be even more distorting and would be so even in a minimal state context. On the latter point see Kliemt (1993); for a general treatment of the Pigouvian margins see Buchanan (1969), chs 4–5.
6. For a reappraisal of the contribution method in financing the federal government, see Sobel (1999) and the literature quoted therein.
7. I use tax share as a proxy for public/private mix.
8. See Tsebelis and Garrett (1997).
9. Cutting expenditures could involve a reduction in services while government's political rent remains unaffected. On this see Edwards and Keen (1996).
10. Cf. Frey and Eichenberger (1999) and for a more general perspective Brennan and Eusepi (2000).

11. McGuire (1991) supports the destructive role of fiscal competition because her reasoning does not consider the role played by constitutional rules. At any rate her reasoning refers to relationships among local governments and therefore cannot be extended to the relationships among national governments and *a fortiori* to the relationships that national govenments have with a supranational government such as the EU.
12. Of course, the breaching of the contract might still be a consensual agreement. For a general discussion see Eusepi (2002).
13. Brennan and Eusepi (2000) suggest that rather than of exchange, one should talk of trust. This is fully correct and realistic, but it does not invalidate the argumentation in the text. See also Brennan and Lomasky (1993).
14. In the text a four-year term is implicitly assumed. Hence, at half-term the government takes resolutions neither under the pressure of an immediate voting motive, nor with the aim of gaining a trust credit over the government that has been defeated in the last election. Beginning and ending terms have been omitted because in both circumstances governments might even try to circumvent constitutional provisions – namely budget constraints – by resorting to accounting manoeuvres as the after Maastricht events have confirmed *ad abundantiam*.
15. This can be explained by referring to the concept of locational surplus (see Grewal, 1988).

REFERENCES

Akai, N. and M. Sakata (2002), 'Fiscal Decentralization Contributes to Economic Growth: Evidence from State-level Cross-section Data for the United States', *Journal of Urban Economics*, **52**, 93–108.

Blankart, C.B. and M.J. Neumann (1999), 'Financing the European Union: a constitutional approach', typescript.

Brennan, Geoffrey and James M. Buchanan (1980), *The Power to Tax*, Cambridge, UK and New York, USA: Cambridge University Press.

Brennan, Geoffrey and Loren Lomasky (1993), *Democracy and Decision. The Pure Theory of Electoral Preference*, Cambridge, UK and New York, USA: Cambridge University Press.

Brennan, G. and G. Eusepi (2000), 'Hobbesian and contractarian constitutions', typescript.

Brennan, Geoffrey and Alan Hamlin (2000), 'Nationalism and federalism: the political constitution of peace', in Gianluigi Galeotti, Pierre Salmon and Ronald Wintrobe (eds), *Competition and Structure: The Political Economy of Collective Decisions: Essays in Honor of Albert Breton*, Cambridge, UK and New York, USA: Cambridge University Press, pp. 259–83.

Buchanan, James M. (1969), *Cost and Choice: An Inquiry in Economic Theory*, Chicago: Markham.

Buchanan, James M. and Gordon Tullock (1962), *The Calculus of Consent*, Ann Arbor: University of Michigan Press.

CEPR (1993), *Making Sense of Subsidiarity: How Much Centralization for Europe?*, Monitoring European Integration 4.

Dahlby, B. (1996), 'Fiscal Externalities and the Design of Intergovernmental Grants', *International Tax and Public Finance*, **3**, 397–412.

De Jasay, Anthony (1996), 'Before resorting to politics', in Charles K. Rowley (ed.), *The Political Economy of the Minimal State*, Cheltenham, UK and Brookfield, USA: Edward Elgar, pp. 5-v–5-71.

Edwards, J. and M. Keen (1996), 'Tax Competition and Leviathan', *European Economic Review*, **40**, 113–34.

Eusepi, Giuseppe (2002), 'The calculus of dissent: Constitutional completion and public goods', in Geoffrey Brennan, Hartmut Kliemt and Robert D. Tollison (eds), *Method and Morals in Constitutional Economics. Essays in Honor of James M. Buchanan*, Berlin: Springer-Verlag.

Feld, L.P. and G. Kirchgässner (2001), 'Does Direct Democracy Reduce Public Debt? Evidence from Swiss Municipalities', *Public Choice*, **109**, 347–70.

Frey, Bruno S. and Reiner Eichenberger (1999), *The New Democratic Federalism for Europe. Functional Overlapping and Competing Jurisdictions*, Cheltenham, UK and Northampton, MA, USA: Edward Elgar.

Grewal, Bhajan S. (1988), 'Locational surplus and its relevance for subnational taxation and inter-governmental grants in a federation', in Geoffrey Brennan, Bhajan S. Grewal and Peter Groenewegen (eds), *Taxation and Fiscal Federalism. Essays in Honour of Russell Mathews*, Canberra: Australian National University Press.

Kirchgässner, Gebhard (2002), 'The effects of fiscal institutions on public finance: a survey of the empirical evidence', in Stanley L. Winer and Hirofumi Shibata (eds), *Political Economy and Public Finance*, Cheltenham, UK and Northampton, MA, USA: Edward Elgar.

Kliemt, H. (1993), 'On Justifying a Minimum Welfare State', *Constitutional Political Economy*, **4**, (2), Spring/Summer, 159–72.

McGuire, Therese J. (1991), 'Federal aid to states and localities and the appropriate competitive framework', in Daphne A. Kenyon and John Kincaid (eds), *Competition among States and Local Governments*, Washington, DC: The Urban Institute, pp. 153–66.

Sobel, R.S. (1999), 'In Defense of the Articles of Confederation and the Contribution Mechanism as a Means of Government Finance: A General Comment on the Literature', *Public Choice*, June, 347–56.

Tsebelis, George and Geoffrey Garrett (1997), 'Why power indices cannot explain decision-making in the European Union', in Dieter Schmidtchen and Robert Cooter, *Constitutional Law and Economics of the European Union*, Cheltenham, UK and Lyme, USA: Edward Elgar.

COMMENT

Giuseppe Vitaletti

Eusepi's thesis is that the present EU approach of tax harmonization through intergovernmental agreements between nation-states lays the groundwork for the inevitable establishment of an oversized, uniform public sector with the usual undesirable side-effects of crowding-out of the market, proliferating bureaucratic rents from monopolistic management of the state, and the fiscal Leviathan under the false pretence of maintaining social rights and welfare. Instead he calls for a constitutional approach setting a ceiling on tax revenues as the premise to a streamlined state, a flourishing market, limited bureaucratic rents thanks to competition between administrations, and thus, in the final analysis, reinforced democracy.

I agree on the adverse repercussions of tax harmonization and the likely tendency to convergence on the marginal state, that is, at the highest prevailing tax rates. My main perplexity concerns the adequacy of the arrangements that would be produced by the constitutional approach as formulated in Eusepi's chapter, namely the setting of tax ceilings. This approach may in fact entail the setting of very narrow differentials in tax rates on the various items, putting the centre of gravity below present standards while safeguarding certain distributive equilibria. On this hypothesis it is possible (but not certain) that bureaucratic rents would be cut and that administrations would be more sensitive to the principle of 'value for money' for users and taxpayers. In any event, national independence in decision making would be gravely compromised just as a situation emerged (namely, acceptable efficiency of the public administration) that could prompt voters to make increased, and highly differentiated, demands for public services. For example, the demand might be for joint services to businesses, in countries where small firms predominate; or for pay-as-you-go pension provisions in countries where the stock markets are least reliable; for health care, education or other local public goods, in countries that elect to foster the powers of local government.

As an alternative, tax ceilings could take the form of a limit on total tax revenue or, in more diversified fashion, maximum tax rates for specific types of income or wealth. This would attenuate the force of the critique of 'uniformity', even though the crucial ban on going above the ceiling would remain. Yet one cannot help observing that given free-riding by the holders of mobile incomes, the public sector dimension desired by the majority of voters may be unsustainable, or sustainable only at the cost of severe distortions of the tax structure (overtaxation of less mobile incomes).

Moreover, assuming unrestricted downward fiscal competition in the context of the single currency, taxpayer free-riding can easily be wedded to attempts at fiscal dumping on the part of individual states. For regardless of the level of public spending, they can direct taxation above all to consumption, so that production taxes are lower than the value of the public services to producers.

However, the foregoing criticism does not invalidate the constitutional approach, whose fundamental idea is sound: making tax arrangements depend on 'basic institutions' rather than 'day-by-day' decisions, with attention to procedures rather than to the content of individual measures. Research on the matter should go further into the concept of tax price. Eusepi uses the notion to endorse the kind of public sector that emerges under the constraint of tax competition and limited resources, because competition implies the need for efficiency in order to gain electoral consensus, which would be accorded depending on the results achieved by different public administrations providing similar services.

In Italian public finance economics the concept of tax-price as used by its principal spokesman, De Viti de Marco, also carries other connotations. First of all, it designates a preference for a tax base that is a good indicator of the public services that taxpayers receive. In complex, diversified economies and administrations like those of any modern country, a natural further implication designed for the greatest possible transparency is the need to define macro-areas for the private sector and for public services and to institute specified financial relations between them.

An obvious way of proceeding is to distinguish, within the private economy, the three moments of production, income distribution, and final demand, the last dominated, especially in the long run, by the consumption component. Moreover, it is now standard practice in all the advanced countries to divide public services into central government, social security institutions and local government. The first mainly provides services to production (economic and regulatory policy, major infrastructure, and certainly a good part of expenditure on justice, law and order, and foreign policy); the second mainly serves the dominant component of distributed incomes, namely salaries and self-employment; and the third is clearly dominated by services relating to taxpayers' social life (health care, education, environment, local infrastructure), one of whose most important aspects is consumption.

Therefore, a natural coupling of the tax base to segments of public spending would be: (1) taxation of the added value on the production side (tending to take over corporate income tax and social security taxes on payroll employment), with most of the revenue going to the central government and the rest to local government; (2) taxation of consumption as VAT under rules permitting most of the revenue to go to local government and a smaller part to central government departments; and (3) allocation of the proceeds of individual income tax to social security institutions, where the portion of revenue deriving from non-labour income would make explicit and transparent the social solidarity transfer towards labour incomes. (As an alternative, given that at least in Europe labour now accounts for virtually all personal income tax revenue, solidarity could be provided by transfers from central and local government out of their own tax revenues.)

There is no impediment, technical or in principle, to such a transformation. The tax bases, while becoming subject to price taxes (the benefit principle), would continue to be those now in effect (production, income, consumption), and would thus conform to the ability-to-pay principle. Many different production taxes are already in being (in Italy, for example, the regional tax on productive activities), and in the proposed new framework it would be easy to extend them. Personal income tax is already becoming, in practice, a tax on labour incomes only, which is devastating for the present tax system but would be easily compatible with the proposed new approach. As for consumption taxes, the economic literature has devised mechanisms, in the case of VAT too, that permit decentralization and geographical flexibility of revenue.

This is not the proper place for a discussion of other aspects of the tax-price approach. It should at least be pointed out that in an international framework this approach would require a constitutional phase to guarantee: (a) the coupling by all countries of the ability-to-pay principle with the benefit principle; (b) the common criteria for estimating the proportional allotment between production and social life of services furnished by central and local government that have effects on both simultaneously; and (c) on this basis, the ceilings on transfers between sectors (for example, those in favour of social security). However, each country would retain full freedom of action on tax rates, hence on the overall dimensions and organization of the public sector. Efficiency would be assured by transparency, accountability and competition, perhaps even more so than in Eusepi's vision. But the arrangements suggested here would promote not only efficiency but also the freedom of the individual member states, and specifically the liberty to provide for different total size and composition of the public sector, in line with the wishes of their different electorates.

4. The political economy of regulation: a prolegomenon

Geoffrey Brennan

1. BACKGROUND

The point of departure for the current chapter can be said to consist of five Ps: a perception; a proposition; two predictions; and a prejudice.

The perception is that in virtually all Western economies over the last 30 years tax dollars have become increasingly scarce. What I mean by this observation is that the political price of increased taxes has risen. Or to put the same point in equivalent terms, the political rewards from reduced taxes are now greater than they were, relative to alternative political actions, of which spending increases and debt are the two most notable. The reasons for this development are various. It partly reflects independent shifts in political theorizing at the academic level, partly changes in the marginal excess burdens of taxation associated with reduced tax compliance and scope for avoidance activities, and partly a general increased scepticism about what the public sector can deliver. These various factors are, of course, reflected in shifts in what passes as prevailing ideology. Pretty well all parties of whatever stripe have moved somewhat 'to the right' in relation to fiscal matters. And this move has, among other things, placed the fiscal system under considerable pressure: tax dollars have become increasingly scarce.

The first prediction is that this pressure on the fisc will intensify. My grounds for believing so are not based on predictions of shifts in public opinion as such. I have no crystal ball on public opinion. However, it does seem likely that there will be continued erosion of tax bases associated in part with increased globalization. Capital – including human capital – is likely to become yet more mobile internationally, making it harder and harder to tax. And it will become more and more difficult to make up the lost revenue elsewhere, because as tax revenue on a shrinking base rises, marginal excess burdens and incentives to evade tax altogether also tend to increase. At the same time, increases in quasi-contractual commitments under underfunded public retirement schemes mean that revenue available for discretionary purposes will decline. A shrinking tax capacity combined with an expanding social security commitment is a sure recipe for increased fiscal pressure.

The proposition is that, at least as a first approximation, regulation and fiscal operations represent roughly equivalent ways of securing policy objectives. More specifically, any given regulation is equivalent in its effects to *some* tax/expenditure operation, although to achieve equivalence might require that different individuals face different tax rates. To put the central point better, we can think of budgetary operations and regulation as alternative technologies for the securing of particular policy objectives. So, for example, a particular level of environmental improvement can be achieved either via a subsidy for pollution abatement activities or via a legal restriction on effluent release. A certain level of individual security against industrial accident or disability can be provided either through a publicly funded government scheme or via a regulation that requires all individuals to acquire insurance coverage. A particular level of educational attainment might be secured by subsidized education (possibly provision of publicly funded schools) or by a regulation that requires all individuals to attend school up to a certain age. In all these cases, the regulatory outcome and the budgetary alternative will differ in significant ways. But their aggregate effect in many cases will be quite similar – similar enough, in any event, to justify the thought that the broad policy objective involved is the same.

This is a point familiar to those who make international comparisons of public sector size (or public sector growth rates). It is widely recognized that the level of government 'intervention' in the economy can be very considerable even where formal tax rates are low. For example, the Australian public sector appears small in part because much of its social welfare, including retirement support and industrial accident insurance, is provided via compulsory 'private insurance' and superannuation contributions rather than via a publicly funded scheme. Australia achieves by regulation what most other countries achieve via direct government provision. The aggregate level of insurance cover might well be more or less the same in Australia as elsewhere, despite the fact that the apparent 'size' of the public sector seems very different. Whether government provides n units of a good free to all or whether it passes a law that requires everyone to acquire n units, the objective of securing a given level of overall consumption will be met. This means that measuring the economic impact of public sector activities by the share of GDP that goes through the public sector can be deeply misleading. This is a point that is widely acknowledged in principle in undertaking international comparisons or time series analysis of public activity, though it is more acknowledged in theory than in practice. When large-scale empirical exercises that involve inter-country comparisons of 'government activities' are undertaken, aggregate tax levels or expenditure levels are usually wheeled out, as if these measures did indeed tell us what we want to know.

The three foregoing 'ps' – the perception, the prediction and the proposition – taken together, imply that in periods of fiscal pressure, we ought to expect more extensive reliance on policy instruments that are 'revenue-saving' or 'revenue-neutral' compared with policy instruments that are revenue-using. In particular, we ought to expect greater reliance on regulation. This is the fourth 'p' – the second prediction. It is that, over the next 20 or 30 years, there will be considerable increased pressure to substitute regulatory for budgetary instruments.

Finally, the prejudice. I believe that any such shift in policy technology is in general a bad thing, that is, that other things equal, budgetary measures are to be preferred to regulatory ones as a method of securing public policy objectives. I have referred to this belief as a prejudice, however, because it is neither an obvious nor a professionally well-established claim. On the other hand, it is a claim that I think most public finance scholars would be inclined to support, without necessarily having done much serious thinking about it. More personally, it is a claim that I find myself intuitively inclined to accept – without ever having done the kind of conceptual or empirical work required to establish that the claim is well grounded.

This brings me to the object of the project of which this chapter is a part. My general aim in this project is to interrogate the prejudice. Simply put, is it the case that substituting a regulatory for a budgetary technology in the securing of policy objectives is a bad thing? Or, more generally, what are the pros and cons of any such substitution?

It should perhaps be emphasized that this line of enquiry – this final 'p' – would remain interesting, even if the four earlier 'ps' were false. Accordingly, I am not going to try to defend those earlier claims here. I mention them to explain my motivation; they are not a key part of the basic argument. Nevertheless, I believe that the issues at stake in evaluating regulation as a means of delivering policy outcomes are indeed more significant now than they have been in the past, and will become yet more significant in the next few decades.

While dealing with motivational aspects, I should also mention one final consideration. My interest in what may loosely be called the 'political economy of regulation' arises, in part, out of a personal desire to contribute to a very much larger enterprise currently being pursued within the Research School of which I am a member. This enterprise, under the banner REGNET, aims to deal with regulation in all its guises. The REGNET project is presided over by a criminologist and is expressly multidisciplinary in its ambitions. However, the main players so far have been lawyers, criminologists and sociologists: the contribution from economists to this point has been small and primarily focused on that part of the regulatory system that deals with 'economic issues', rather narrowly conceived. These more focused economic issues are, of course, entirely worthy of exploration. They include the usual suspects: competition policy; the regulation of 'privatized' public monopolies; and some aspects of tax compliance. There is, however, also scope for an 'economic enquiry' of a broader kind – one that aims to develop an economic account of regulation *tout court*. It is just such a broader economic account that I would like to contribute.

2. THE GENERAL SHAPE OF THE EXERCISE

The purpose of this chapter is as much to lay out the broad shape of the enquiry as to deliver substantive results. I shall develop one specific line of enquiry in the final section. First, however, I want to underline certain aspects of the approach I will be taking; and try to indicate some planned lines of attack that I intend to pursue in the broader exercise but will not be developing in this chapter.

Compared to What?

There is a substantial literature on the 'economics of regulation' that comes mainly out of the Chicago school of industrial organization (see, for example, Stigler, 1971; Peltzman, 1976 and so on). This literature is relevant to my concerns here but has a rather different focus. Essentially, the question at issue in that literature is whether regulation can plausibly be explained by reference to 'public interest' considerations – understood in terms of the policy objective outlined in the political rhetoric that putatively justifies the regulation. The claim is that a better explanation lies in the interests of the bodies subject to regulation. The point of departure in this literature is that regulation typically serves to redistribute income from consumers of the regulated product to producers (occasionally from producers to consumers). So much follows from standard economic analysis of markets. The further, more contentious claim is that this redistribution serves to explain the existence and/or maintenance of the regulation. In other words, the redistributional consequences of the regulation are not merely an incidental result of the policy, but a critical feature of any proper explanation.

The central implication of this line of analysis seems to be that regulation is just after all a tool for redistributive politics; and that the policy rationales offered for regulations are therefore not to be taken at face value. Implicitly, the regulatory regime is being compared with a *laissez-faire*, zero-regulation alternative. And since the redistributions that are the central causal feature of the regulations in place are not themselves normatively justified, a zero-regulation regime is to be preferred. In fact, no such conclusion necessarily follows. Even if all regulations were implemented to secure particular redistributions to powerful political groups, it could still be the case that the availability of a plausible rhetorical defence operates as a crucial constraint in most instances. In that event, even if the redistributions were the primary motivating factor for the key policy-determining players, the policy goal would still be an (explanatorily) incidental by-product of the regulation. There seems to be an assumption implicit in this argument that there is an infinite supply of rhetorically plausible defences available for any regulation that meets the relevant redistributive test. But a more plausible line would surely be that both considerations are in operation. To be sure, the conclusion would be that many regulations that might in principle be desirable would not be implemented because they failed to redistribute in a politically relevant manner. But equally, many politically expedient redistributions would never be implemented because no tolerably persuasive normative defence for the regulation that secures them can be found. If this were so, then the zero-regulation regime could well be worse than the prevailing one: virtually every regulation would have a normative defence, even if it were true that normative defence could not adequately explain the regulation's presence.

In any event, in the framework I shall assume, I shall be deliberately finessing the issue of the desirability of the policy objective. The comparison I want to foreground is that in which the stated policy objective is secured by fiscal as distinct from regulatory means. I shall still want to include broad political economy/'public choice theory' elements in the analysis. The redistributions that occur when tax-expenditure operations are replaced by regulatory ones will remain an important consideration in the broad explanatory scheme. However, other considerations will also play a role. Moreover, I shall be interested, among other things, in the effects that the choice of policy technology has on the extent to which various policy objectives are pursued. Throughout, the basic comparator in evaluating regulation will be an appropriate fiscal 'equivalent'. The 'equivalence' in question is in inverted commas because that equivalence will be only approximate. Just how approximate, and what is at stake in the approximations in question, are of course precisely the objects of analysis in my conceived project.

One further aspect of the comparative approach should be emphasized. This is that the comparison occurs 'at the margin', as we might put it. That is, I shall not be concerned here with more cosmic questions as to whether a 'regulation-free' regime is imaginable, or whether fiscal operations might substitute for all regulations whatever their domain or scope. These are issues that cannot be entirely avoided when one attempts to develop measures of the extent of regulation, or an analysis of regulation *tout court*. However, I hope to be able to finesse them here by focusing just on those cases where substitution appears most natural.

In particular, I want to avoid the charge that my approach involves an implicit claim of 'rough equivalence' between a law against murder and a subsidy to refrain from murder. Perhaps these measures might in principle affect the murder rate in the same direction – but this is not the kind of substitution I have in mind. But as we move from the murder case to, say, the case of drug policy, the issue comes less clear. We can certainly imagine the goal of minimizing substance abuse being pursued through various fiscal means (of which taxation is the most obvious). And when we get to issues like environmental regulation, or late secondary education, the idea of fiscal/regulatory substitution seems yet more plausible. Precisely what is at stake in distinguishing those cases where scope for fiscal/regulatory substitution is highest from those where it is lowest is an important and relevant question. But it is one that I intend to abstract from here.

Macro versus Micro

There are two broad approaches possible in effecting the fiscal/regulatory comparison. These can be broadly characterized as 'macro' and 'micro' respectively.

The macro approach involves examining international comparisons involving large samples of countries. The method would involve comparing the effects of heavy regulation and large public spending shares respectively on parameters that might be construed as normatively significant. So, for example, we attempt to explain rates of growth, or per capita levels of GDP, or the distribution of income, or measured 'freedom', or measured levels of corruption, or whatever, in terms that include the extent of regulation. This method is not the one that I shall be pursuing here; but the general thrust of the results should be noted. For example, it appears that in explaining differential GDP growth rates, public sector share (whether measured on the taxation or the spending side) tends to be either not significant at all or of relatively small explanatory power, whereas regulation levels tend to be significantly negatively related to GDP growth, and to have non-negligible explanatory power.

In some suggestive preliminary work, Waterman (2003) has matched information from comparative international rankings of corruption with the international Economic Freedom Index (Gwartney and Lawson et al., 2002). His results suggest that there is virtually no relation between corruption and public sector size (with the latter as measured in the Economic Freedom Index), but that there is a quite high positive relation between corruption and regulation.

In short, the empirical evidence at the macro level does suggest that the substitution of regulatory for budgetary technology in the delivery of policy outcomes has undesirable effects – presuming, that is, that higher growth rates and lower corruption levels are desirable things. The macro approach does not, of course, provide any economic explanation of why these relations between regulation and lower growth/higher corruption prevail. It does provide *prima facie* evidence that there is something to the public economist's prejudice. But explaining why such relationships are plausible depends on a finer-grained microeconomic analysis. And it is that kind of analysis that the resources of conventional public economics are best equipped to provide.

Micro – Public Finance and Public Choice

The micro account of the choice between regulation and budgetary measures takes as its point of departure the implications of the two instruments for individual choice. The general context for choice needs of course to be specified, but the ambition would be to do this in terms that are as broad as possible. So consider a familiar case. Pigou's smoke-emitting factories are pouring dirt onto the washing of nearby laundries. The amount of smoke so emitted is larger than would be emitted if the factories and the laundries were owned by the same entrepreneur. Or (more or less equivalently), smoke emissions are larger than if the resource 'clean air' were priced, so that laundries and factories had to pay to get the services that clean air provides. There is in other words an 'externality' involved here. The output of the factories will be too large and that of laundries too small *vis-à-vis* the notional optimum. There are significant problems at stake in knowing what the optimal level of air-cleanliness is in such cases and/or whether better solutions to the problem might be found by one of the parties moving or via some other adjustment. But let us suppose that the policy solution found is to moderate the output of smoke from the factories. The question of interest here is how this might be done. In particular we want to examine three possible alternatives: a tax on smoke output; a direct regulation that would specify the amount of smoke emission permitted; or a subsidy for smoke reduction. And we stipulate, as part of the analytical framework, that the amount of smoke emitted in the wake of the policy is the same in each case.

The standard analysis here would involve the derivation of the equilibrium in each case, and specifically the distributive effects of the various policy instruments as among the main groups of players: taxpayers; consumers of factory product; owners of factories; and specific factors in the production of factory product. In the conventional public finance analysis, the resultant redistributions are evaluated by appeal to 'equity' criteria, with a general presumption in favour of policies that give most benefit to the poorest.

However, there is a specific issue that arises in this example that is worth noting – namely, the efficiency effects of greater or lesser reliance on public revenues. The effect of regulation is to redistribute between consumers and producers of the regulated product: apart from the efficiency considerations involved in the determination of the optimal level of smoke, there are no further 'externalities' to be incorporated. But once taxation is involved, whether directly or as a means of providing the revenue required to finance the subsidy, there is an additional 'externality' involved – that embodied in the changed incentives to free-ride on the provision of public goods (of which clean air is one). Individuals will rationally attempt to minimize their individual tax payments, notwithstanding any general benefits they derive from public activity. This kind of avoidance/evasion activity is an increasing function of the level of tax take. So when taxes rise, additional distortions are introduced between heavily taxed and lightly taxed activities. In that sense, revenue-saving instruments are to be preferred over revenue-neutral instruments; and *a fortiori* over revenue-using ones. On this basis, in short, there appears to be a general efficiency presumption in favour of tax solutions over regulation; and regulation over subsidy. Note that this presumption seems to run directly in the face of the macro-empirical results in relation to growth rates. Noting the distortions introduced in, say, labour markets by income tax, one might have thought that at least over some range regulation might be a more growth-enhancing option than increased income taxation. Though this will not be a direct focus of concern in this chapter, there is an apparent inconsistency between this thought and the macro-evidence. That inconsistency demands an explanation.

As we noted earlier, within the 'public choice' framework, the redistributions involved under alternative policy instruments perform an explanatory rather than a normative role. Attention focuses not on the poorest but on those groups that seem likely to have the most political power, or the greatest stakes in the outcome. This perspective introduces an additional range of considerations into the analysis – an additional set of quasi-market relations to be incorporated – namely those associated with the 'political market' in all its variants.

The particular orientation that any such analysis invites depends of course on general presumptions about what factors in political processes are most significant, and on what drives those processes. Specifically, there are three questions that seem especially relevant here:

1. What is the relative importance of electoral, as distinct from lobbying, elements in determining policy decisions?
2. Within electoral politics what assumptions about voter motivation are most appropriate? In particular, are voters best modelled as driven by their individual interests (as public choice orthodoxy claims) or do moral and/or symbolic considerations play a disproportionate role (as I have argued in various places – see Brennan and Lomasky, 1993 and Brennan and Hamlin, 1998, for example)?
3. How significant is the role of the 'supply side' in determining political outcomes – that is, the preferences and/or judgements of political agents, whether elected, as in the case of politicians, or institutionally privileged, as in the case of judges or bureaucrats?

The answers to these questions influence what one looks to in both trying to explain and to evaluate broad policy outcomes. Different answers to these questions might plausibly be given. In the next section, I want to offer a brief characterization of my own position. Then in section 4, I shall pursue one aspect of the regulation/budget trade-off that seems to me to be of some interest and importance.

3. THE CENTRAL ELEMENTS OF 'POLITICAL ECONOMY'

If the questions posed immediately above are a good checklist for describing one's approach to political economy, then answering them in my own case will provide a fair sense of the approach.

The first point to be made in this connection is that, in my view, the considerations that weigh in electoral competition are distinct from those that weigh in the lobbying process. In the latter case, it seems reasonable to think of the transactions that take place between political agents and lobbyists as direct *quid pro quo* transactions of the same basic kind as occur in markets. This is not to say that it is entirely obvious precisely what the objects of the transactions in question are – neither what it is that the lobbyist provides; not what it is that the political agent undertakes to deliver. In the simplest cases, the lobbyist might provide campaign contributions in return for quite specific policy that the lobbyist desires. But this kind of transaction is not the only one possible and may not be all that common. The political agent may, instead, be offering privileged access in the future – a preparedness to listen to complaints, rather than to act in accordance with the lobbyist's wishes. And the lobbyist may offer not (merely) campaign contributions but (also) support of other kinds, such as positive endorsement or campaign assistance or 'inside information' or rhetorical ammunition for speeches on topics of special concern. Sometimes the offer may take the form of a threat not acted upon – refraining from supporting an opponent, say. Nevertheless, in broad terms, the relation between political agents and lobbyists is best thought of in terms of negotiating common interests broadly conceived – that is, in terms of a conventional exchange, much like that which routinely occurs in markets. In that sense, the focus in the 'economic theory of regulation' seems to me to be broadly appropriate: industry-specific redistributions that advantage particular well-organized interests seem to be the kind of currency in terms of which campaign contributions can be bought.

On the other hand, I do not think that electoral politics operates primarily in this mode. The large-number electoral setting is such that voters are unlikely to vote according to their individual interests. To use an analogy that I have explored in detail elsewhere (Brennan and Lomasky, 1993), voting in the typical democratic setting is more like cheering at a football match than choosing an assets portfolio. On this reading, the best strategy for candidates is to render themselves in terms that induce maximal cheering. And while in some cases voters are likely to cheer for their interests, they are rather more likely to cheer for highly symbolic things that speak to their identities, or are seen as intrinsically desirable. For example, voters are more likely to cheer for candidates that can be identified as 'responsible', 'decent', 'honest', 'warm-hearted', 'morally upright' than for the reverse. Each candidate will therefore have an incentive to seek policies that reveal her as having those characteristics.

Public choice orthodoxy often describes itself as 'politics without romance', to use the title of one of Buchanan's most aptly named papers. The object of this self-description is precisely to distinguish the public choice view of politics from that which sees politics as a quest for the 'true', the 'beautiful', the 'admirable'. But at the purely descriptive level, the latter version seems to me to be closer to the mark. Each candidate wants to be associated with the true, the beautiful and the admirable because these are things that are likely to induce voters to find the candidate appealing – and candidates seek policy platforms that are consistent with that picture.

There may be much to be said for insisting on a rather prosaic view of politics, with an appropriately sceptical view of the high-flown claims that politicians routinely make for it. But justification for this kind of deflationary posture is more normative than descriptive. Indeed, that posture makes most sense when the essentially 'romantic' character of electoral politics is accepted and understood. Electoral competition just *is* better characterized as wooing (or 'romancing') voters than as buying votes. And the best evidence for this claim is that the candidate who self-describes as formulating policy in order to buy office is likely to lose votes by that description. Voters are likely to see any offer to do 'whatever the electorate wants' as a form of prostitution – and prostitution is not in general something that the electorate seems likely to cheer for.

Developing plausible rhetorical defences of policy is, as I see it, a crucial part of what electoral politics is all about. In that sense, there is an irreducible element of 'spin' involved. But plausible rhetorical defences, to be convincing, must be offered in a way that makes everyone think that the candidate proposing those defences is convinced. And it may be that the best way to ensure this is if the candidate is in fact convinced. So politics may select for candidates with convictions rather more than it does for used-car-salesmen types, or clever liars.

None of this need disarm the political sceptic. The idea that many politicians may actually believe much of what the dispassionate scholar sees as romantic clap-trap may be seriously scary rather than reassuring. But the fact remains that the description of electoral politics as essentially a scramble over rival interests is seriously defective as a description. Voters will not recognize themselves in such terms; and they will not recognize their would-be 'leaders' in such terms; and their would-be leaders may not even recognize themselves in such terms.

Furthermore, it should not be assumed that developing a plausible rhetorical defence is entirely independent of the policy platform to be defended. Spin may be crucial; but not everything is equally spinnable. It is easier to defend a policy as admirable if it is indeed admirable, or if it is likely to look admirable to most people. This constraint is not sufficient to ensure that all policies will actually be admirable, but it is a constraint! And that constraint is rather different in kind from those operative in markets and in analogous settings (special interest lobbying, for example) where interests predominate.

The picture of politics I have in mind can be depicted conveniently in matrix form as in Table 4.1. The rows represent the extent to which a policy is rhetorically defensible – the extent to which it generates 'expressive benefits' to voters. The range is divided into three categories, corresponding to the cases where expressive benefits are: positive, neutral and negative. Policies that fall in the first row are amenable to rhetorical defence and are therefore electorally attractive. Those that fall in the third row are not amenable to rhetorical defence and are in that sense electorally infeasible.

Analogously, the columns represent the extent to which policies serve to

Table 4.1 Electoral and lobbying constraints

	Lobbying effects		
Electoral effects	Positive	Neutral	Negative
Positive	*f*	*f*	*f*
Neutral	*f*		~*f*
Negative	~*f*	~*f*	~*f*

Note: *f* = feasible; ~*f* = infeasible (see text).

redistribute from diffuse and largely impotent groups to concentrated and powerful groups. Policies that fit that categorization fall into the first column. Those that are neutral in this respect fall into the second. And those that are 'perverse' in this dimension – that redistribute away from potent groups to impotent ones – fall into the third column.

Policies that fall into the top left-hand corner of the matrix satisfy both relevant constraints. They are amenable to rhetorical defence; and they serve to redistribute in an appropriate fashion to concentrated and potent interest groups. As we move towards the lower right-hand corner of the matrix we increasingly confront political feasibility constraints of both electoral and lobbying kinds. The cells labelled '*f*' are feasible; those labelled '~*f*' are, I assert, infeasible. It will be noted that the upper right-hand cell is labelled feasible, while the lower left-hand cell is not. This signifies my reckoning that electoral-relevant constraints of rhetorical defensibility are more binding than lobbying constraints. I base this view on the fact that there is only one relevant electoral episode, which is more or less a winner-takes-all competition. With lobbying, by contrast, there are alternatives to any one source of campaign funds. Moreover, campaign funds are likely to be less useful when one has a policy platform that is relatively difficult to defend.

However, the formulation in Table 4.1 probably serves to overstate the extent to which lobbying considerations and electoral ones are likely to conflict. The dimensions of policy that are relevant for electoral justification are in many cases rather different from those relevant for making strategic redistributions towards special interest groups. A policy of increased military expenditure in the face of some perceived increased threat is amenable to persuasive rhetorical defence. But that policy can be finely tuned to secure specific transfers to special interest groups without such fine-tuning necessarily undermining the general rhetorical effect. Consider decisions such as where the military bases will be located, what precise mix of inputs will be used, how the specifications for those inputs will be framed. All of these aspects of policy delivery may be made with an eye to favouring the relevant special interests, without much in the way of implications for the general policy. Or, to take up again the smoky factories case, the general policy of environmental protection may be rhetorically defended in terms that leave largely open whether the appropriate instrument for the pursuit of that policy will be taxation, subsidy or regulation. In other words, the lobbying account of political process as interest-based and the electoral account of politics as expressive can often exist reasonably contentedly side by side.

Indeed, in some ways, the expressive account of electoral processes is more hospitable to the 'private interest' account of regulation than public choice orthodoxy would be. The standard public choice line would see all of politics in terms of strategic redistributions. The fact that electoral processes enable negatively affected consumers to combine their opposition to regulations that redistribute away from them means that the advantages of concentration in allowing special interests to secure regulations in their own favour would be diminished, whereas on the expressive voting account, the more micro-oriented interest-based aspects of the lobbying process are seen to operate mainly in a different domain.

So far in this section I have focused on the first two of the questions I posed at the close of the last section. Let me engage the final question now. Although I do not intend to defend the claim in this chapter (it is defended in Brennan and Hamlin 1999), I do think that the expressive account of voting is hospitable to a truly representative conception of democratic processes. By this I mean to distinguish representative democracy both from direct democracy and from a 'delegate' conception of representative institutions. Elected governments and/or presidents are, as a matter of fact, given substantial scope for discretion over policy once elected. Indeed it is not even clear that policy platforms are to be understood as contracts between those elected and voters: those platforms may be more designed to illustrate the kinds of commitments, and to suggest the general values, of those who are elected. The thought here is that electors may be more capable of assessing the personal qualities of alternative candidates than the likely effects of alternative policies, and that they recognize this fact both in the design of their institutions and in their actual voting behaviour. This is not an implausible claim. Nothing in ordinary life equips ordinary individuals to assess the effects of alternative policies – matters which are often enough the object of contestation among experts. But all of us have experience of other persons, and it seems likely that we may as a species have evolved to be reasonably accurate in our assessments of their qualities.

In any event, if voters believe themselves to be better judges of persons than of policies, then they are likely to prefer institutions that give those whom they elect a fair amount of discretion. And this means in turn that the 'supply side' of politics will be quite significant. That is, the particular beliefs, preferences and values of political agents will tend to play a significant role in political decision making – a rather more significant role certainly than median-voter models of constrained policy convergence might lead one to believe.

It is, in any event, on this basis that I come at last to a piece of substantive analysis. As will be clear, there is a larger project involved in spelling out the analytical details of the foregoing sketch. However, in the final section of this chapter I want to focus on just one aspect of the political economy of regulation – that attached to the effects of increased reliance on regulation on the extent of public activity.

4. REGULATION VERSUS BUDGETARY POLICY IN BUREAUCRATIC STRATEGY

Consider the following scenario. You are a policy adviser at a high level. You find yourself sitting around the table at a meeting of Cabinet, preparing the annual budget. Your minister has a pet project, which he would like to have endorsed as policy by his Cabinet colleagues. However, he knows, and you know, that his Cabinet colleagues all have pet projects of their own. And all these projects require significant amounts of public money. If even one of these projects were to be funded, then tax levels (or debt levels) would have to increase non-negligibly. And that tax increase would have serious political fall-out – a fact that everyone recognizes. To put the point in the kind of expressive terms outlined above, the government has made its best guess as to the general expressive costs and benefits of increased taxes and increased spending, and has come to a broad judgement as to what the balance of those considerations requires. The size of the budget is not exactly cast in stone: if Cabinet colleagues can be persuaded of the electoral merits of your minister's pet project, then perhaps it can go ahead. But it will have to compete against all the other pet projects around the table, and even if it is highly ranked, none of them may actually win support. Tax increases are just not electorally popular, and you will need pretty good arguments for any tax increase, even if Cabinet can be persuaded that your policy is a 'great idea', and indeed the 'best idea' around the table.

This last is a serious challenge. All these ministers have king-sized egos. They are all disposed to think that their own project is best. And anyway, this is a competitive game and they all want to win. Moreover, they all have their own advisers, who are also clever people good at inventing persuasive arguments. And all those ministers, and all their advisers, recognize the essential competitiveness of this game. They know, as you do, that the opportunity cost of your getting support for your project is their own forgone. So they will already have developed clever and persuasive arguments as to why your project should not proceed. And you will have spent a lot of effort doing the same with respect to their pet projects.

As the debate proceeds, you hit upon a thought. You pass your minister a note. You have thought of a way that his project could be achieved without any fiscal cost at all. All you need is an appropriate regulation. Your minister offers that thought. And immediately, the politics around the table changes. For, under the regulation alternative, it is no longer the case that your project is competitive with others: the opportunity cost of your regulation is not some other minister's pet project forgone, because the reformulated project doesn't call for any fiscal resources at all. And when the opportunity cost of any project falls, it is more likely to receive endorsement.

The idea is catching. Other ministers and their advisers see that their chances of success lie in reformulating their projects in regulatory form. In this way, all can finesse the intrinsically competitive character of the budgetary process. Of course, regulations also have some political costs. The policy will need to be rhetorically defensible. And there is presumably some limit to the amount of regulation that can be achieved in any parliamentary session. So even under regulation there will be some competition at that margin between the various Cabinet players. But there is not the additional 'economic' constraint, embedded in the budget process. The fiscal constraints simply don't come into play.

I have sketched this scenario in the context of the modified Westminster system with which I am most familiar. The contextual details could, however, be modified without in any way affecting the basic thrust. For I take it that it is a characteristic feature of the budget process that some general aggregative judgement is made on budget size and that total spending is made to fit that aggregative judgement – even if there is some *tâtonnement* between that aggregative judgement and more decentralized processes. Put another way, if processes for decision making on expenditure levels were taken in an essentially decentralized way, there would by necessity be a question as to whether the resultant aggregative spending programme could be financed at all. And if the programme could be financed, the question would still remain whether the level of taxation to which the spending programme would give rise would be politically viable. At some level, an aggregative determination will have to be made – and budgetary activities will have to be rationed within the resultant aggregate constraint.

But what are we to make of the effective removal – or substantial weakening – of such constraints when regulatory instruments are used? It is, after all, rather a good thing, one might have thought, that any policy that is finally implemented (or appears in a party's platform) has been subject to intense and somewhat adversarial scrutiny. A system that creates incentives for others to knock down your projects seems superior to one in which that kind of competitive element is lacking.

Moreover, one of the strengths of representative government is that it is forced to confront aggregative economic constraints in a way that individual voters do not have any incentive to do. One could certainly imagine cases in which the net expressive advantages of an expanded public sector are positive, but where the level of public activity that secures the most cheering from the electorate is simply fiscally infeasible. The specified level of activity requires more tax revenue than the system can deliver. In other words, an expressive enthusiasm for some project on the part of the voter–citizen does not necessarily imply a preparedness on the part of that voter, and others like her, to create the additional taxable capacity that would make that project viable. It is a characteristic feature of the expressive account of voting that the 'economic' costs of taxation and the electoral costs of taxation will not in general be the same. What this observation implies is that the capacity of assigned tax instruments to raise the revenue that electoral popularity demands operates as an independent 'reality check' on government activity. The removal of that reality check seems highly unlikely to be a good thing.

Suppose we agree. There remains a problem: namely, whether preserving this 'good thing' is itself likely to be politically feasible. In other words, it is one thing to argue that the discipline of budgetary operations is a 'good thing' overall. It is another to show how the interaction of more or less rational agents within the political structure might ensure that that 'good thing' survives. After all, the prediction one might make on the basis of our 'scenario'-story is that budgetary technology for the delivery of policy is obsolete: all the political pressures are towards wholesale replacement of fiscal operations by regulatory ones. And this in turn raises a question: why do we observe budgetary operations at all in the first place?

One possible answer to this is that at least some politically relevant players recognize the problems associated with any 'takeover' by regulation, and are motivated by moral considerations to do something about those problems. I do not reject this possibility. The expressive voting account is hospitable to the idea that moral motivations of all kinds may play a disproportionate role in electoral politics. All the same, one might feel somewhat reassured if there were some players in the political arena who had a clear and reasonably well-defined interest in budgetary over regulatory operations.

Who might those players be? Well, at least within the public choice tradition, the most obvious contenders would seem to be bureaucrats. In the classic public-choice-theory statement of bureaucratic behaviour (Niskanen, 1971) bureaucrats are modelled as possessing the power to appropriate the entire economic surplus from the provision of public goods in the supply of which they exercise a characteristic monopoly. However, in the original model, the entire surplus so generated is spent on expanding the supply of the public good. The apparent rationale for this assumption is that this additional spending is to be seen as the means whereby bureaucrats actually get possession of the rents available.

The public choice literature on bureaucracy has developed a long way from its Niskanen origins, and the basic model has been considerably refined (Mueller, 2003, ch. 16). However, the general thrust of this literature is that the quasi-monopoly power of the bureaucratic structure does provide some capacity for bureaus to create rents. And although some of these rents may be spent on augmenting the quality and quantity of the bureau's services, some proportion of these rents will also accrue to the bureaucrats themselves as direct benefits.

Consider a simple model. The utility function of the bureau manager can be written as:

$$Ub = f(q;r) + g(\ldots),$$

where q = level of policy achievement
r = rents acquired from bureau expenditure, and
$g(\ldots)$ all non-bureau-related things that add to the manager's utility.
The last plays no role in the analysis.

There are two policy technologies: regulatory, which generates increased 'output' understood as policy achievement; and budgetary, which generates both rents and policy achievement in what we shall take to be fixed proportions. There are political limits on the level of both budgetary and regulatory activity. We take these limits to be exogenously fixed. The issue at stake is the bureau's choice over the policy technology mix.

Consider on this basis Figure 4.1. In this diagram we show on the horizontal axis the level of policy achievement, q; and on the vertical axis, the rents that the bureau manager enjoys. The line *OR* shows the $r{:}q$ share that is given by regulation. It lies along the horizontal axis, indicating that it generates no fungible resources from which rents might be extracted. *R* indicates the amount of policy achievement that can be secured if the bureau devotes all its energies to securing regulation. The ray, *OB*, represents the combinations of r and q associated with the budgetary technology for policy pursuit. If the bureau devotes all its energy to budgetary activity, it can secure a maximal amount of rent and policy achievement given at *B*.

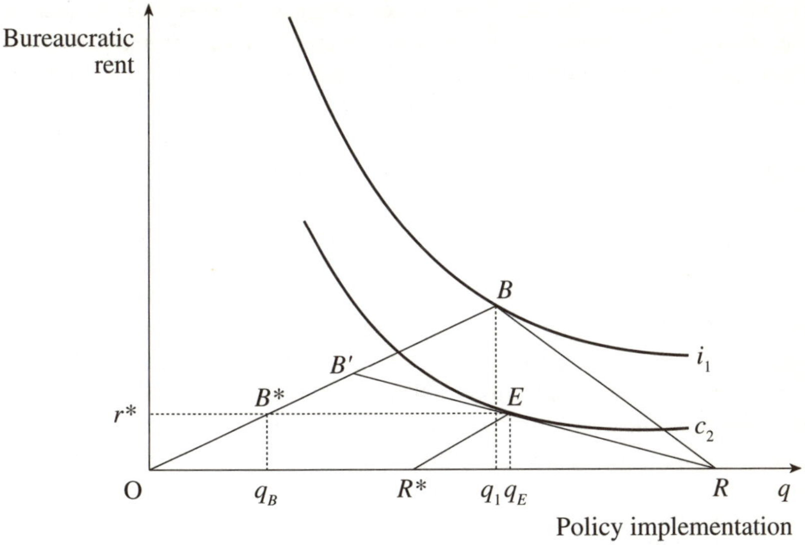

Figure 4.1 Bureaucrat choice between rents and bureau output

Because the political constraints affecting budgetary operations are more severe than those applying to regulation, *B* lies to the left of *R*. Accordingly, the maximal set of combinations of *r* and *q* feasible is given by the line *BR*.

In Figure 4.1, I have assumed that the amount of rent extraction possible under budgetary activity is rather small: the slope of *OB* is shallow. On this basis, and given the bureau's preferences as indicated in the indifference curves, i_1, and c_2, the initial equilibrium is at *B*. The bureau will put all its energies into securing budgetary policies. Think back to our Cabinet-room scenario. Although the possibility of a regulatory alternative to the budgetary project occurs to me, I will not bother to mention this possibility to my minister: there is not enough in that possibility to make it worth my while. Better for me to hang out for the budgetary alternative, because then I stand to have some extra resources to play with.

Our chief interest here is with a comparative static exercise of a different kind. Suppose that external pressures are such that the capacity to get budgetary policies implemented is reduced. The share of rents accruing to the bureau from any public expenditure operation remains the same, but the political price of taxation increases. Then the maximal amount of rent/policy that the bureau can achieve through budgetary means is reduced to *B*′, and the new feasible set is given by *B*′*OR*, as depicted in Figure 4.1.

The new equilibrium is now at *E*, with a budget level corresponding to *B**:

the level of rents is r^* and the amount of policy achievement via budgetary means is q_B. The level of regulation is at R^* and total policy achievement at q_E, which in this example is greater than originally at q_1. The reason that the level of policy achievement in the new equilibrium is higher is attributable to the fact that 'rents' have become relatively more expensive. The consequent shift to policy achievement involves a corresponding substitution towards the mechanism that is more efficient in generating policy achievement.

This simple model serves then to illustrate two general points. The first relates to why there might be extensive (indeed predominant) reliance on budgetary operations in any political equilibrium. Budgetary operations produce surplus for the suppliers of public sector output; regulations do not. Moreover, it is notable that the reliance on budgetary mechanisms will tend to be greatest, *ceteris paribus*, when the capacity of suppliers to derive rents from public expenditures is somewhat limited.

The second point, however, is that when the political price of budgetary operations becomes too high – when the fisc is under maximal pressure – then bureaucrats may support a substantial shift towards the regulatory alternative. The natural support for the budgetary technology embodied in the interests of bureaucrats may largely evaporate. When that happens, there is likely to be an increase in total public activity. This increase is not necessarily bad in itself; but it comes about essentially because the intense scrutiny of public activity characteristic of budgetary processes is removed. In that sense, increased reliance on regulation is disturbing.

5. SUMMARY AND CONCLUSION

My object in this chapter has been to do two things. First, I have sought to provide a broad-brush account of what the ingredients into a full 'political economy of regulation' would look like, and what I see as the critical prior questions that any such exercise would need to answer. In that sense, the chapter is a preliminary probe into this territory. It is better described as a prolegomenon – a 'discursive introduction', as the OED has it – than as itself the required analysis. Second, however, I have attempted to provide a simple piece of analytics designed to throw some light on the issue of bureaucratic response to changes in the terms of the regulatory/budgetary trade-off.

I conclude with a brief list of what I see as the main claims I have made:

1. Any analysis of regulation ought to be conducted in 'comparative mode'. That is, the regulation in question should be compared with a clearly stipulated alternative.
2. Whereas much economic analysis proceeds by comparing the cum-

regulation situation with the zero-policy alternative, it is also useful to compare the cum-regulation situation with one in which the policy end in question is achieved via budgetary action. That is the comparison with which I deal here. So the issue can be thought of in terms of the consequences of substituting regulatory for budgetary technology in the pursuit of 'policy goals'.

3. An important element at stake in that substitution is its redistributional effects. There is, however, a question as to whether those redistributional consequences are important primarily for explanatory purposes or for normative reasons.
4. A further relevant difference between regulatory and budgetary instruments is the effect that changed revenue levels have on the overall 'excess burden' of the tax system: in that respect, regulation is superior to revenue-using policy instruments.
5. The substitution itself can be thought of either as a matter of broad electoral relevance or in the more instrumental terms relevant for lobbying activity. I claim that the conceptual frameworks for analysis, and specifically the motivational assumptions, in these two settings are different.
6. Budgetary processes have certain features that regulatory processes lack. In particular, alternative revenue uses are subject to a kind of competitive scrutiny that is lacking in the regulation case. Further, the budgetary technology invokes narrowly 'economic' revenue constraints that operate in addition to, and potentially somewhat independently of, electoral constraints.
7. Some internal support for budgetary policy-technology can be expected from bureaucrats. However, under more or less conventional assumptions about bureaucratic motivation, that support will be responsive to the political cost of revenue. Indeed, we can explain the substitution of regulation for budgetary operations in part by appeal to the rational response of bureaucrats to increased fiscal pressure – whether 'political' or 'economic' in origin.

I return finally to my point of departure. It may seem as if the topic involved here and the particular way in which it is formulated are slightly bizarre. My concerns seem to run in the face of the fact that, in most places, the last 20 years or so have seen more 'progress' in deregulation than they have in winding back the size of the fisc. To worry about the substitution of regulation for budgetary measures in the face of that experience may seem ill judged. Perhaps that is so. However, 'at the margin', as we economists say, the kind of substitution that I have been concerned with here does seem to be an emerging issue. And as I have observed, the forces that seem to be promoting such substitution also seem likely to gather in intensity over the next few decades.

REFERENCES

Brennan, Geoffrey and Loren Lomasky (1993), *Democracy and Decision*, New York: Cambridge University Press.

Brennan, G. and A. Hamlin (1998), 'Expressive Voting and Electoral Equilibrium', *Public Choice*, **95**, 149–75.

Brennan, G. and A. Hamlin (1999), 'On Political Representation', *British Journal of Political Science*, **29**, 109–27.

Gwartney, J. and R. Lawson et al. (2002), *Economic Freedom of the World*, Vancouver: Fraser Institute.

Mueller, D. (2003), *Public Choice III*, Cambridge: Cambridge University Press.

Niskanen, W. (1971), *Bureaucracy and Representative Government*, Chicago: Aldine.

Peltzman, S. (1976), 'Towards a More General Theory of Regulation?', *Journal of Law and Economics*, **19**, 211–40.

Stigler, G. (1971), 'The Theory of Economic Regulation', *Bell Journal of Economics and Management Science*, **2**, 137–46.

Waterman, A. (2003), 'Political Corruption and Economic Freedom', mimeo, University of Manitoba, Canada.

PART II

Becoming EURO: internal stability and international crises

5. EMU as an evolutionary process[1]

Pier Carlo Padoan

INTRODUCTION

Early critics of European Monetary Union (EMU) argued that the project had two major drawbacks, one economic and the other institutional. From the economic point of view, they argued that the euro would not meet the requirements of an optimum currency area and, therefore, that costs would exceed benefits for its members. Second, they argued that EMU would be plagued by an institutional disequilibrium between a supranational, unaccountable central bank and national governments. If these arguments were proved to be valid, EMU would probably fail.

This chapter examines the two critiques, and interrelated issues, in an evolutionary perspective. It argues that both points are misplaced because the evolution of the economic structure of EMU as well as its economic policy machinery will eventually bring forward an efficient, viable European economic and institutional model. We discuss the optimality of the monetary union by referring to the concept of 'endogenous currency areas,' in which monetary integration spurs transformations in the integrating economies that make the adoption of a single currency more suitable. We provide some evidence with respect to several aspects discussed in the optimum currency area literature, such as cyclical convergence, regional convergence, specialization and labor markets. We consider the evolution of these aspects under different monetary regimes in Europe since the introduction of the European Monetary System (EMS) in the late 1970s.

We discuss the relationship between the European Central Bank (ECB) and national governments by referring to the concept of policy spillover. We argue that centralization of monetary policy in Europe leads to changes in other policy areas, such as coordination between the single monetary policy and national budget policies, coordination of national budgets, and convergence towards a 'stable budget regime' (understood as the fulfillment of the requirements of the Stability and Growth Pact). Convergence in other policy areas, such as tax policy and labor market policy, may also be expected to increase over the foreseeable future.

This chapter also argues that, over the past decades, economic policy regimes in Europe have evolved under the pressure of macroeconomic and structural integration. The transformation of economic structures has created a configuration more supportive of monetary union (we refer to this process as endogeneity). The transformation of the European policy regime toward a new model of EU governance holds the promise of improving policy outcomes. These two transformative processes have mutually influenced and possibly reinforced each other and will probably continue to do so in the future.

COSTS AND BENEFITS OF MONETARY UNION

Collignon (1997) provides a simple yet useful approach, based on the literature on monetary unions, for analyzing the impact of these processes on the costs and benefits of the euro area. Benefits from monetary union increase with the expansion of the union, in terms of either the number of participating countries or of economic size. This arises from the fact that the larger the union, the greater the benefits accruing to each member from the elimination of transaction costs and exchange rate uncertainty, besides those stemming from lower variability of interest rates (Collignon, 1997).[2] These advantages, furthermore, increase with the degree of openness of the member economies. If these two elements are applied to the European case, it follows that EMU's benefits grow with (a) the number of member countries, (b) the EMU's GDP and (c) the degree of integration of the Single Market.

Costs increase with dispersion in the preferences of the area's policy makers regarding stabilization policies. In other words, the costs of union membership for a country with a high preference for containing inflation increase if other union members hold a strong preference for output-stabilization-oriented monetary policies. In general, the higher the convergence of the member countries' preference for low inflation and stability-oriented monetary policy, the lower the costs. From this point of view, EMU's composition becomes crucial, but it is equally evident that the process of convergence towards the Maastricht criteria suggests that the costs of EMU will be quite moderate. Even the least disciplined among the Union's members have implemented rigorous anti-inflationary and fiscal reform policies.

Graphically, costs (see Figure 5.1) rise with the value of A, which indicates the propensity of the Union's members to use monetary policy for output stabilization. Increasing values of A fuel the Union's inflation and hence diminish monetary stability. Benefits rise as S, the extension of the Union, grows because of economies of scale from the use of a common

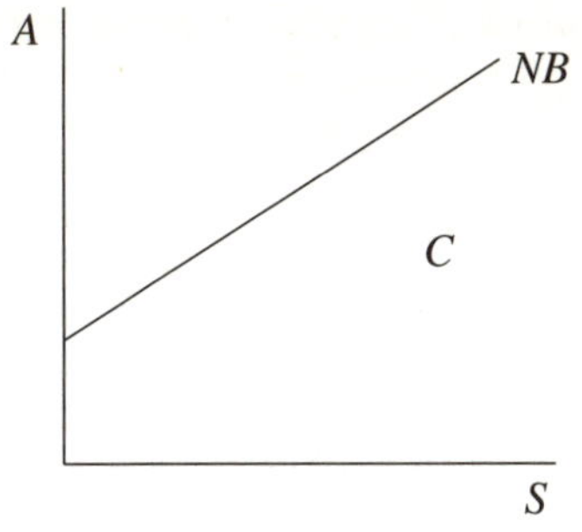

Figure 5.1 Costs and benefits of a monetary union

currency. Line *NB* is the locus of the points where benefits and costs offset each other (net benefits equal zero). *NB* is increasing because more monetary activism may be offset by an expansion of the Union's size. The slope of *NB* reflects the degree of integration of the Union's member economies. Points above *NB* indicate net negative benefits: there is no incentive to create a monetary union. The opposite occurs below the line. Increasing propensity towards monetary activism for a given size of the Union clearly results in net negative benefits and must be offset by enlarging the Union and/or by a growing degree of integration (increasing slope of *NB*) in order to raise the scale benefits.

EMU is 'successful' as long as it is described by a point below the *NB* schedule, such as point *C*. That success depends on two variables: intensity of integration and convergence of policy preferences towards stability. As long as EMU is endogenous in terms of the intensity of integration, point *C* will move to the right, while policy convergence will move point *C* downwards.

While Figure 5.1 is useful in providing an intuition of the general point, it must be supplemented in many respects. Both extension of the Union and policy convergence are variables with multiple dimensions. The first variable relates to the evolution of national economic structures towards an 'optimal' configuration from the point of view of optimum currency area theory. The second variable relates not only to macroeconomic convergence but, more importantly, to the definition of a coherent and well-functioning structure of governance of EMU, in short, an EU-wide model of economic policy. Indeed, the weakness of the euro during its second year of life and the first half of the third is frequently attributed to unsatisfactory performance in both aspects: a still not fully integrated and inflexible economy, a fragmented and often non-coherent system of governance, plagued by excessive conflicts among member states (a sign of non-converging policy preferences). We will consider both aspects at some depth in the rest of the chapter.

EMU's ENDOGENEITY: GROWTH, CONVERGENCE AND SPECIALIZATION

The most serious doubts regarding the sustainability of a common exchange rate policy in Europe are based on the traditional approach to optimum currency areas. According to the basic tenets of this theory, the changeover to a single currency delivers net benefits only if the countries involved are not subject to asymmetric shocks. Whenever such a condition does not apply, the optimal choice is maintenance of independent monetary policies that can offset the lack of synchronism of business cycles and absorb country-specific shocks.

The conclusions drawn on the basis of the theory of optimum currency areas may, nevertheless, be questioned regarding (a) the correctness of the methodologies and (b) the practical relevance of the issues raised. With respect to the first point, Frankel and Rose (1996) emphasize that trade integration and synchronization of business cycles will most likely increase with monetary integration, so that the criteria suggested by the literature on optimum currency areas would be met *ex post* by the countries joining EMU.

The literature on 'endogenous currency areas' is still in its infancy, yet it represents a useful approach to assessing the perspectives of EMU. In what follows, we provide some further evidence of the endogeneity of EMU as a currency area, looking at macroeconomic and regional convergence. In reviewing the evidence, an important caveat must be kept in mind. The evidence covers a period during which two integration processes have taken place: monetary integration (from the introduction of the EMS to the run-up to EMU) and real integration accelerated by the Single Market process. It is extremely difficult, if not simply impossible, to disentangle the effects of the two processes. Because the two processes are complementary and mutually reinforcing, however, disentangling them may not be necessary.

Convergence of Economic Cycles

One of the preconditions for sustainability of a monetary union is convergence of national economic cycles. Different cyclical patterns would point at differences in sensitivity to exogenous shocks, which would produce asymmetrical consequences (Bayoumi and Eichengreen, 1998). The endogenous currency area approach suggests that monetary integration deepens trade integration and leads to converging cyclical profiles. Some evidence is already available in this respect (Frankel and Rose, 1996).

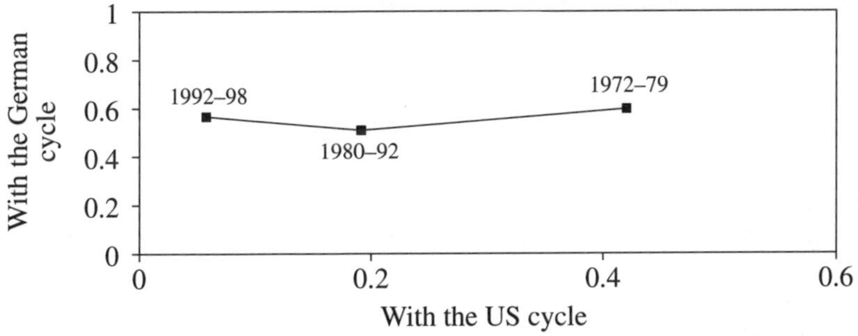

Source: Based on Padoan (2000b).

Figure 5.2a Cyclical correlation in the EU (German cycle)

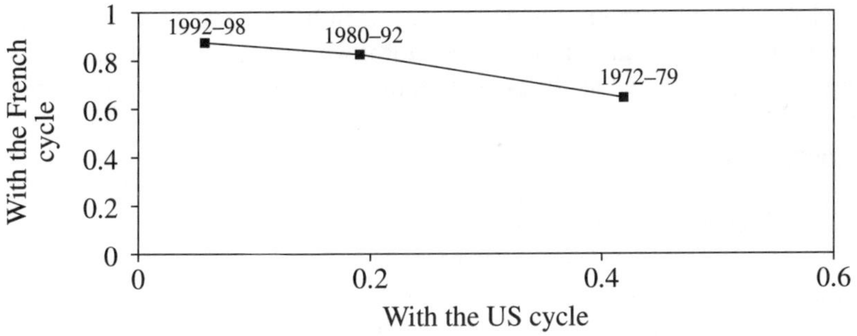

Source: See Figure 5.2a.

Figure 5.2b Cyclical correlation in the EU (French cycle)

Figures 5.2a and 5.2b present some further evidence. Correlation coefficients among European GDP cycles are compared for three different subperiods. Specifically, the cycles of Euroland's largest countries are compared to Germany and to the USA.[3] Furthermore, as the evolution of the German cycle is distorted by the process of unification, the correlation with the French cycle is also presented. Points shown on the curves indicate a marked diversification over time with respect to the US cycle. Note that, in the case of correlation with the French cycle, the curve shifts upwards, indicating a higher coefficient of correlation with the other European economies. This is not present in the German case because of the consequences of unification.

The data confirm the presence of an 'emerging' European economic cycle as a consequence of deepening monetary integration. The three periods considered relate to different economic policy regimes in Europe: an initial period of flexible exchange rates following the collapse of Bretton Woods (1972–79), the EMS years (1980–92) and the final period (1992–98), marked by the substantial depreciation of several currencies but also by an acceleration of convergence towards the single currency.

The relevant point, however, is that convergence was obtained towards declining, not rising, growth rates. The European GDP growth rate declined over the period in question (average growth rates were 3.3 percent in 1972–79, 2.4 percent in 1980–92 and 1.6 percent in 1992–98). This suggests that the countries with initially higher growth rates gradually converged to the German economy's slower rate: while the French and Italian GDP grew, respectively, at 3.3 and 3.7 percent in the 1970s as against 2.9 percent in Germany, the German economy expanded faster in 1980–92, when the Italian economy was growing more slowly.

In the immediate aftermath of the introduction of the euro, GDP cycles have begun to diverge, suggesting a separation between fast-growing small economies and slow-growing large economies. During 2000, however, convergence has increased as the large economies have started to grow faster.

Exchange Rates and Growth

In a currency area experiencing increasing trade integration such as EMU, two factors need to be examined to assess its sustainability: the sensitivity of growth to exchange rate changes and the elasticity of employment with respect to exports and growth. The sensitivity of growth to exchange rate changes is one of the topics commonly discussed in connection with the evaluation of costs and benefits of a single currency. It is usually assumed that there are differences among the EMU countries' preferences for exchange rate management that could create coordination problems in the management of the common monetary policy. To the extent that the growth model of the 'Mediterranean' members of EMU is relatively more dependent on the exchange rate, for example, these countries would be suffering higher costs in terms of growth and employment by giving up the exchange rate. In other words, currency unification would be biased by a structural divergence in policy preferences.[4]

Evidence reported in Padoan (2000b) sheds some light in this respect. In the first place, the elasticity of exports to intra-European exchange rates is highest in Germany and lowest in Italy. This implies that, contrary to what is often believed, the German economy will benefit from the creation of the single currency as it interrupts the real long-term appreciation of the D-mark. At the same time, the cost to Italy of giving up intra-European exchange variability is limited as the elasticity of its exports to this variable is relatively small (less than 0.5).

Germany, next to Spain, also displays the highest export elasticity to the real extra-EU exchange rate. An appreciation of the euro would depress German exports more than those of France and Italy. On the other hand, Italy displays the highest export demand elasticity *vis-à-vis* both the European aggregate and the rest of the world. A demand shock would thus affect Italy to a proportionally greater extent. The relevance of these has been confirmed in 1999 and in 2000 as the depreciation of the euro has largely benefited German growth through exports.

Table 5.1 Exports and economic growth in selected countries: Granger causality tests

	Germany	France	Italy	Spain	UK
Exports > employment	11.3*	0.7	1.5	4.2**	1.7
Exports > gross fixed capital formation	7.9*	0.5	2.7***	0.1	1.5
Exports > productivity	0.0	1.6	0.7	0.8	2.0
Gross fixed capital formation > exports	0.6	0.1	1.6	1.6	0.1
Productivity > exports	8.6*	0.3	0.2	0.8	3.5**
Gross fixed capital formation > productivity	3.0***	0.2	4.7	2.6	1.3
Productivity > gross fixed capital formation	8.4*	1.2	6.3*	1.4	4.6**

Note: Asterisks indicate cases for which the null hypothesis of non-causality is rejected.

Source: Padoan (2000b).

Nonetheless, export elasticities are only a partial confirmation of an export-led model. Table 5.1 reports some causality tests between employment, exports and growth in the four large euro countries as well as in the UK[5]. With the important exception of Germany, there does not seem to be a causal link between exports and employment, nor between exports, investments and productivity. These links are, on the contrary, observable in the case of Germany, suggesting that an export-led growth model is applicable only in the center economy of EMU.[6] In this respect as well, Germany's economy would be the most negatively (positively) affected by an appreciation (depreciation) of the euro.

As a whole, evidence reported above suggests that, for most of the

European countries, the loss of the exchange rate instrument would not seriously affect long-term growth, as we find little evidence of export-led growth and little evidence of exchange rate sensitivity of exports. While these results support the idea of a sustainable EMU, however, other results presented above suggest that convergence towards the German cycle has not favored investments and employment. Further evidence reported in Padoan (2000b) provides additional insights. Deceleration of investment in Europe, which can be seen, to some extent, as the cost of monetary and cyclical convergence, has been accompanied by an increase of the labor-saving (capital-deepening) share of capital accumulation over total capital formation, implying that, partially at least, a cost of (getting to) monetary union might be foregone employment opportunities.

Regional Catching-up

An additional set of evidence relates to regional catching-up.[7] Using a standard model (Barro and Sala-i-Martin, 1992), we report tests of the hypothesis that monetary convergence has a positive effect on regional catching-up in Europe. A measure of the rate of convergence in a neoclassical model of exogenous growth is obtained by log-linearizing the movement of the capital stock around its steady state; in the case of a Cobb–Douglas production function, the rate of growth of income per capita is a fixed proportion of the rate of growth of the per capita capital stock, so that the convergence parameter can be estimated within the following equation:

$$D\,log\,y \cong -\beta \log\left(\frac{y}{y^*}\right),$$

where $D\,log\,y$ is the rate of growth of per capita income over the period, y indicates the per capita income of the ith region at the beginning of the time interval (in our case, 1980–95), y^* is the per capita income of the richest region, and β is the measure of regional convergence. The method of estimation is non-linear least squares. We report the values of β, the convergence parameter (see Table 5.2). We first look at convergence over the whole sample period. We obtain a significant, but very small, convergence parameter.

We then consider the effect of the exchange rate regime for the convergence process, that is whether, and to what extent, the introduction of the EMS in 1979 may have affected the regional convergence process in Europe. For this purpose, we consider three separate periods: the first EMS period (1980–87), the 'hard EMS' period (1987–92), and the period following the 1992 crisis.

Over the 1980–87 period, which was marked by a regime of fixed, yet

Table 5.2 Regional convergence in selected periods

Period	β	*t*-value
1980–95	0.009510	5.026860
1980–87	0.001615	1.079498
1987–92	0.014207	10.21923
1992–95	−0.00334	−2.316057

Source: Padoan (2000b).

adjustable, exchange rates, there is no evidence of income convergence among the European regions as parameter β is not significantly different from zero. Conversely, regional convergence is not rejected during the period of the 'hard EMS', 1987–92, featuring strict nominal exchange rigidity. The value of β is not significantly different from that obtained from the equation covering the entire period. In the following period, 1992–95, which was marked by a more flexible exchange regime and by several devaluations of currencies participating in the exchange rate agreements, the opposite seems to have occurred, that is, divergence among regional growth rates.

The results reported above should not be overemphasized, however, they should be taken as additional evidence of the effect of monetary integration on output convergence, hence of partial endogeneity of another of the criteria suggested by the optimum currency area literature, increasing similarity among regions and thus reducing exposure to asymmetric shocks.

Specialization

Changes in industry specialization across the EU over the past two decades clearly reflect both the effects of the implementation of the Single Market project and of monetary integration. In a report prepared for the EC Commission, Midelfart-Knarvik et al. (2000) show that industrial specialization in EU countries decreases from 1970 to 1980 and increases from 1980–83 to 1994–97, especially in small countries. More specifically, high return-to-scale, high-skill and high-tech industries are increasingly located in core regions, pointing to the growing importance of economic geography factors in determining location, while skill-intensive industries are more widespread and also show higher rates of growth. To the extent that national specialization increases risks of asymmetric shocks, it carries negative consequences for the sustainability of EMU. However, other evidence (Paci and Pigliaru, 2000; Verspagen, 2000; Padoan, 2000b, ch. 8 and references therein) shows that specialization in the EU increases at the regional rather than national level.

Increasing regional specialization has a number of implications for the functioning of EMU. Institutional differences among national labor markets become less important while regional policies appear to be an essential tool for the performance of economic and monetary union. Padoan (2000b) offers a description, based on cluster analysis, of different regional specialization patterns and their relationship with unemployment. This work finds a positive relationship between specialization in advanced manufacturing sectors and employment. Regions with a relative intensity of advanced service sectors, that is, sectors closely integrated with industry, are associated with low unemployment. The opposite occurs in regions with a high intensity of traditional services and commerce. Over the period between 1981 and 1991, which covers most of the period of the EMS, regional specialization increases.

Financial Markets

EMU is changing the European financial landscape and has the potential to continue to do so in the future, both in terms of performance and of pressure on policy makers. Danthine et al. (2000) show that several important changes in European financial markets have emerged after the introduction of the euro. A corporate euro bond market has developed to the point where issues in 1999 exceeded issues in the dollar market. Portfolios are increasingly being allocated along pan-European lines rather than on a country basis. The banking industry is undergoing rapid transformation through mergers and acquisitions. Other direct effects of EMU include standardization and transparency in pricing, the shrinking of the exchange market, the elimination of currency risk, the elimination of currency-related regulations, and the homogenization of the public bond market and bank refinancing procedures. Indirect effects include lower costs of cross-country transactions, increasing depth and liquidity of European financial markets, better diversification possibilities and decreasing importance of the home-bias effect in investment. In addition, the emerging euro financial market has prompted new pressures on policy makers to harmonize legislation, taxation and standards. The establishment of TARGET and EURO1, the settlement systems for large transactions of the European System of Central Banks and the European Banking Association respectively, and the implementation in 1999 of the EU Directive 97/5/EC of January 1997 on cross-border credit transfers are some visible examples. Kraus (2001) provides additional evidence that investment in the euro area increasingly follows sectoral rather than national criteria, indicating a gradual elimination of country risk.

One relevant implication of the process of financial integration will be an increasing convergence in national monetary policy transmission mechanisms, thus making the management of supranational monetary policy more effective.

LABOR MARKETS

European labor markets have often been considered as the major stumbling block to the success of EMU. Critics have repeatedly claimed that excessive rigidity in EU labor markets would simply be inconsistent with monetary union. Two aspects have to be considered here, one macroeconomic and the other microeconomic. The macroeconomic aspect concerns the relationship between the centralization of monetary policy and the wage bargaining process. The microeconomic aspect relates to pressure on labor market legislation arising from the loss of the exchange rate.

Macro Aspects: Labor Markets and Monetary Stability

Economic and Monetary Union rests on the fundamental principle of monetary stability, and one of the main pillars of EMU is the independence of the central bank, according to the widely held view that central bank independence is a necessary and sufficient condition for price stability.[8] This principle has been (partially) challenged[9] on the ground that the correlation between central bank independence and inflation has to be assessed taking into account the characteristics of industrial relations and of the wage bargaining process in particular. More precisely, one result of these analyses is that the higher the level of wage bargaining coordination, the more efficient and less costly in terms of unemployment is (independent) monetary policy in curbing inflation.

Hall and Franzese (1998) advance, and test, the following three hypothesis: (a) there is a negative relationship between inflation and central bank independence (the traditional view about central bank independence and monetary stability); (b) the level of wage bargaining coordination has a direct effect on inflation irrespective of the role of central bank independence; and (c) in cases where the level of wage coordination is low, central bank independence lowers the rate of inflation only at the costs of higher rates of unemployment. Taken together, these three hypotheses determine a structure of monetary independence and wage bargaining arrangements leading to differentiated patterns of macroeconomic performance. Based on the average performance of the OECD countries over the period 1955–90, Hall and Franzese's findings are summarized in Table 5.3.

At first glance, the implications are a source of concern. EMU introduces

Table 5.3 Monetary policy and wage bargaining regimes and results

	CBI low	CBI high
CWB low	High unemployment with high inflation	High unemployment with low inflation
CWB high	Low unemployment with high inflation	Low unemployment with low inflation

Notes:
CBI = central bank independence.
CWB = coordinated wage bargaining.

Source: Hall and Franzese (1998).

no incentive to increase the degree of wage bargaining centralization to match the degree of centralization and independence of monetary policy. As a matter of fact, the establishment of EMU and of the European Central Bank reduces the centralization of wage bargaining as it leaves it, in the best case, at the national level. The straightforward implication is that EMU will achieve price stability at a higher cost in terms of unemployment compared to cases where wage bargaining centralization was higher. In addition, according to this view, higher unemployment would be unevenly distributed among countries according to the levels of wage bargaining centralization. Facing the same degree of central bank independence, countries where wage bargaining is more decentralized will suffer from higher unemployment.

By contrast, Bertola (1999) argues that wage bargaining within the euro area as a whole should be made less rather than more centralized. Given relevant differences in productivity, not only between countries but especially between regions, wage bargaining structures should be kept at the lowest possible level (at least regional). Decentralization would also take into account the fact, addressed above, that regional specialization has been increasing over the recent past. Regional wage bargaining structures would therefore represent a partial substitute of low labor mobility within EMU (Bertola, 1999). An issue to be watched closely, therefore, is to what extent monetary integration increases (or reduces) the amount of wage bargaining centralization or, to put it differently, to what extent national trade unions across Europe coordinate wage bargaining. Some initial evidence suggests, however, that European trade unions are increasingly taking into account the EMU dimension in their bargaining strategies (European Foundation for the Improvement of Living and Working Conditions, 2000).

Micro Aspects: The Evolution of Labor Market and Welfare State Institutions

The view just presented may be further specified, however. Another view[10] holds that the amount of unemployment, for a given level of monetary policy independence, is inversely correlated with the degree of labor market flexibility, itself dependent on the characteristics of the institutions regulating labor markets. In addition, given a supranational central bank, unemployment costs of monetary stabilization will be a function of the level of structural unemployment (that is, the rate of unemployment not dependent on cyclical factors) which is the average of national levels of structural unemployment. In such a case what improves the smooth operation of monetary union is an increase in the level of labor market flexibility, itself dependent on national institutional characteristics.

A comprehensive review of this issue is presented in Nickell (1997), who studies the impact of labor market regulations on unemployment. Drawing on labor market data for a number of OECD countries, he finds that continental European countries exhibit different degrees of labor market rigidities and they are generally higher than in the UK and the USA. He regresses his indicators of labor market rigidity against total, long-term and short-term unemployment. The unemployment rate is positively affected by (unrestricted) unemployment benefits, especially if associated with lack of incentives to accept jobs; lower pay rates in different sectors; a high level of union militancy without a high level of coordination with employers' associations in wage bargaining (which is equivalent to a low level of wage bargaining centralization as discussed above); high labor tax rates, especially if associated with high minimum wages; and a low level of workers' skills. The same analysis, however, shows that other labor market institutions do not affect the rate of unemployment, such as workers' protection legislation and labor standards; unemployment benefits, if they are accompanied by appropriate job search incentives; and high union militancy rates, if associated with high levels of coordination with employers' associations in wage-setting procedures (thus confirming evidence reported in the previous section).

These results are relevant to our discussion especially from one point of view. While some labor market institutions may affect unemployment more than others, their interaction plays a potentially important role. We can, therefore, draw some additional implications: increased 'flexibility,' understood as the appropriate combination of different labor market institutions, may increase employment for a given degree of monetary policy independence.

The Road to More Flexibility: Institutional Competition or Social Dumping?

What are the implications for the endogenous approach to EMU? The priority of a national as opposed to a European dimension in labor market policies and the relevance of the labor market institutions for employment have led many analysts and policy makers to predict 'institutional competition' or, in some cases, 'social dumping' under EMU. Deeper international integration and 'globalization' increase competition between product and factor (especially labor) markets, they reason. Elimination of exchange rate movements clearly increases such competitive pressures. To the extent that labor market regulations affect labor costs and hence competitiveness, absent a supranational labor market regulation, national (and subnational) regulatory bodies, often with the agreement or under the pressure of workers' and employers' representative bodies, can be expected to loosen labor market regulations in order to increase competitiveness. Better competitive positions, and hence better employment opportunities, could be the result of cheaper domestic production costs and increased foreign capital inflows attracted by them. As a consequence, a 'race to the bottom' might result in labor regulations. This concern has been raised especially with respect to the EU's future enlargement to Central and Eastern European countries, which typically have much lower labor costs compared to current EU members.[11]

How real is this possibility? As of now, evidence is still too limited to offer a final verdict. Here we can report evidence regarding the impact of international competition on employment and wage levels and evidence on the recent evolution of social institutions in Europe.

A first set of evidence looks at the effects of international competition on employment and wage levels in manufacturing sectors in the core EU countries (Padoan, 2000b).[12] This is useful in assessing the degree of exposure of these economies to competition from low-wage countries. Estimation results show that labor markets in continental European countries, irrespective of the manufacturing sector considered, react to international competition more through changes (decreases) in employment levels than through wage cuts. The reverse is true in the UK and the smaller Nordic countries. This can be taken as evidence of a generalized 'labor market rigidity' in continental Europe.

Second, international competition exerts a stronger (negative) pressure on both wages and employment levels in sectors where the country exhibits a trade comparative disadvantage, while such pressure is much weaker or absent in sectors where the country enjoys a comparative advantage. This implies that the widespread assertion that international competition, which may be increased by forms of social dumping, will hurt especially unskilled-labor-intensive sectors must be qualified. (For instance, Italy, which has a comparative advantage in traditional labor-intensive sectors, does not show strong pressures on its labor markets in these sectors.) One implication is the following. The role of labor market institutions which affect performance of both wage and employment levels cannot be separated from the role of other factors (most notably, cumulated learning, scale effects and specific knowledge) which determine the overall trade performance of a sector.

A second set of evidence looks at changing labor market institutions. Boeri (2000) provides a detailed analysis of institutional changes in labor market regulation and social security legislation in Europe over the past 15 years, a period of increasing monetary integration. His relevant findings are four. First, there is no evidence of a race to the bottom in social security contributions. Quite the contrary, a 'race to the top' may be identified, especially in the D-mark zone countries (that is, those where monetary integration has been more intense and prolonged). Second, there is some evidence of convergence in pension schemes towards the middle range. Third, some evidence of declining generosity in unemployment benefits exists, but this trend has not been uniform and has been only marginal in the D-mark zone. Finally, there is some evidence of a decline in the extent of employment protection legislation.

The author concludes that we cannot find any clear evidence of a tendency towards one model of European social legislation or of increased labor market flexibility. Participation in currency agreements (the D-mark zone) does not seem to matter much for the direction and intensity of changes in social legislation. In addition, the hypothesis of social dumping (race to the bottom) is not supported, although the two Iberian countries and the Netherlands have recently introduced 'major' reforms in employment protection legislation.

INTERACTIONS BETWEEN POLICY AREAS

The evidence that we have reviewed in the previous paragraphs is mixed. In some cases, such as cyclical convergence or integrating financial markets, the evolution of the EMU area is pointing toward a strengthening euro zone. In other cases, such as the evolution of national specialization, words of caution are in order. Evidence on the evolution of social and labor market institutions, in addition, does not show any clear sign that a euro-zone model is emerging. Nonetheless, over the past two decades, under the impact of the Single Market and monetary integration, the EU economy has been changing in ways that facilitate adjustment. An increasing convergence towards an optimal currency area configuration, however, would represent only a necessary and not sufficient condition for a successful EMU. A convergence of national economic policies towards a coherent European model of governance is needed.

The issue of policy convergence covers two aspects. The first deals with policy spillovers (interactions), while the second deals with policy convergence strictly defined. In the case of markets, the mechanism leading to endogenous change is deeper monetary integration. In the case of policies, the driving force is centralization of monetary policy at a supranational level. Once the shift is made from several national monetary policies to a single, supranational policy and institution, other policy areas and institutions are affected and face pressures to adjust.

The interaction between policy areas is a more complex issue than can be fully explored here. Let us nonetheless consider the extent to which outcomes in one policy area influence outcomes in another.

Monetary and Fiscal Policy

Cooperation between the single monetary policy and national budget policies increases benefits in terms of improved performance. Spillovers between monetary and fiscal policy support the idea that coordination is beneficial. OECD (1999) simulations show that switching to a common monetary policy increases the effectiveness of monetary stabilization to the extent that common monetary policy is geared to average and not country-specific inflation rates. However, as Bini-Smaghi and Casini (2000) stress, after the establishment of the European Central Bank (ECB) the exchange of information between monetary and fiscal policy authorities has become much weaker compared to, say, the EMS period, when national monetary and fiscal authorities in the ERM interacted on a permanent basis with tangible benefits for macroeconomic management. The implication is that centralization of monetary policy requires a strengthening of the so-called 'euro group' (former euro-11) (Jacquet and Pisani Ferry, 2000).

Cooperation among National Fiscal Policy Authorities

There are other reasons to favor a stronger 'euro group'. OECD (1999) shows that losses in the stabilization power of budget policies decrease when the number of countries allowing automatic stabilizers to operate increases. This number, in turn, increases as budget flexibility is restored.[13] The extent to which budget cooperation in the euro group increases the speed of convergence towards a 'stable budget regime' (understood as the fulfillment of the requirements of the Stability and Growth Pact) is an important issue. In a low-growth situation in the core euroland countries (notably Germany, Italy and partly France) such as the one prevailing at the early start of EMU, fiscal stabilization measures are harder to obtain. Budget coordination increases, if marginally, the overall growth rate, making it easier to converge to the 'stable budget regime'. Benefits from coordination increase if externalities can be exploited. Informal evidence suggests that these externalities are present. Within euroland, incentives for a coordinated policy action are larger in the core countries. At the outset of EMU, for example, peripheral countries (notably Ireland, Portugal, Spain) experienced higher growth and would have preferred a more restrictive policy stance. In this situation, the peripheral countries could tighten fiscal policy beyond the requirements of the Stability and Growth Pact while others could be somewhat more relaxed within the limits of the Pact.

Budget Policy Composition

Once financial and monetary stabilization are obtained, attention can be shifted towards a 'qualitative approach' to budget policy focusing on the composition of expenditure and taxation becomes more relevant. As discussed in the EC Commission document on public finances in EMU (EC Commission, 2000), as financial equilibrium approaches and growth resumes in Europe, the room for tax cuts increases. However, the Commission has reiterated that tax cuts are justified only when corresponding expenditure cuts are implemented, especially in light of unfounded pension liabilities. Under this approach, new attention is given to the composition of taxation with an eye toward its implications for long-term growth in particular. Once attention is shifted from aggregate revenues and expenditure to their composition, the allocation function of economic policy comes to the fore and the interaction between the macroeconomic and the microeconomic dimensions deepens. This is becoming particularly relevant for the exploitation of the opportunities offered by information and communication technologies (ICT).[14]

Tax Policy Cooperation

A widely held view is that monetary union requires tax harmonization to operate effectively under a regime of full capital mobility. An alternative view is that tax competition is beneficial as it stimulates policies to attract mobile capital and enhance the efficiency of financial markets. To the extent that tax competition produces effects on national budgets, it may interfere with cooperation among national fiscal authorities. It is not clear to what extent an 'optimal' tax regime can be designed in a monetary union. Different views and incentives are present. Core EU-12 countries have favored some form of tax harmonization. At the Feira European Council meeting in June 2000, a compromise agreement was reached under which countries will continue to set their own, different tax rates but national authorities will exchange information to prevent tax evasion. In practice, all major continental European governments (Germany, France and Italy) announced in 2000 major tax cuts favoring both households and business. This may suggest that a 'mixed regime' of tax harmonization and competition is emerging.[15]

These linkages between monetary unification on the one hand and other economic and structural reform on the other illustrate a more general point. The launching of monetary union and the introduction of a supranational central bank lead to a growing interconnection between macro and micro (structural) policies. This makes the issue of policy convergence much more complex than generally assumed.

POLICY CONVERGENCE

Policy convergence in EMU is really another name for a more complex and ambitious goal: a new model of EU economic governance. In discussing this point, one has to come to terms with the unique features of EMU, the coexistence of different levels of economic sovereignty – supranational, national and local – in which the community and intergovernmental dimensions coexist.

To understand the features of the EU policy regime, it is useful to distinguish between the macro and the microeconomic domains. It is not just a question of different policy domains, however; it is rather an issue of different mechanisms and rules, that is, different, yet interacting policy regimes. In what follows, we will look at the macroeconomic (monetary–fiscal) regime and at one specific microeconomic regime, employment policies (which is dealt with at the Community level under the so-called 'Luxembourg process'), one of the few areas where some evidence of performance is available.

The stability of policy regimes is a central question. Are regimes based on a structure of incentives that leads to mutually consistent behavior by actors involved, both policy and market agents? Are agents' behaviors consistent with monetary union specifically? This question should be evaluated in an evolving framework. As we have discussed above, monetary union generates pressure for change in both markets and policies. So we have to consider whether the response of agents to the pressures arising from EMU supports monetary union itself.

The Macroeconomic Regime

The discussion on policy interaction in the previous section leads to two implications. First, the creation of a supranational institution in one policy area generates pressures for change in other policy areas, in all of which at least some degree of supranationality is introduced. This suggests that a model of pure supranational monetary policy and pure national policies in other areas is unstable. Second, to the extent that a 'mixed' model of economic policy emerges, it must be based on a coherent set of policy incentives to produce consistent and stable outcomes. Policy convergence should be examined within this context. To discuss the point, it is useful to reconsider the evolution of macroeconomic policy regimes in place under the EMS, before EMU. This because one of the main (economic) justifications for the move from the fixed exchange rate regime to a single currency was that the former was becoming increasingly unsustainable in the presence of full capital mobility.[16]

The EMS can be described as a 'weak hegemonic regime,' based on asymmetric adjustment obligations between the key country, Germany, and the periphery. The main incentive for Germany's partners was the importation of monetary discipline, the exploitation of the public good of monetary stability provided by the center economy. The incentive for Germany to participate in the regime was, given domestic price stability, the support of its international competitiveness by preventing or limiting exchange rate devaluations in the periphery. The stability of the regime was obtained to the extent that national policies converged towards the German monetary policy stance. The regime collapsed when, after German unification, the core country was not willing to bear the cost of supporting the weaker (more inflation-prone) economies and the periphery was not willing to make the (deflationary) adjustment necessary to support the exchange rate regime in light of high capital mobility. The policy regime proved to be effective as an anti-inflationary mechanism, but it produced limited, if any, policy spillovers towards other areas (especially fiscal policy). The ERM crisis of 1992–93 showed that policy convergence had to extend to other areas beyond monetary and exchange rate policy, if it were to pass the test of the markets. As long as it succeeded, it proved that an 'intergovernmental' approach to macroeconomic policy requires leadership; its failure demonstrated that weak hegemonic leadership may be insufficient when market integration deepens beyond some critical threshold.

The decision to move forward from the EMS to EMU has led to a major change in the policy regime and in the policy convergence process. Policy convergence has been witnessed with respect to both monetary and fiscal policy. More importantly, it has shifted towards a more symmetric configuration.

The greater symmetry has in turn required two additional conditions in order to be effective: (a) the move from a hegemonic leadership structure to a supranational one; and (b) the imposition of high entry costs (fulfillment of the Maastricht convergence conditions under the threat of exclusion) as well as high exit costs (the costs associated with the possibility of one country leaving the single currency). In this respect, monetary union can be described as a club good (Padoan, 1997).

The Microeconomic Regime

The Stability and Growth Pact guarantees that, once monetary convergence has been obtained and a single monetary policy becomes feasible, national fiscal policies are managed according to common guidelines (and hence fiscal policy convergence is also obtained). However, the sustainability of monetary union requires some movement towards the configuration of an optimum currency area. Consequently, as one cannot rely on market forces alone to produce this convergence, monetary union requires the adoption of appropriate microeconomic (structural) policies to overcome labor and product market rigidities. The extent of harmonization or convergence of microeconomic policies towards common standards required by EMU remains to be seen and evidence discussed above shows little recent movement in this respect.

To accelerate policy reform, the EU has launched three sets of consultative procedures, known as the Cardiff, Luxembourg and Cologne processes. The Cardiff process involves the adoption of measures aimed at improving the performance of product markets. The Luxembourg process deals with employment policies. The Cologne process calls for enhanced interaction between microeconomic and macroeconomic policies. The voluntary, consultative approach taken in these processes is very much still in its infancy and, in many respects, lags behind the degree of cooperation that we observe even for budget policies.

To explore the implications of this approach, consider the case of employment policies within the Luxembourg process in more detail. Because no 'institutional dumping' process seem to be at work in the EU, as concluded above, any convergence of social policies is likely to take the form of a 'race to the top.' It is interesting to ask, therefore, whether the existing policy framework can support such a process.

In a nutshell, the EU employment policy framework operates as follows. Each year, every EU member state sets out its National Action Plan (NAP), which contains the policy actions it has taken to improve employment. The general philosophy of the approach is that flexibility in European labor markets can be obtained by moving away from 'passive' employment policies, such as unemployment benefits, towards 'active' policies, such as welfare-to-work schemes and active learning and retraining. Within the process, however, a wide range of policies is considered, including those supporting small and medium enterprises.

Policies are implemented at the national level, as only national governments have jurisdiction over such policies, and are classified according to a (long) list of 'policy guidelines' established by the Commission. These guidelines are grouped under four headings: employability (employment policies in the strict sense of the term, such as the creation of job placement agencies), adaptability (policies aimed at adapting workers to the new market conditions, such as retraining policies), entrepreneurship (policies aimed at improving the demand side of the labor market, such as incentives for small business), and equal opportunity (policies aimed at increasing the employment opportunities for women).

Each year, the NAPs are presented to the Commission and are reviewed by member states through a 'peer review' procedure. A final 'score' is assigned to each government, indicating the degree of fulfillment of the policy guidelines and identified 'best practices.' Policy recommendations are then directed to each member country by the Commission and the Council.

Retaining full control of policy, national governments are not subject to any explicit obligation.[17] Failure to follow recommendations brings no punishment or threat of exclusion, as was the case before the creation of the monetary union. In other words, as we move away from policies in which the supranational element prevails, the strength of the convergence process weakens.

Even in areas where there is no explicit obligation to adjust, however, there are substantial incentives for national governments to change policies. Two distinct sets of incentives operate: a 'competition' incentive and a 'cooperation' (regime-building) incentive. The competition incentive derives from both the policy arena and from the market. A country that performs poorly in improving its employment policies would see its reputation weaken and, consequently, its leverage in the design and implementation of EU policies at large diminish. This would be particularly worrying whenever the intergovernmental dimension is relevant. In addition, markets would punish a poor performer to the extent that inefficient policies make that country less attractive for investment, while good performers would presumably enjoy greater profitability and thus increased investment. The competition incentive will be increasingly relevant in a world of high capital mobility. In short, institutional competition will not go away; rather it may well produce a healthy improvement in EU economic performance, provided that it takes the form of exchange of best practices and provides content to the principle of subsidiarity.

The cooperation incentive is relevant to the extent that poor performance in any member of EMU weakens the performance and attractiveness of the euro area as a whole *vis-à-vis* the rest of the world. Poor policy and economic performance in any one member of the club decreases the quality of the club good (monetary union), generating a negative externality on the other club members. This will presumably lead to a strengthened peer pressure on the poor performer from the rest of the club members (and from the Commission). In this case, the supranational pressure might be more important that the intergovernmental pressure. To the extent that such an incentive structure strengthens, therefore, policy convergence could well be the result of the interaction of intergovernmentalism and supranationalism.

CONCLUSIONS

EMU is endogenous, to some extent, and derives from two complementary viewpoints. As suggested by Collignon's (1997) approach to currency areas, first, benefits from monetary union increase with the degree of economic integration for a given distribution of policy preferences among countries. Second, given the degree of integration, convergence in the distribution of policy preferences is necessary for net benefits to be generated by monetary unification. Pre-EMU monetary convergence has led to deeper integration, thus increasing net benefits. This has been obtained because the process of monetary integration in Europe has produced (or rather 'forced') convergence in 'revealed' policy preferences. However, while observed convergence relates to preferences for financial stability, the same is not yet clear for preferences and policies for more flexible product and labor markets. It remains to be seen whether the incentives to implement polices more consistent with an optimum currency area will be effective enough to produce the necessary policy adjustments. To the extent that the convergence of economic preferences and convergence of policy preferences are self-reinforcing, however, EMU is indeed a self-fulfilling, evolutionary mechanism.

Finally, if EMU can be considered to be a substantially endogenous process, one should ask what are the exogenous forces that are also contributing to adjustments in markets and policies that could underpin a more viable currency union.[18] A short answer is that the exogenous forces are the same ones that drive the EU integration process at large. Three main factors are particularly important.

The first factor can be understood as a regional response to the excess demand for international public goods (Padoan, 2000c), which in turn is the consequence of the collapse of the postwar hegemonic system. Regional agreements have been strengthened as a response to external threats. As Henning (1998) suggests, whenever the USA has behaved 'aggressively' in its macroeconomic and monetary relations with Europe, European countries have increased the degree of monetary cooperation among themselves in order to stem such 'aggressiveness.' Periods of 'benign' attitudes on the part of the American authorities saw a retardation or even backsliding in European monetary integration.

Henning's framework can be adapted to the EMU phase, which represents the highest degree of European monetary cooperation, and broadened. An 'aggressive' US attitude towards Europe would favor a European attitude of 'non-cooperation' *vis-à-vis* the USA, and perhaps even foster an attempt to redirect abroad factors of instability inside the EU.[19] Conversely, a benign American attitude would favor adoption of a similar attitude by Europe. Such a pattern of response would constitute 'tit-for-tat' behavior, which, as Axelrod (1984) shows, could lead to more cooperation by raising the costs of defection.

The second exogenous factor is related to the traditional European strategy of deepening integration to support its overall performance and to close the competitiveness gap with the USA. The most notable examples are the launching of the then Single Market as a response to 'eurosclerosis' and the 'Lisbon strategy' to make Europe the 'best knowledge-based economy in the world.'

The institutional response to the enlargement of the EU to perhaps 27 members represents the third exogenous factor. The Nice Intergovernmental Conference has delivered a clear message: the way forward for EU integration is 'reinforced co-operation,' that is, through initiatives taken by a subset of members, a restricted club, to move further on towards deeper integration. EMU will most likely be the most relevant example of this new institutional model and, to the extent that EMU membership increases, it would both signal the success of monetary union and represent a major engine for deeper European integration in areas beyond economic and monetary union.

NOTES

1. I acknowledge financial support from the University of Rome, 'La Sapienza.'
2. Costs and benefits of monetary unions are amply discussed in the literature. For an overall evaluation, see, for example, De Grauwe (1992).
3. A similar analysis was developed by Artis and Zhang (1995).
4. In a long-term perspective, export-led growth should matter less than productivity-led growth. However, for a number of European countries the advent of flexible exchange

rates presented the possibility of competitive devaluations, which provided a temporary boost to exports and growth and, to the extent they were unanticipated, significantly influenced business attitudes towards investment.

5. The same tests have been used in Belke and Gros (1997).
6. There is here a clear difference from the Bretton Woods system, which was focused on the central country's (the USA's) trade deficit.
7. Evidence reported in this paragraph also draws on Padoan (2000b). Lack of available data on regional per capita output prevented us from carrying out the estimation beyond 1995.
8. For a recent reassessment of the issue see Eijffinger and De Haan (1996).
9. See Iversen (1998) and Hall and Franzese (1998).
10. See, for instance, Center for Economic Policy Research (1995) and Nickell (1997).
11. Central and Eastern European countries have hourly labor costs which are from one-third to one-tenth of the EU average. See CEPR (1998), table 4.4.
12. Based on a model suggested by Neven and Wyplosz (1996).
13. On the implications of cooperation for economic policy in EMU see Buti and Sapir (1998).
14. Exploiting such technology requires more efficient and flexible product markets as well as more investment and integration in innovation activities. Success in these tasks can be expected to reduce unemployment accordingly. This is the focus of the so-called 'Cardiff Process'.
15. It has been argued that tax competition has led to excessive labor tax loads, which in turn may explain a large part of European unemployment (Daveri and Tabellini, 1997). So it may be that tax competition, to the extent that it leads to excessively low taxation on capital, may lead to more labor market competition and thus adjustment.
16. Eichengreen (1994) argues that, once full financial integration is achieved, only two monetary regimes are sustainable, monetary union or fully flexible exchange rates. Intermediate regimes such as pegged exchange rates come under heavy pressure and are likely to eventually collapse.
17. In some areas, of course, national governments must fulfill obligations emanating from Commission Directives such as those related to the prohibition of implementing state aids.
18. I thank Randy Henning for raising this issue.
19. Reference is the scenario explored by Benassy et al. (1997).

REFERENCES

Artis, M. and W. Zhang (1995), 'International Business Cycles and the ERM: Is There a European Business Cycle?', CEPR Discussion Paper no. 1191, August.

Axelrod, R. (1984), *The Evolution of Cooperation*, New York: Basic Books.

Barro, Robert J. and Xavier Sala-i-Martin (1992), *Economic Growth*, Cambridge: MIT Press.

Bayoumi, T. and B. Eichengreen (1998), 'Shocking Aspects of Monetary Unification,' CEPR Discussion Paper no. 643, March.

Belke, A. and D. Gros (1997), 'Estimating the Costs and Benefits of EMU: The Impact of External Shocks on Labour Markets,' CEPR Discussion Paper no. 9795.

Benassy, A., M. Benoit and J. Pisani-Ferry (1997), 'The Euro and Exchange Rate Stability,' presented at the Fondation Camille Gutt, Imf Seminar on EMU and the International Monetary System, Washington, 17–18 March.

Bertola G. (1999), 'Labor Markets in the European Union,' EUI Working Papers 99/24.

Bini-Smaghi, Lorenzo and Claudio Casini (2000), 'Monetary and Fiscal Policy Co-operation: Institutions and Procedures in EMU,' *Journal of Common Market Studies*, **38** (September), 375–91.

Boeri, T. (2000), 'Social Europe. Dramatic visions and real complexity,' CEPR Discussion Paper no. 2371.

Buti, Marco and André Sapir (eds) (1998), *Economic Policy in EMU. A Study by the European Commission Services*, Oxford: Oxford University Press.

Center for Economic Policy Research (1995), *Monitoring European Integration 5: Unemployment Choices for Europe*, London.

Collignon, S. (1997), 'European Monetary Union, Convergence and Sustainability,' Association pour l'Union Monétaire en Europe.

Danthine J., F. Giavazzi and E. von Thadden (2000), 'European Financial Markets after EMU. A First Assessment,' CEPR Discussion Paper no. 2413.

Daveri, C. and G. Tabellini (1997), 'Unemployment, Growth, and Taxation in Industrial Countries', CEPR Discussion Paper no. 1615.

De Grauwe, P. (1992), *The Economics of Monetary Integration*, Oxford: Oxford University Press.

Eichengreen, B. (1994), *International Monetary Arrangements for the 21st Century*, Washington, DC: Brookings Institution.

Eijffinger, S. and J. De Haan (1996), 'The Political Economy of Central Independence,' Special Paper in International Economy 19, Princeton: Princeton University Press.

European Commission (2000), 'Public Finances in EMU,' May.

European Foundation for the Improvement of Living and Working Conditions (2000), 'The "Europeanisation" of collective bargaining,' http://www.eiro.eurofound.ie/1999/07/study/TN9907201S.html.

Frankel, J. and A.K. Rose (1996), 'The Endogeneity of the Optimum Currency Area Criteria,' NBER Working Paper no. 5700, August.

Hall, P. and R. Franzese (1998), 'Mixed Signals: Central Bank Independence, Coordinated Wage Bargaining, and European Monetary Union,' *International Organization*, **52** (summer), 505–35.

Henning, R. (1998), 'Systemic Conflict and Regional Monetary Integration: The Case of Europe,' *International Organization*, **52** (summer), 537–74.

Iversen, T. (1998), 'Wage Bargaining, Central Bank Independence, and the Real Effects of Money', *International Organization*, **52** (summer), 469–504.

Jacquet, P. and J. Pisani-Ferry (2000), 'La coordination des politiques économiques dans la zone euro: bilan et propositions,' *Conseil d'Analyse Economique. Questions Européenes*, Paris: La Documentation Française.

Kraus, T. (2001), 'The Impact of EMU on the Structure of European Equity Returns: An Empirical Analysis of the First 21 Months,' IMF Working Paper WP/01/84.

Midelfart-Knarvik, K., H. Overman, S. Redding and A. Venables (2000), 'The Location of European Industry,' report prepared for the Directorate General for Economic and Financial Affairs, European Commission.

Neven, D. and C. Wyplosz (1996), 'Relative Prices and Trade Restructuring in European Industry,' CEPR Discussion Paper no. 1451.

Nickell, S. (1997), 'Unemployment and Labor Market Rigidities: Europe versus North America,' *Journal of Economic Perspectives*, **11**, (3), 55–74.

OECD (1999), *EMU. Facts, Challenges and Policies*, Paris: OECD.

Paci, Roberto and Francesco Pigliaru (2000), 'European regional growth. Do sectors matter?,' in John Adams and Francesco Pigliaru (eds), *Economic Growth and Change*, Cheltenham, UK and Northampton, MA, USA: Edward Elgar.

Padoan, Pier Carlo (1997), 'Regional agreements as clubs, the European case,' in E. Mansfield and H. Milner (eds), *The Political Economy of Regionalism*, New York: Columbia University Press.

Padoan, Pier Carlo (2000a), 'The role of the Euro in the international system: A European view,' in Randall Henning and Pier Carlo Padoan (eds), *Transatlantic Perspectives on the Euro*, Washington, DC: European Economic Studies Association and Brookings Institution.

Padoan, Pier Carlo (ed.) (2000b), *Employment and Growth in European Monetary Union*, Cheltenham, UK and Northampton, MA, USA: Edward Elgar.

Padoan, P.C. (2000c), 'Globalization, regionalism, and the nation state. Top down and bottom up,' in Maurizio Franzini and Roberto F. Pizzuti (eds), *Globalization, Institutions, and Social Cohesion*, Berlin and Heidelberg: Springer.

Verspagen, B. (2000), 'European regional clubs: do they exist and where are they heading?', in John Adams and Francesco Pigliaru (eds), *Economic Growth and Change*, Cheltenham, UK and Northampton, MA, USA: Edward Elgar.

COMMENT

Peter Bernholz

In his chapter Padoan rightly states that the European Monetary Union is presently not an optimal currency area. But he stresses that endogenous factors are pushing the system in that direction, though some doubts are still entertained as to whether this will be sufficient to maintain EMU without further supranational policy measures. A valuable overview of several relevant empirical results is presented which mostly support the latter hypothesis.

My critical remarks refer to two points. First, since there has never been an optimal currency area in history, how much of an approach towards such an ideal type in the sense of Max Weber is really necessary? Second, Padoan has not addressed the issues raised by public choice theory and constitutional economics. Closely related to this second point is the question of how far 'countries' preferences' for 'containing inflation' versus 'output-stabilization-oriented monetary policies' have and should converge.

As regards the first question, historical evidence for federal states like the USA, Switzerland and Germany before 1900 shows that a common currency could exist for decades without much of a federal system and central economic policies. All these nations had no federal income taxes during that time, and their very limited revenues stemmed mainly from import duties. The USA and Switzerland didn't even have a central bank during that period, though they enjoyed a metallic monetary standard with full convertibility of banknotes and checking accounts at fixed parities.

This immediately leads to the gold standard before 1914, which was in fact a common worldwide monetary system, perhaps somewhat directed by the Bank of England, but certainly with negligible government fiscal and economic policy cooperation. And within the gold standard there had existed for decades the Latin Monetary (with France, Belgium, Italy, Switzerland and Greece as members) and the Scandinavian Monetary Unions, which were only abolished because of World War I. As for the latter, exchange rates were not even quoted among the member countries' currencies. Also, although the Latin Monetary Union faced crises from time to time, these were mainly – apart from some periods of inconvertibility of Italian banknotes – caused by efforts to maintain bimetallism of gold and silver, which was finally abolished (Lexis, 1900).

Now it can be argued that all these experiences were based on metallic commodity money, whereas the euro is a discretionary paper money standard. This is certainly true, but the optimal currency arguments are not directed to this difference. Moreover, the Maastricht Treaty has put in its place an independence of the European Central Bank (ECB) which is legally much stronger than that of other independent central banks, including the German Bundesbank (Bernholz, 1999). And from the literature it seems to follow that independence of central banks works in favour of monetary stability (Eijffinger and de Haan, 1996). This argument leads directly to the question of public finances and the Stability Pact. Padoan is certainly right that if its conditions were met (over business cycles), this would put less pressure by certain member states on the ECB to follow a more expansionary policy. But the ECB could withstand such pressures, the Treaty even forbids financing any deficits. Now assume as a worst-case scenario that one country, because of increasing deficits, was no longer able to serve its debt. Then, if the other member states were not prepared to come to its rescue, and if the ECB stuck to its policy of monetary stability, this country would have to declare open bankruptcy. The losses would have to be borne by creditors instead of taxpayers. This would be a welcome innovation. For after one such case had happened the financial markets would take up their monitoring functions by asking for high-interest premiums for additional debts of highly indebted countries. This would certainly make governments more reluctant to accumulate debt. Let us recall that a return to such conditions has historical precedents. Philippe II led Spain into three open bankruptcies without touching the Spanish silver currency, which went on to circulate, especially in the 'piece of eight', the precursor of the dollar, for centuries as an international currency.

This brings us to the second critical point. Public choice theory has shown for decades that democratic governments have a strong tendency towards ever-increasing government expenditures (as a share of GDP) and regulations (Bernholz, 1982; Weede, 1986; Tanzi and Schuknecht, 1997), with negative consequences for GDP growth and employment. This is also in tune with Padoan's statement that 'there is no evidence of a race to the bottom in social security contributions. Quite the contrary, a 'race to the top' may be identified . . .' On the other hand, it is now well known that the present level of the social security system cannot be maintained in the future, especially in Germany, France and Italy. Given these tendencies and the reluctance of politicians, depending on incompletely informed voters for their re-election and pressured by interest groups, it seems that only systems competition within open markets for labour, capital, goods and services in the EU will force governments to take the necessary reforms earlier than with harmonization of taxes and social security systems. The same is true for rigid labour markets. I therefore doubt that 'one cannot rely on market forces alone to produce this convergence . . .', provided, however, that systems competition among the member states is fully permitted.

Padoan, in a sense, also seems to agree with this statement. For he explains that

> A country that performs poorly in improving its employment policies would see its reputation weaken and, consequently, its leverage in the design and implementation of EU policies at large diminish. . . . In addition, markets would punish a poor performer to the extent that inefficient policies make that country less attractive for investment . . .

It follows from this arguments that it may be true 'that a model of pure supranational monetary policy and pure national policies in other areas is unstable'. But apart from the fact that this statement should not refer to a model but to reality, it is exactly the question of to what extent supranational policies will be necessary. And here the above arguments seem to show that less is probably better than more.

I would like to add that a strict limitation of the jurisdiction of the European Centre is also preferable, first, to prevent the ever-rising share in public expenditures and in the power to regulate which has until now always been observed in federal states, and second, to ensure the principle of citizens' sovereignty that the decision-making powers are devolved as far as possible to the lowest feasible level (European Constitutional Group, 1993).

I conclude with two minor points. First, it is an exaggeration to say that the 1992/93 crisis of the European Monetary Union was only caused by the conflict about adequate monetary policies in the wake of German unification, after free capital mobility had been introduced. Several currencies, like those of Italy, the UK and Ireland, were already heavily overvalued in the 1980s (Bernholz, 1999, pp. 765ff.). Second, I do not understand Figure 5.1. Why is it that *NB* is the line 'where benefits and costs [of integration] offset each other?' Why should *NB* be a straight line? And why does its slope reflect 'the degree of integration of the Union's member economies'? I can understand that benefits rise with *S*, the extension of the Union, because of economies of scale. But why should costs and in what sense rise with *A*, 'the propensity of the Union's members to use monetary policy for output stabilization'? But if all the members agreed on such a policy, would they not count such policies as beneficial? Or are the costs measured in terms of rates of inflation? And dA/dS signifies the change of *A* if *S* rises, which would mean that the costs rise with *S*, from which it would follow that a steeper rise of *A* with *S* would reduce but not increase the set of points *C*, which, by contrast, according to the author would raise the incentives to create a monetary union. But perhaps I have just misunderstood the figure and its explanation.

REFERENCES

Bernholz, Peter (1982), 'Expanding Welfare State. Democracy and Free Market Economy: Are They Compatible?', in Rudolf Richter and Hans F. Zacher (eds), *Social Policy in a Free Market Economy*, Zeitschrift für die Gesamte Staatswissenschaft (Journal of Institutional and Theoretical Economics), **138**(3).

Bernholz, Peter (1999), 'The Bundesbank and the process of European monetary integration', in Deutsche Bundesbank (ed.), *Fifty Years of the Deutsche Mark. Central Bank and the Currency in Germany since 1948*, Oxford: Oxford University Press, pp. 731–89.

Eijffinger, Sylvester C.W. and Jacob de Haan (1996), 'The Political Economy of Central Bank Independence', *Special Papers in International Economics*, **19**, Princeton, NJ: Princeton University.

European Constitutional Group (1993); *A Proposal for a European Constitution.* Brussels/London: European Policy Forum. See also, 'A Proposal for a European Constitution (Summary of Main Features)', extract from the Report, August, 1997.

Lexis, Wilhelm (1900), 'Muenzbund (lateinischer)', in J. Conrad, L. Elster, W. Lexis and E. Loening (eds), *Handwoerterbuch der Staatswissenschaften*, Jena: Gustav Fischer, 2nd edn, vol. 5, pp. 893–8.

Tanzi, Vito and Ludger Schuknecht (1997), 'Reforming Government: An Overview of Recent Experience', *European Journal of Political Economy*, **13**, 395–417.

Weede, Erich (1986), 'Catch-up, Distributional Coalitions and Government Growth or Decline in Industrialized Democracies', *The British Journal of Sociology*, **27**, 194–220.

6. The role of international monetary institutions after the EMU and the Asian crises: some preliminary ideas using constitutional economics*

Friedrich Schneider

1. INTRODUCTION

The realization of the euro as the single currency (or European Monetary Union, EMU) promises to be one of the great economic events in modern history. It will certainly be the most important change in the international monetary system since President Nixon took the US dollar off the gold standard in 1971, which resulted in the world monetary system adopting flexible exchange rates. The introduction of the euro in 2002 will have important economic consequences for the EU countries (see section 2) and will challenge the status of the dollar in the international monetary system (see section 3.1). It will also lead to a change of the monetary power configuration, because the monopoly situation of the dollar will be ended. For this and other reasons (such as the Asian crisis) the introduction of the euro will be the most important development since the dollar replaced the pound sterling as the dominant international currency during World War I. The international monetary institutions (such as the IMF, the World Bank and so on) will thus face new challenges and should rise to them (see section 3.2). In section 4 some theoretical ideas are put forward relating to how a new international monetary institution should operate. With the help of constitutional economics it will be shown how such a monetary institution should be configured in order to operate much more efficiently and react more appropriately to major financial economic crises such as the Asian one. In section 5 some elements of a 'new' institutional design of an international monetary system are developed, from which a new structure will be derived regarding what the major tasks should be and how this 'reformed' institution should operate. Section 6 summarizes the main results and draws some conclusions.

2. THE CONSEQUENCES OF THE MONETARY UNION FOR THE EU COUNTRIES

European Monetary Union has been an economic as well as a political project. This means that the idea of EMU has not been derived solely from an economic perspective and in particular is not a straightforward implementation of the theory of optimum currency areas, as the EU cannot be regarded *ex ante* as an optimum currency area.[1] Instead EMU, which is at least partially justifiable in terms of modern economic theories,[2] has fulfilled positive as well as negative expectations. These are shown in Table 6.1.

Table 6.1 Positive and negative expectations of the EMU

Expectations	Economic theory
Positive	New growth theory
(1) Economic growth (in general)	
(2) (Faster) development/convergence of less-developed EU countries	
Negative	
(1) Higher inflation, especially in low-inflation EU countries	New stabilization theory Theory of optimum currency areas
(2) Increased (and permanent) one-sided transfer payments	

2.1 Positive Expectations of the European Monetary Union

Economic growth

The scientific economic justification for the expectation of economic growth rests mainly on the following hypotheses: the realization of monetary union leads to a reduction of exchange rate uncertainty, and hence to a decrease in the risk premium of the interest rate and a decrease in the economy's real interest rates. Furthermore, it leads to a decrease in transaction costs, in particular in costs of exchanging currencies and of insuring against risks of exchange rate fluctuations. In addition, it increases price transparency and thus leads to more competition and therefore also to price reductions, with the consequence that demand for consumption and investment increases. By using the results of new or endogenous growth theory, it is possible to derive not only positive income-level effects but also some important long-run growth effects. Thus a reduction of real interest rates is supposed to lead not only to a substitution effect from labour to capital, thereby increasing per capita income (this is the typical effect, derived from traditional neoclassical growth theory[3]), but also to create a learning effect, which leads to permanent increases in per capita income. This mechanism has been developed by new growth theory,[4] which operates as follows: capital accumulation from the substitution effect leads to an increase in labour productivity, caused by learning effects and generated by additional knowledge embodied in the capital accumulation process. This process is extended by the public-good aspect of knowledge, which is effective across firms, sectors and countries, and is embodied in interfirm, intersectoral and international spillovers.

Faster growth of less-developed EU countries

The less-developed EU member countries have been most supportive of EMU and want to participate in it as soon as possible, because they believe it will foster their economic development.[5] One can differentiate between direct and indirect development-enhancing effects of EMU. The former are:

- the removal of exchange rate uncertainties;
- (the expected) rise in direct foreign investment; and
- a possible increase of financial transfers to the less-developed EU countries.

The most important effect is the expected rise in direct foreign investment as a response to the elimination of exchange rate uncertainty. Here again, the expectations of substantial growth effects have been supported by new growth theory. This approach argues that the decisive development-enhancing factors are technology transfer from the more developed countries and investment in infrastructure, in particular education and training (human capital), in the less-developed EU countries. The main hypothesis is that EMU would increase foreign direct investment in less-developed member countries, these direct foreign investments would bring in the technology needed for development. Based on this hypothesis, one can derive positive spillovers to other sectors, which will lead to an increase in human capital in the whole economy. Indirect development-enhancing effects include all the positive stabilization effects that can be expected for less-developed countries, but also for developed countries due to spillover effects from the prospect of entering the EMU. The main stabilization effects are:

- the discipline forced by the convergence criteria,
- the credibility gained from the European Central Bank; and
- an increase in political stability.

These stabilization effects function to support the intended convergence, because the necessary sustainable growth process will probably occur in a situation of political and economic stability.

2.2 Negative Expectations

The negative expectations of EMU, on the contrary, relate mainly to the following two aspects:

- higher inflation in the low-inflation EU countries; and
- conflicts between EU members because of large, one-sided transfer payments.

Higher inflation

Particularly in Germany, Austria and the Netherlands, one of the main reasons for opposition to EMU by the population has been the fear of increasing inflation in these low-inflation countries. There are different theoretical arguments for such a development. The main one refers to structural differences between the member countries, which are: differences in the preferences about inflation and unemployment of the voting population, differences in market institutions, and differences in fiscal systems.[6] The main hypothesis with respect to the derivation of inflation effects is: the price stability reputation of the newly established European Central Bank (ECB) will be lower than that of the former German Bundesbank, and consequently inflation expectations will tend to be higher for the previously low-inflation countries, at least temporarily. Inflationary tendencies of EMU for the low-inflation countries can be derived from this line of reasoning, when the following hypothesis is valid: different 'optimum' inflation rates of the single member countries will lead to compromises in the EMU, so that the political pressure from countries with high 'optimal' inflation rates will produce a kind of 'average' inflation rate in the EMU that is higher than the desired rate of countries with lower optimal inflation rates.

Transfer payments

After the introduction of the euro, the exchange rate policy of the EU member countries is eliminated and cannot be used as a shock absorption mechanism. Price (wage) flexibility and labour mobility are not sufficiently effective and developed in Western Europe, so that the great fear is that the job of shock absorption has to be done mainly through financial transfers. As long as there is no constitutional EU arrangement with respect to regional redistribution, such as the Austrian or German system of 'Finanzausgleich', political conflicts will arise, because of the fear of enforced discretionary redistribution associated with financial transfers in crisis situations.[7] Thus an EMU which tends to produce political conflicts about the amount of fiscal redistribution will destabilize itself. The worst possible consequence will then be a failure of or withdrawal from the EMU, which would incur large costs for the EU and its member countries.

2.3 Institutional Precautions/Arrangements of the EMU

As politicians and their advisers were largely aware of the possible negative aspects associated with the EMU, they set up a number of institutional precautions/arrangements in the Maastricht Treaty and in the subsequent EU summits; these are shown in Table 6.2.

Table 6.2 Institutional precautions/arrangements of the EMU

1. The Maastricht Treaty	
1.1. Statute of the ECB	(i) Commitment to price stability
	(ii) Independence of the ECB
	(iii) Prohibition of government deficit financing
1.2. No bailout clause	
1.3. Fiscal convergence criteria	(i) Government budget deficit
	(ii) Government overall debt
1.4. Monetary structural convergence criteria	(i) Inflation convergence
	(ii) Long-term interest rate convergence
	(iii) Exchange rate stabilization
2. At recent summits	
2.1. Stability Pact	(i) Fiscal and budgetary discipline

There are three areas of economic policy in which the Maastricht Treaty introduced important institutional arrangements. These are:

- monetary policy
- fiscal policy; and
- structural adjustment policy.

Monetary policy

Here, the statute of the European Central Bank is of particular relevance.[8] In order to minimize the inflation risk, the ECB has been assigned a strong position. This can be seen in the following three features:

(i) commitment of the ECB to price stability as its main goal (article 105 treaty establishing the European community, ECT);

(ii) institutional independence of the ECB and independence of its employees (article 107 ECT); and
(iii) prohibition of government deficit financing by the ECB (article 104 ECT).

Fiscal policy
In the fiscal policy area two aspects are important:

(i) the 'no bailout' clause (article 104 ECT); and
(ii) the fiscal convergence criteria, which restrict the government budget deficit and the overall government debt to certain (politically accepted) levels.

Structural adjustment policy
Further criteria set out in the Maastricht Treaty are designed to ensure that the structural convergence process has gone far enough. Countries that want to participate in EMU are obliged to fulfil the inflation, the interest rate and the exchange rate criteria as laid out in the Maastricht Treaty.

Recent summit agreements
Here the provisions of the so-called Stability and Growth Pact agreed in Dublin in 1996 and confirmed in Amsterdam in 1997 are particularly important. This Pact provides a framework for maintaining and enforcing the Maastricht fiscal criteria after EMU has begun. It restates the commitment to a maximum budget deficit of 3 per cent of GDP and, except in special circumstances, applies sanctions to countries whose deficits exceed this level. Whether such sanctions can really be enforced is an open question, but at least an attempt has been made.

3. THE NEW TASKS OF THE INTERNATIONAL MONETARY INSTITUTIONS AFTER THE EMU AND AFTER THE ASIAN CRISES

3.1 The Euro and the US Dollar as the Two Main Currencies

If one assumes that the euro will continue to be a stable currency, a new situation arises in the financial world. Whether the euro can compete with the US dollar depends on whether it will continue to be a stable currency; the stability of the euro depends, among other things, on the following four factors:

1. size of the transaction domain;
2. stability of monetary policy;
3. stability of the political system; and
4. fall-back value.

Size of the transaction domain

It is obvious that a currency used by a hundred million people is much more liquid than one used by one million people. The larger the single currency area, the better it can act as a cushion against shocks. Comparing the size of the GDP of the EU's 11 or 15 member countries with that of Japan and the USA immediately makes the EU into a monetary 'player' in the same league as the USA and Japan. Over time, as other EU member countries join, as the per capita incomes of the poorer members of the EU catch up, and as the EU expands into the rest of Central Europe, the EU will have a substantially larger GDP than the USA. This size of market is attractive not only for domestic, but also for foreign, investors, mostly because of the stability and the size of the new currency.

Stability of monetary policy

As already argued in section 2.3, European monetary policy has the primary goal of price and monetary stability. This is especially evident if one analyses the institutional design of the European Monetary System, in which all forseeable steps have been undertaken to promote a stable currency.

Stability of the political system

Monetary stability, of course, depends on monetary policy, and monetary policy is in turn affected by political stability. Strong international currencies have always been linked to strong and stable governments. How strong the European political union will be in future, from a purely political perspective, depends on whether the EU is able to undertake major reforms in its political and economic policy organizations. There are some first (hopeful) signs, but this process has just started and it is an open question how successful the EU will be in this respect.

The fall-back factor

Most modern currencies have no real fall-back factor as the older currencies had, which were either gold or silver standards or convertible into one or both of those metals; hence, unlike the modern paper currencies, the former currency had a fall-back value if the state collapsed. However, most EU member countries have a considerable amount of reserves in US dollars and in gold, which can be treated as a fall-back factor. Thus the euro should stand up against the US dollar, especially as it has two great strengths: first, a large and expanding transaction size, and, second, a culture of stability surrounding the ECB in Frankfurt. Initially the EU-11 member countries will be smaller than the dollar area, but as other members enter, as the EU expands and as the poorer countries catch up, the euro area will eventually be larger than the dollar area. From the standpoint of monetary policies, there is also not much to choose between the two areas. Information is globally mobile and there is no reason why the ECB should not become as efficient as the Federal Reserve System in the USA. However, the euro has still two weaknesses: it is not backed by a European Federal Union and it has no real fall-back value. In an unstable world these weaknesses could be dangerous.

It is unrealistic to argue that the realization of the euro leaves other things constant. If one assumes that the euro is successful, it will probably be adopted by the remaining four members of the EU. Then countervailing steps might be taken by the USA, including perhaps the expansion of the dollar area into Latin America. Whatever the forecasts, the US dollar–euro exchange rate will in future be the most urgent focus of management. As the world has moved from monetary unilateralism to monetary bilateralism, policy coordination has become much more important. Under unilateralism, other countries were comparatively free to fix or change their currency against the dollar, with a kind of benign neglect of exchange rate on the part of the USA. That is now no longer possible with the existence of the euro. If intervention is required, it should be cooperative. In view of the long period of transition from a mainly dollar world into a world in which the dollar and the euro are quasi-equal partners, it may be necessary to develop new institutions capable of dealing with this problem.

Earlier it was shown that for most Western European countries it was worthwhile to shift domestic monetary policy to a transnational (European) level. The expectation was that a better monetary policy would be the outcome, that is, a stable hard currency and low inflation rates, but also better predictability of monetary policy. Hence such a change from a domestic institutional monetary arrangement to a transnational one may also be worth considering for the development or industrial countries, if they face financial crises and are not able to cope with it, as we have seen in the Asian crises. In the next two sections a preliminary attempt is made to develop a new international financial institution with much increased intervention rights as well as more flexible and more incentive-oriented instruments than the IMF.

3.2 The Difficulties of Crisis Prevention by International Monetary Institutions

The Asian financial and economic crisis is one of the best examples of an unexpected event which had been foreseen neither by private rating agencies nor by the international monetary organizations. The crisis resulted in a contraction of output, and employment and poverty began to rise sharply. Negative spillover effects have affected numerous other countries. As a consequence of this crisis, the growth in world output was projected at just 2.5 per cent for 1999, about 2 percentage points below the projection made before the outbreak of the Asian crises – a loss of some US$800 billion in 1998 alone. The question arises as to what can be done better and what can be done by the international monetary institutions in future. The latter will be discussed – as an example – with respect to the reaction of the IMF, so far the only international monetary institution which has some experience in dealing with financial crises.

During the past two decades the IMF's surveillance has relied on indicators, especially in the periods between consultation discussions, to monitor economic developments and to draw conclusions about their likely future trends. While crisis prevention is mentioned nowhere specifically as one of the IMF's main objectives, there is an urgent need to undertake reforms, so that the IMF can react more quickly and appropriately to events such as the Asian crisis. Thus, while the aims of the IMF are clearly more ambitious than mere crisis prevention, the latter can be said to be a prerequisite for the achievement of these objectives. Indeed, crisis prevention should be indeed a core function of the IMF, and surveillance should be the IMF's principal tool for crisis prevention. Hence it is no surprise that the surveillance activities, broadly defined, absorb the largest share of the IMF's human resources. Surveillance over the funds of 182 member countries is, however, a continuous process, and the executive board meets about once a month in informal country-matter sessions that aim to facilitate early identification of emerging financial tensions by focusing on potential problems and providing additional empirical material on a selective basis. The staff informs management each month on important country developments, but also as and when necessary. Beyond the usually annual consultation visits, formal financial arrangements, precautionary arrangements, informal staff-monitored programmes and enhanced surveillance provide additional channels for more intensive contact between the staff and country authorities. The closer monitoring in the context of a quantitative framework that accompanies these modes of IMF involvement tends to reassure interested third parties, such as donors, creditors and financial markets, and thereby can contribute to crisis prevention.

It should be briefly mentioned that the IMF has also undertaken regional and multilateral surveillance. The former, which is becoming increasingly important in the surveillance of the European economies, complements bilateral surveillance in areas where policy responsibilities have been shifted to the supranational level. Executive board discussions of regional surveillance reports provide guidance to the staff in conducting bilateral surveillance with the countries affected. In the future, this is expected to increase with respect to monetary policy in the euro area, and for consultation missions to both EMU participants and countries, which have close links with the euro era. The multilateral surveillance exercise provides valuable input for bilateral surveillance, for example in the form of projections for the growth of trading partner markets or market assessments of country financing prospects.

The eruption of the Mexican crisis in late 1994 and especially the outbreak of the Asian crisis two and a half years later raised urgent questions about the effectiveness of IMF surveillance. The issue of relevance today is not so much whether this crisis could have been prevented. Of course, it could have been avoided through better economic policies or subsequently mitigated by the readiness on the part of the government in the crisis countries to deal swiftly and decisively with the emerging panics.

If one examines the record of surveillance in the Asian region, the IMF appears to have been more aware of the risks in Thailand's economic policy course than had most market observers. In other cases in Asia, however, the IMF, despite having identified critical weaknesses, particularly by the financial sector, had been taken by surprise, owing in part to lack of access to required information and also to an inability to see the full consequences of the combination of structural weaknesses in the economy and contagion effects. In particular, in the case of Korea, the IMF had not reacted quickly enough to the financial tensions that had begun developing in early 1997.

From this brief survey of the ability of the IMF to react to severe economic and financial crises it can be seen that there is a need either to undertake major reforms of the IMF, so that it is better able to fulfil its tasks, or to create a new international monetary institution. Both steps require, however, a much wider remit than that of the IMF. It will be shown, with the help of constitutional economics, that the new monetary institution will only be successful in handling these policies if it can (re)act (at least for a certain time span) like an independent central bank, with the additional rights to discipline governments and other actors in those countries. This new monetary institution can only act successfully if it is truly independent; this means that no pressure from major countries should be put on it or that it could be misused as a lender of last resort. An attempt to develop and justify such a framework will be undertaken in the next two sections.

4. SOME THEORETICAL IDEAS ABOUT A NEW INTERNATIONAL MONETARY INSTITUTION

4.1 The Economic and Political Independence of Monetary Institutions

The modern theory of financial institutions (like central banks or international monetary institutions) stresses the importance of the independence of these institutions and of the incentive structures of the decision makers responsible for monetary policy. According to Grilli et al. (1991), the monetary institution can be defined by its political and economic independence. Economic independence is defined as the ability of the monetary institution to determine the use and choice of its monetary (and if necessary other) policy instruments to act autonomously and without interference from national governments or national organizations.[9] Economic independence may be adversely affected by the monetary institution's obligations to finance national governments, to supervise commercial banks and by a lack of freedom to set interest rates.[10]

Political independence is defined as the ability of the monetary institution to choose monetary policy goals autonomously and without interference from the government. The basic determinants of this ability are found in personal independence (for example procedures for appointing and dismissing managers (and prescribing their terms of office)), in the national government's rights (or international institution's rights) to give instructions to the international monetary institution, as well as the right to veto, to suspend or to fire the top executives (of such international monetary institutions).

4.2 Institutional Solutions to the Time Inconsistency Problem

A starting-point for the theoretical foundations of an independent monetary institution might be that the behaviour of politicians is also greatly influenced by the existing rules of the political game.[11] Even for the simple case that we have either benelovent policy makers (that is, policy makers who behave like social planners) or we assume selfish policy makers who are opportunistic and have partisan preferences, the existing incentive constraints can lead to suboptimal policies. The fundamental reason for this is that policy makers operate in a discretionary regime; that is, monetary policy decisions are taken sequentially over time in a second-best world and therefore a socially desirable monetary policy may suffer from a lack of credibility caused by time inconsistency.[12] According to Blanchard and Fischer (1989), a policy is time inconsistent when a future policy decision which forms part of an optimal plan formulated at an initial date *ex ante* is no longer optimal at the time the policy is implemented *ex post*, although there is no relevant new information.[13] Various economic decisions are based on agents' expectations of future monetary policy, if we assume that a monetary authority is able to influence the inflation rate. For instance, when deciding on labour supply, wage contracts, investments or portfolio allocation, agents have to form expectations of the future inflation rate. In a discretionary regime, policy makers can make revisions of *ex ante* announced policy decisions and therefore create more inflation than forward-looking agents expect. One possible way to deal with this 'credibility' problem consists in removing all discretionary power from the government – this is, however, quite an unrealistic assumption. The establishment of an independent (international monetary) authority would then be unnecessary, if a strict, legally embedded simple *x* per cent money supply rule were used. Government would then only have to pass a law requiring it to fix the growth of money supply at a steady rate. However, studies on the employment motive for monetary expansion show that when stochastic shocks are taken into account, the optimal monetary policy does not conform to a simple rule but also includes an optimal shock absorption mechanism.[14] By following a simple rule, the government might be able to eliminate the inflation bias, but would produce suboptimally high output fluctuations. On the other hand, statutory entrenchment of the optimal state contingent rule appears to be extremely difficult, because it is hard to imagine how all contingencies might be described *ex ante* and verified *ex post*. What remains is a choice between simple rules, which are inflexible, and discretionary policies, which lead to an inflation bias. It is this trade-off between credibility and flexibility which has led to a game-theoretic foundation for the independence of monetary institutions (like a central bank). In principle, two approaches can be differentiated: on the one hand, Rogoff's (1985) approach to delegate monetary policy to an independent 'central' banker and, on the other, the contracting approach by Walsh (1995a,b). What both theories have in common is that they propose the establishment of monetary institution structures which permit monetary policy to react to economic disturbances independently, that is, without interference from the government.

In the following some basic guidelines for a new monetary institution are developed using the contracting approach, which seems more suitable for such a new framework.[15] However, they differ in their policy advice regarding the determination of central bankers' objectives and incentives. Starting from a principal–agent approach, Walsh (1995a) and Persson and Tabellini (1997) come to the conclusion that even though the government should transfer the control of a monetary policy instrument to an independent monetary institution, it should also provide this institution with incentives to optimize a social welfare function. This will be done in the form of a (performance) contract between the government (as the principal) and the monetary institution (as the agent). On the assumption that the preferences of the government and the monetary institution coincide, Walsh (1995a) shows that a simple contract which makes the central banker's remuneration linearly dependent on a realized rate of inflation eliminates the inflation bias without any sacrifice of stabilization efficiency. In addition, he shows that the incentive structures of optimal performance contracts can also be generated through the implementation of inflation-dependent dismissal rules (Walsh, 1995b). Such dismissal rules come close to the corresponding rules of price-targeting agreements practised, for example, in the New Zealand Central Bank System (ibid.).

As incentives in the traditional approach depend exclusively on deviations of realized inflation from the socially desirable rate of inflation, performance contracts are frequently interpreted in the sense of direct inflation targeting as well. Svensson (1997) shows that, under conventional assumptions, the result of an optimal monetary institution contract can also be achieved when the government imposes an inflation target of the international monetary institution which is below the socially desirable inflation and other monetary targets.

However, an optimal monetary institution contract becomes considerably more complex if we consider 'distorted' or selfish preferences of governments. If optimal contracts are very complex, problems with regard to their implementation are raised, because it becomes more difficult to review the compliance and the design in the incentive structures. Walsh (1995a) also shows, for example, that the incentive structures of an optimal monetary organization contract are not solely dependent on inflation but also on output, if the managers of this international organization try to maximize their income (ibid., pp. 158ff.). Svensson (1997) highlights the importance of persistence in the labour market, which, among other things, leads to a discretionary monetary policy not only entailing an increased inflation bias but also a stabilization bias. The reason for this is that surprise inflation also leads to real economic effects in subsequent periods.

In general, these theoretical considerations show that it is quite difficult to derive from the monetary theory an optimal framework under which an international monetary organization should operate. However, some of the guidelines of the contract approach can be used for modelling an institutional design of an international monetary organization.

5. SOME IDEAS ABOUT THE INSTITUTIONAL DESIGN OF A NEW INTERNATIONAL MONETARY INSTITUTION

Having experienced the Asian crisis, the existing international monetary institutions were not able to deal adequately with the problems that arose. Either they gave the wrong advice or they were under considerable pressure from the major donor governments to behave in a way that was of no use to the affected countries (such as Indonesia or Korea). To lay down the right policies *ex ante* so that such a major crisis can be overcome in the foreseeable future or even might be avoided in other countries is an extremely difficult task. With the current structure of the IMF and especially the weak instruments this organization has to achieve its goals, one should be thinking of a completely different (new) institution with much more enforceable instruments.

The following suggestion may sound 'wild' and normative, but on the other hand if one realizes what happens in such major financial and economic crises, as in Indonesia, Thailand or South Korea, it might indeed be necessary to create a new monetary institution. If a financial crisis emerges in a country and this country calls on the new institution for help, such help should be specified in a contract between the affected country and the institution so that the latter may act as a completely independent central bank, coming from outside. For a certain period of time (say one or two years) this monetary institution (new IMF) would perform such a task, with all the influence of a central bank. The idea behind this suggestion is that, on the one hand, the moral hazard problem of the IMF (that is, the IMF is a lender of last resort and bails out these countries) is considerably reduced and that this new monetary institution has a strong incentive to undertake policies for the affected country that are suited best for it, because it now has full responsibility with respect to monetary policy for this country so that it can act promptly. As the financial help from the donor countries depends on success in overcoming the crisis in this country, there are strong incentives for this new institution to act accordingly. On the other hand, there are now considerably higher costs for affected countries; because the governments in these countries lose a great part of their (monetary and fiscal policy) power, strong pressure can be put on them by the new financial institution to undertake necessary reforms, and (perhaps most important) the 'easy' bailout option no longer exists! When creating such an institutional design for the new international monetary organization two aspects are very important: the institutional design and policy tasks of this new institution; and the implementation problems.

5.1 The Institutional Design and Policy Tasks of a New Monetary Institution

A two-tier banking system

An important requirement of autonomous and successful central banking is the establishment of a two-tier banking system.[16] This means that there should be a strong and independent central bank, and the new monetary institution could play this role for a certain time, until it has reformed or built up such an institution together with a number of competitive commercial (private) banks. Once we have such a type of banking system, in which the central bank sets out clear policy guidelines in controlling the private banking system (with minimum reserve and other monetary policy guidelines), some stabilization can be expected. But even when establishing such a two-tier banking system, the new international monetary organization should be able to do more and to undertake a reform of the economic and financial environment of the affected state. In the following fields, in particular, major reforms are necessary: thorough restructuring of the banking system, a stable legal and administrative framework and the establishment of control mechanisms on the fiscal authority.

Thorough restructuring of the banking system

A main precondition for an efficient conduct of monetary policy is a well-functioning market-based banking system. It is not enough to commercialize state-owned banks and to give them new tasks and in addition allow a number of new private banks to emerge. In order to enable commercial banks to function effectively under market conditions, deregulation and sometimes privatization of these institutions might be necessary. An adequate supervisory capacity is also absolutely necessary, because a weak and inefficient banking system hinders or even prevents successful monetary policy. It distorts the transmission mechanism of monetary policy, because unsound banks that are unable to control the balance sheets are less responsive to changes in reserve money or interest rates. In addition, the central bank (or the international monetary institution) may come under pressure to give credits for bailing out banks and to loosen monetary conditions, thereby undermining their monetary control. Moreover, there are additional problems with unsound banks. There is a general consensus among economists that indirect instruments of monetary policy are more effective than direct instruments, which promote more efficient financial intermediation.[17] In the presence of unsound banks, however, introducing indirect instruments such as a credit auction or similar market-based facilities may induce adverse selection and moral hazard effects, because unsound banks may be willing to borrow at any cost to avoid illiquidity. What is needed are institutional innovations such as specific supervisory policies and bank restructuring schemes.[18]

A stable legal and administrative framework

A stable legal and administrative framework is extremely important for market economies to function, as we have seen in the financial crises of some of the Asian states where such an institution is missing! The establishment of an independent legal system, however, usually takes a great deal of time. During this period, the investment process in the real sector as well as in the financial sector is hampered by great uncertainty. As long as a stable legal framework has not been established, private investments are regarded as very risky by potential investors. Thus private domestic investments tend to be very low and urgently needed foreign investments are delayed. However, it is not only the legal environment that counts; the administrative and moral environments are important, too.[19] Administrative inefficiency and corruption inevitably impose restrictions on the feasibility of projected monetary policy, rendering the assesment of the international monetary institution's performance very difficult.[20] During such a transition period this new financial institution can help to instil confidence in domestic and foreign firms to invest in this 'crisis' country with a reliable monetary policy which restores monetary stability.

Establishment of control mechanisms on the fiscal authority

The domestic monetary institutions are more or less permanently under pressure of the fiscal authorities to ease their restrictive (anti-inflationary) monetary policy. In the public choice literature, central banks are regarded as exposed to strong political pressures to behave in accordance with government preferences.[21] The point is that restrictive monetary policy aggravates the budgetary position of the government. Since a (temporary) slowdown of economic activity, induced by restrictive monetary or disinflationary policy reduces tax income and receipts from seigniorage and since a short-term increase in interest rates means an additional burden on public debt that worsens the deficit, the government may prefer 'easy money' and hence canvass public support to push the central bank in this direction. Some evidence exists that the relatively independent US Federal Reserve and the German Bundesbank have often complied with such pressures.[22] Hence it seems to be very likely that the relatively independent monetary institution will have difficulties in withstanding such a pressure over a longer time. Such pressures from the fiscal policy side can make the commitment of the international monetary institution to follow a steady anti-inflationary policy unconvincing since the sustainability of such a policy is doubted. This problem can only be overcome if some control mechanisms on the fiscal authority are established, as in the Maastricht Treaty in the case of EMU

5.2 Implementation Problems

In a perfect world all of the above-mentioned institutional changes would be implemented instantly – and hence it would also be desirable to implement all reform elements simultanously. This, however, is wishful thinking. The problem of sequencing and of making a wrong decision respecting the sequence of reform steps cannot be ignored. For example, it is not sufficient to have formerly independent monetary institutions in such crisis countries if they have not the institutional and political support for such a step. In order to strengthen the position of the monetary institution and to enhance the credibility of its announcements, there are two ways to improve the situation: the first is to implement appropriate institutional control mechanisms to deal with the inflation driving authorities or groups (such as the fiscal authority and wage-price-setting groups). Or one could propose the introduction of constitutional restriction of government debt. The second way is to choose an appropriate nominal anchor in order to conduct monetary policy successfully. The question of nominal anchors is important because the credibility of the monetary policy strategy eventually determines the success of the monetary institution. Credibility, however depends not only on the classical time inconsistency aspects (namely the incentives of the monetary institution to deviate from its goal) but also on the expected implementability of the strategy that is a function of the reform stage.

6. SUMMARY AND CONCLUSIONS

In this chapter an attempt has been made to demonstrate that we have a completely new situation after the introduction of EMU and the experience of the Asian crisis. The European Monetary System (EMS) has become a legal institutional framework from which a stable currency so far has emerged. This changes the picture of the world financial system because two major currencies operate in it that are competitors, and where the rate between the euro and the US dollar is a crucial factor. In the light of these new developments a first attempt has been made to propose a more powerful and effective new international monetary organization. It is argued that the policies of this organization will only be successful if it is really independent, especially from its major donors, and hence can act independently if it is 'called on' for help in certain countries. Then it was shown that various instruments should be developed for this new organization, giving it the status of an independent central bank in an affected country for a certain time period, so that this organization can control monetary policy and has the appropriate instruments to interfere with elements of the country's fiscal policy, so that the goals of this institution can be achieved. In general this chapter should be seen as a first attempt to suggest new international monetary institutions relating to two major world currencies, the US dollar and the euro, after the experience of the Asian financial and economic crisis.

NOTES

* Earlier versions of this chapter were presented at the annual US Public Choice meetings, New Orleans, 12–14 March 1999, at the European Public Choice meeting in Lisbon, 8–11 April 1999 and at the 55th IIPF congress in Moscow, Russia, 23–26 August 1999. The author thanks Keven Grier (University of Mexico), Bill Niskanen (Cato Institute), Zeljko Bogetic (IMF), Jorn Rattso (Norwegian University of Science and Technology) and Vito Tanzi (IMF) for critical and stimulating comments.

1. See, for example, Ishijama (1995) and Eichengreen (1993).
2. See, for example, Alesina and Grilli (1992), Cukiermann (1996), De Haan (1997) and Eichengreen et al. (1995).
3. See the classical contribution of Solow (1956).
4. See Romer (1994), Jones and Manuelli (1997).
5. See, for example, Alesina and Grilli (1992), Alesina and Roubini (1997) and Cukierman et al. (1993).
6. See, for example, A. Wagner (1997).
7. For first thoughts for an EU federal constitution see Schneider (1996) and Schneider and Wagner (2000).
8. See A. Wagner (1997).
9. This definition of economic independence is very similar to the meaning of instrumental independence introduced for example by Debelle and Fischer (1994). These authors distinguish between instrumental independence and global independence. See ibid., p. 197.
10. See, for example, Alesina and Grilli (1992), p. 56.
11. In the public choice literature the selfish behaviour of politicians is extensively analysed and the importance of institutional arrangements is stressed. See Mueller (1987) and Schneider (1994).
12. See Persson and Tabellini (1997) and H. Wagner (1997).
13. See Schaling (1995), p. 25.
14. Compare Rogoff (1985) and King (1996).
15. It should be noted that Rogoff's approach of a conservative central banker is also an attractive approach. Rogoff shows that social welfare can be improved if the government delegates monetary policy to a conservative central banker who agrees with the social preferences regarding the target values of inflation and output, but places a greater weight on the inflation targets than the government. Once appointed, the conservative central banker operates with discretion and is independent to pursue an activist policy. By appropriate choice of the degree of conservativeness, a society realizes a better equilibrium position than the government itself can achieve following inflexible rules or discretionary policy. See further Rogoff (1985), Fischer (1994) and, for an extension of this approach assuming a partisan interest of politicians, see Alesina and Gatti (1995). For a treatment in the context of the EU, see Wagner (1997).

16. See, for example, Romer and Romer (1997), Sahay and Vegh (1995) and IMF (1997).
17. See, for example, Alexander et al. (1995) or Demileux and Denizer (1997).
18. For example Enoch and Breen (1997) demand this.
19. See Freyhold et al. (1995) and Frey and Eichenberger (1994).
20. See the work by Schneider and Enste (2000), who deal with corruption and the rise of a shadow or underground economy in developing states like the Asian ones.
21. See for the USA Akhtar and Howe (1991) and Havrilesky (1995); for Germany: Frey and Schneider (1981) and Berger and Schneider (2000); for a survey see Cukierman (1996).
22. See, for example, Allen (1986), Alesina (1989) and Berger and Schneider (2000).

REFERENCES

Akhtar, M.A. and H. Howe (1991), 'The Political and Institutional Independence of U.S. Monetary Policy', *Banca Nazionale del Lavoro, Quarterly Review*, **178**(3), 343–89.

Alexander, W., T Balino and C. Enoch (1995), 'The Adoption of Indirect Instruments of Monetary Policy', IMF Occasional Paper 126, Washington, DC: International Monetary Fund.

Allen, S.D. (1986), 'The Federal Reserve and the Electoral Cycle', *Journal of Money, Credit and Banking*, **18**(1), 57–98.

Alesina, A. (1989), 'Politics and Business Cycles in Industrial Democracies', *Economic Policy*, **8**(1), 55–98.

Alesina, A. and R. Gatti (1995), 'Independent Central Banks: Low Inflation at no Cost?', *American Economic Review*, **85**(1), 169–200.

Alesina, A. and V. Grilli (1992), 'The European Central Bank: Reshaping monetary politics in Europe', in M.B. Canzoneri, V. Grilli and P.R. Masson (eds), *Establishing a Central Bank: Issues in Europe and Lessons from the U.S.*, Cambridge, MA: Cambridge University Press, pp. 49–77.

Alesina, A. and N. Roubini (1997), *Political Cycles and the Macroeconomy*, Cambridge, MA: MIT Press.

Berger, H. and F. Schneider (2000), 'The Bundesbank's reaction to policy conflicts: Evidence and implications', in Jacob de Haan (ed.); *The History of the Bundesbank: Lessons for the European Central Bank*, London and New York: Routledge, pp. 43–66.

Blanchard, D. and S. Fischer (1989), *Lectures on Macroeconomics*, Cambridge, MA: MIT Press.

Cukierman, A. (1996), 'The Economics of Central Banking', paper prepared for the 11th World Congress of the International Economic Association, Tunis; also published as Discussion Paper No. 3631, Center for Economic Research.

Cukierman, A., P. Kalaitzidakis, L.A. Summers and S.B. Webb (1993), 'Central Bank Independence, Growth, Investment and Real Rates', *Carnegie-Rochester Conference Series on Public Policy 39*, autumn, pp. 95–145.

De Haan, J. (1997), 'The European Central Bank: Independence, Accountability and Strategy: A review', *Public Choice*, **93**(3), 395–426.

Debelle, G. and S. Fischer (1994), 'How Independent should a Central Bank be?', in J.C. Fuhrer (ed.), *Goals, Guidelines and Constraints Facing Monetary Policy Makers*, Boston: Federal Reserve Bank of Boston, conference serial number 38, pp. 195–221.

Demileux, M. and C. Denizer (1997), 'Monetary Policy During Transition: An Overview', Policy Research Working Paper 1706, Washington, DC: World Bank.

Eichengreen, B. (1993), 'European Monetary Unification', *Journal of Economic Literature*, **31**(3), 1321–57.

Eichengreen, B., J. Frieden and J. von Hagen (eds) (1995), *Monetary and Fiscal Policy in an Integrated Europe*, Heidelberg and New York: Springer, pp. 12–37.

Enoch, C. and J.H. Green (eds) (1997), *Banking Soundness and Monetary Policy: Issues and Experiences in the Global Economy*, Washington, DC: International Monetary Fund.

Fischer, S. (1994), 'Modern central banking', in: F. Capie, Fischer C. Goodhart and N. Schnadt (eds), *The Future of Central Banking*, Cambridge, MA: Cambridge University Press, pp. 262–78.

Frey, B.S. and R. Eichenberger (1994), 'The Political Economy of Stabilization Programs in Developing Countries', *European Journal of Political Economy*, **10**(1), 169–90.

Frey, B.S. and F. Schneider (1981), 'Central Bank Behavior: A Positive Empirical Analysis', *Journal of Monetary Economics*, **7**(3), 291–316.

Freyhold, H.V., V. Gessner, E.L. Vial and H. Wagner (1995), 'Cost of Judicial Barriers for Consumers in the Single Market', A report for the European Commission (DG XXIV), Brussels.

Grilli, V., D. Masciandaro and G. Tabellini (1991), 'Political and Monetary Institutions and Public Financial Policies in Industrialized Countries', *Economic Policy*, **13,** 341–92.

Havrilesky, T. (1995), *The Pressures on American Monetary Policy*, Dordrecht: Kluwer.

International Monetary Fund (1997), 'Status of Market-Based Central Banking Reforms in the Countries of the former Soviet Union', report prepared for the 10th Coordination Meeting of Cooperation Central Banks and International Institutions, Basel, Switzerland.

Ishijama, Y. (1995), 'The Theory of Optimum Currency Areas: A Survey', *IMF Staff papers*, **42**, 120–76.

Jones, L. and R. Manuelli (1997), 'The Sources of Growth', *Journal of Economic Dynamics and Control*, **21**(1), 75–114.

King, M. (1996), 'Direct inflation targets', in Deutsche Bundesbank (ed.), *Monetary Policy Strategies in Europe*, München: Verlag Vahlen, pp. 45–74.

Mueller, D. (1987), *Public Choice II*, Cambridge, MA: Cambridge University Press.

Persson, T. and G. Tabellini (1997), 'Political Economics and Macroeconomic Policy', NBER working paper no. 6329, Cambridge, MA.

Rogoff, K. (1985), 'The Optimal Degree of Commitment to an Intermediate Monetary Target', *Quarterly Journal of Economics*, **100**(3), 1169–90.

Romer, C.D. and D.H. Romer (1997), 'Institutions for monetary stability', in C.D. Romer and D.H. Romer (eds), *Reducing Inflation: Motivation and Strategy*, Chicago: The University of Chicago Press, pp. 307–34.

Romer, P. (1994), 'The Origin of Endogenous Growth', *Journal of Economic Perspectives*, **8**(1), 3–22.

Sahay, R. and C. Vegh (1995), 'Dollarization in Transition Economies: Evidence and Policy Implications', IMF Working Paper 9596, Washington: International Monetary Fund.

Schaling, E. (1995), *Institution and Monetary Policy. Credibility, Flexibility and Central Bank Independence*, Brookfield, US and Aldershot, UK: Edward Elgar.

Schneider, F. (1994), 'Public Choice – Economic Theory of Politics: A Survey in Selected Areas', in H. Brandstätter and W. Güth (eds), *Essays on Economic Psychology*, Heidelberg: Springer, pp. 243–69.

Schneider, F. (1996), 'The design of a minimal European Federal Union: Some ideas using the public choice approach', in J.C. Pardo and F. Schneider (eds), *Current Issues in Public Choice*, Cheltenham, UK and Brookfield, US: Edward Elgar, pp. 203–22.

Schneider, F. and D. Enste, (2000), 'Shadow Economies: Size, Causes and Consequences', *Journal of Economic Literature*, **38**(1), 78–120.

Schneider, F. and A. Wagner (2000), 'Subsidiarity, federalism and direct democracy as basic elements of a federal European constitution: Some ideas using constitutional economics', in R. Mudambi, G. Sobbrio and P Navarra (eds), *Constitutional Political Economy*, Cambridge, MA: Cambridge University Press, pp. 78–104.

Solow, R. (1956), 'A Contribution to the Theory of Economic Growth', *Quarterly Journal of Economics*, **70**(1), 65–94.

Svensson, L.E.O. (1997), 'Optimal Inflation Targets: Conservative Central Banks and Linear Inflation Contracts', *American Economic Review*, **87**(1), 98–114.

Wagner, A. (1997), *Geldpolitik in der Europäischen Wirtschafts- und Währungsunion*, Linz: Trauner.

Wagner, H. (1997), 'Rechtsunsicherheit und Wirtschaftswachstum', in S. Behrends (ed.), *Ordnungskonforme Wirtschaftspolitik in der Marktwirtschaft*, Berlin: Duncker und Humblot, pp. 227–53.

Walsh, C.E. (1995a), 'Optimal Contracts for Central Bankers', *American Economic Review*, **85**(1), 150–67.

Walsh, C.E. (1995b), 'Is New Zealand's Reserve Bank Act of 1989 an Optimal Central Bank Contract?,' *Journal of Money, Credit, and Banking*, **27**(4), 1179–91.

COMMENT

Marcella Mulino

I found Schneider's chapter a stimulating contribution to the widespread debate on the need to build a new architecture of the international monetary system. Such a debate gained particular strength after the currency and financial crises of the 1990s, as they were perceived not simply as the outcome of national policy mistakes, but also of shortcomings in current international arrangements.

To draw up an institutional design for a new (or a reformed) international monetary organization is not an easy task. Part of the difficulty of deriving from theoretical models an optimal framework for an international monetary organization arises from the fact that, in an open economy framework, there are additional specific issues to be taken into account. In my opinion, they are likely to modify (at least to a certain extent) the outcomes of the theoretical analysis. Moreover, some theoretical frameworks and practical experiences, like the one linked to the European Monetary Union (EMU), are bound to be more or less unfit for emerging countries.

I think that Schneider's chapter also suffers partly from such limits. His proposal is to entrust an international monetary organization (the 'new' IMF) with the task of handling financial crises, temporarily acting as (and in the place of) the country's central bank, fully independent and with the additional right to impose fiscal discipline on national governments. To this purpose, the statute of the 'new' IMF should openly state commitment to price and currency stability, as its main goal, the 'no bailout' clause, and institutional independence from donor countries, preventing it from performing the lender-of-last-resort function.

Schneider extends the modern monetary theory, favouring the economic and political independence of central banks, to an international monetary institution. This exercise, however, appears a bit too mechanical, as it does not fully take into account both the open economy framework and the specific features of emerging countries.

In this respect, I would like to propose a few reflections. Nowadays, nearly all countries have been strongly encouraged to liberalize their capital account. Nevertheless, in a framework of liberalization of international capital markets there are limits to an emerging country's ability to follow an independent domestic monetary policy or to pursue its own goals. If the central bank aims at reducing the inflation rate, and follows restrictive monetary policies, domestic interest rates will tend to be relatively high. The more a country succeeds in its stabilization policy, improving its access to international financial markets, the more interest rate differentials (corrected for the possibly decreasing expected rate of devaluation) will attract large volumes of foreign capital. Owing to the likely thinness of domestic capital markets, the central bank will probably meet with growing difficulties in trying to sterilize the effects of such inflows on the money supply; either way, it will be forced to further raise the domestic interest rates in order to fight the inflationary impact of big capital inflows.

As stated by Paul Volker (1999, p. 265), we cannot say that misguided national policies produce harmful spillovers; instead, it would be more correct to say that 'national policies produce harmful spillovers, because good national policies can also produce harmful spillovers'. The argument goes as follows: the better a country's policies, the more capital it is likely to attract and the more likely a collapse. For example, most Asian countries have been recording 8 per cent growth rates for nearly 20 years, with price stability, budgetary discipline and sustainable current account deficits. Even Russia, a very different case, showed an impressive anti-inflationary record, from hyperinflation to a bare 7 per cent on a yearly basis.

Another line of reasoning refers to unilateral pegs so often devised to provide a nominal anchor to fight domestic inflation. They pose risks inasmuch as they lead to a real exchange rate appreciation, because domestic inflation converges to international levels only gradually. Owing to the anti-inflationary monetary stance, banks and firms usually borrow abroad to finance imports and current account imbalances, as well as economic activity and investment; in this way, the country's vulnerability to shifts in foreign investors' confidence increases. Therefore, in a fixed exchange rate regime coupled with liberalized capital markets, huge capital flows and over-borrowing are likely. On the one hand, such flows (which are partly the result of successful anti-inflationary policies) may hamper the pursuit of domestic monetary goals, set either by a domestic central bank or by the 'new' IMF temporarily acting as the country's independent central bank. On the other hand, they may lead to increasing financial vulnerability and to dangers of a sudden reversal of capital flows. This problem is enhanced where such flows are short-term financial flows, and where a sound bank regulatory framework is lacking, as is the case in most emerging countries.

The need to overcome this institutional weakness is rightly stressed in Schneider's chapter. He considers that building adequate institutions for monitoring emerging nations' financial sectors is a precondition for an efficient conduct of the monetary policy. I would like just to add that following a sound monetary policy may not solve all problems, as its working may be limited by the danger of inconsistencies between fixed exchange rates and capital account liberalization, possibly leading to a currency and financial collapse, thus calling for international financial assistance.

To summarize, domestic monetary and exchange rate policies cannot be planned without taking into account the problems posed by international capital flows and by the fragility of the banking sector. The problem is that, in order to prevent the outbreak of financial crises, it may not be sufficient to have an independent central bank, either domestically based or superimposed from abroad.

REFERENCE

Volker, Paul A. (1999), 'A perspective on financial crises', in Jane Sneddon Little and Giovanni P. Olivei (eds), *Rethinking the International Monetary System*, Federal Reserve Bank of Boston, Conference Series No. 43, June.

COMMENT

Luciano Marcello Milone

Generally, I agree with much of Schneider's analysis in favour of a new international monetary institution which should be more independent from its donor governments and also more powerful than the current IMF. In principle, well-designed institutional reforms in this direction should be welcome. In particular, the creation of a highly independent international financial institution acting without interference from policy makers of its member states could reduce appreciably the well-known time inconsistency and credibility problems usually affecting national government interventions.

However, I have two short observations concerning the specific content of Schneider's proposal to create an institution acting as an international central bank with – as he says – 'a much wider remit than that of the IMF'. Once we accept the idea of an international monetary institution highly independent of its 'donors', we face the problem of defining both its tasks and its policy instruments. As we know, we have at least three different approaches to address this problem.

A first approach tends to minimize the negative consequences usually associated with financial market failures and, at the same time, tends to emphasize the possibility of social costs from public sector failures at an international level. In particular, this approach stresses distortions produced by the IMF acting as an international lender of last resort; IMF bailouts create moral hazard and, consequently, encourage new crises. This is the thesis of the IMF behaving like a sort of pyromaniac fireman. Following this view, the IMF should become a smaller institution, reducing or completely ceasing financial assistance to member countries, while concentrating on collection and provision of economic and financial data for member countries. Basically, the IMF would improve the functioning of markets by reducing the risk of welfare losses from inefficiencies and from costly financial crises related to asymmetric information. In other words, the IMF would become a sort of international agency promoting information.

According to a second approach, the basic structure of the IMF should remain substantially unchanged, but its traditional activities of surveillance, financial assistance and technical support should be readjusted to face major old and new criticisms and, at the same time, to cope with emerging problems due to a globalized world.

A third approach aims at more radical reforms to strengthen the architecture of the international monetary system. The central idea is that, owing to globalization, potential gains from international cooperation are much higher than in the past. In an increasingly interdependent world, serious problems arising from the presence of cross-country macroeconomic spillovers, international externalities and global public goods cannot be solved by the market mechanism or by single countries acting individually and pursuing national interests in a non-cooperative context. Collective action is required. On the other hand, deeper cooperation would imply a growing role of international agreements and international institutions and, consequently, a loss of national economic policy autonomy. In particular, creating a new international financial organization, or remodelling the IMF in order to make it a more powerful as well as a more independent institution, could increase its ability to promote an efficient provision of global public goods such as exchange rate and financial stability and a world system of open markets. However, the directions of reform are completely different according to the different authors.

In my view, Schneider's stimulating proposals fall within this third approach.

My two observations are as follows. The first concerns the degree of realism of the author's proposals. Reforms leading to such a drastic strengthening of international institutions and, at the same time, to such a strong restriction of the discretionary powers of national authorities appear to be politically unfeasible, at least in the near future. A first obstacle arises from the well-known reluctance of the present national authorities to restrict their economic autonomy. Countries facing a crisis should accept, as Schneider suggests, 'losing a considerable part of their (monetary and fiscal policy) power'. It is quite difficult to imagine nation-state governments ready to sacrifice national sovereignty and to reduce their degrees of freedom in regulating domestic economies to such an extent. In the contemporary world context, a second important obstacle to the political feasibility of Schneider's proposal, so deeply interfering with domestic economic policy, may arise from the growing dissatisfaction of wide sectors of the 'civil society', both in the advanced countries and in the developing world, with the role that the main international organizations have been playing in managing the globalization process and coping with its negative consequences. Broad segments of public opinion have been induced to look at globalization as a threat rather than as an opportunity. This erosion of confidence in respect of international organizations has much weakened the political support to reforms promoting a substantial transfer of powers and tasks from national governments to them.

My second observation relates to the desirability of Schneider's proposals. Well-known agency problems involving citizens, politicians and bureaucrats at national level tend to be more complex when applied to the behaviour of international organizations. This higher complexity is due to at least two reasons: first, international organizations are more remote from citizens who are ultimate principals; second, each country (especially a small one) might face high costs *vis-à-vis* low expected returns from a deep involvement in monitoring these organizations. Thus, reforms expanding the authority and independence of international organizations seriously increase the risk of exposure to government failures at an international level, unless effective solutions are offered to these agency problems. Some recent developments of the theory of international organizations contain remarkable efforts in devising incentive mechanisms and systems of rules constraining the behaviour of bureaucrats and managers so that these organizations might actually act according to their task of maximizing social welfare. Schneider, too, formulates interesting suggestions in this direction. In spite of all these efforts, however, it seems reasonable to maintain that we are still faced with many difficulties before we can find fully satisfactory solutions to incentive problems associated with international organization action. On the desirability of Schneider's proposals, a second very critical point, to some extent connected to the previous one, is given by the problem of the political accountability of international institutions highly independent of national governments. Current discussions on how the international financial system should be redesigned have led to a growing awareness that the risk of a democratic deficit is amplified as a consequence of reforms establishing more powerful as well as more independent global governance institutions. Recent contributions attempting to devise viable procedures to ensure that these institutions are democratically accountable and successfully supervised are encouraging. Nevertheless – as in the case of the above-mentioned agency problems – they do not seem as yet to have produced fully convincing concrete solutions.

Despite the unquestionable merits of Schneider's proposals, all in all my observations do not justify optimistic conclusions about their chances of success in the present economic and political environment. With reference to a short time horizon, my opinion is that we should rely on less ambitious but still acceptable reforms which, however, do not clash with the difficulties discussed here.

Focusing on the main critiques levelled at the IMF during and following the Asian, Russian and Latin American financial crises of the turbulent late 1990s, the following aspects are involved:

- the capacity of the Fund to predict and prevent financial crises;
- the Fund as an international quasi-lender of last resort and its role in encouraging moral hazard;
- the effectiveness of the IMF's financial support programmes in

providing liquidity during a country's crisis and in limiting the risks of contagion;
- the fact that the Fund's prescriptions very often pressed countries to adopt too restrictive monetary and fiscal policies, contributing to an increase in social welfare costs due to financial crises.

The rich and articulated debate dealing with these aspects has produced a variety of recommendations which, even if they could appear as second-best solutions, could help significantly to improve the role of the Fund in the government of the international financial system. In addition to this, their implementation does not require such a large redistribution of powers from national institutions to international institutions as Schneider's suggestions would imply.

Apart from these minor remarks, I found Schneider's chapter very useful in presenting ideas and proposals that deserve serious consideration, especially in a longer-run perspective when the above-quoted feasibility and desirability problems may be overcome.

7. A curmudgeon's view of EMU

Gordon Tullock

My one course in economics was taught by Henry Simons, and my views on EMU depend on the particular way in which he taught it: half on the market and half on money. My introduction to Keynesian economics came when Simons told me what was wrong with it. He was so convincing that I never actually read *The General Theory*. Naturally I picked up a good deal of Keynesian economics over time, but I never thought it was a good theory.

Simons was, of course, a believer in monetary measures and in particular the desirability of the stable value of money. The method that he favored, 100 per cent reserve banking, was one that I still have a retrospective admiration for, but it has pretty much dropped out of the literature. Keynesianism, which for a while was dominant, has also largely disappeared. I presume the reason is the simultaneous existence of high and increasing unemployment at a time of rising inflation.

I can remember when most economists thought that the system suffered from a permanent shortage of demand. It was the government's duty to provide additional demand and Galbraith actually suggested that only military expenditures would be politically acceptable in creating that demand.

Today of course all this is dead. European countries do not seem unduly perturbed by unemployment rates much higher than had ever before been experienced except in extremely serious depressions. There is no suggestion that it be wiped out by 'an expansion of demand' or, in other words, a little inflation. Indeed, now the major arguments for the EMU is that there will be only moderate inflation.

But note that no one really wants, or at least calls for, zero inflation, far less a little deflation. Indeed, no one seems to be concerned about the current non-employment. The unemployed themselves, in particular, seem to be unconcerned since most of them are making out all right on unemployment compensation with, in many cases, a supplement from the black economy.

As almost a comic problem, there is the rate of inflation which should be planned for. Professor Sinn of Munich discovered that the original organization of the new bank was to pay Germany much less than their proper share. He re-computed this and the bank partially increased the German payment so that it was not so unfair as originally, but still unfair. The gain to the German government as a result was sizeable and they paid Professor Sinn no compensation or percentage at all. If they had given him even 1 percent of the savings he could have retired.

Professor Sinn, however, has continued his calculations. In each country there are traded and non-traded goods. Traded goods have the same price everywhere but there can be national differences in the price of non-traded goods. This means that they, given the rate of inflation, will affect different countries differently. Using the Balassa–Samuelson effect, Professor Sinn calculated the minimum rate of inflation that would need no single country to have an actual deflation. It turns out to be about 1 per cent per annum.[1]

It is interesting that in this case, as in the previous one, Sinn discovered that the plans had a defect. I don't know if the bank will attempt to follow his suggested policy. If they do not, there could be difficulties.

I would like to turn now from Keynesianism and Fisherian monetarism to another theory which is largely dead today except among orthodox Austrians. I should explain that I'm not an Austrian and I do not approve of this theory, but the observations upon which Von Mises based his theory are I think correct, and similar phenomena are likely to cause difficulty for the EMU.

Mises observed that countries in Europe, in order to stimulate their economy, engaged in activities to lower the interest rate, essentially by pressing their banks to expand credit. He thought, correctly, that such activities led to the currency of the given country falling against gold, with a resulting gold outflow. We today would say that was a consequence of the monetary expansion. In those days the gold standard was sacred and the country found it necessary to contract its money and raise interest rates in order to keep its currencies stable against gold. Their gold reserves were limited and they could not afford a continuous outflow of treasury gold.

At this point Mises permitted his moral standards to come to the fore. The depression caused by the contraction was obvious. Mises, however, favored such a contraction and disliked the preceding expansion. He therefore said that the depression was the result of the previous expansion and not of the contraction made necessary by the combination of the expansion and the gold standard. Austrian economists have stuck to this view and thus are forced to argue such things as that the 1920s in the USA was an inflationary period.

The gold standard held all currencies participating in the system to what amounted to fixed exchange rates. The physical cost of shipping gold meant that the rates were not exactly the same, but the difference was trivial. This system broke down. Why do we expect that a similar fixed exchange rate will not break down today? I think the answer is that the arrangements are supposed to make it impossible for national governments to engage in the kind of misbehavior which central banks and governments engaged in during the period of the gold standard. Note I refer to the genuine gold standard of preWorld War I, not to the synthetic gold standard of the period immediately after World War II.

In the second, post-World War II period, individual governments confronted with foreign trade deficits as a result of mismanaging their home currency simply devalued. This was a painful matter for the government, but less painful than taking domestic deflationary measures. It is hoped that the UN will deprive governments of the possibility of this kind of activity.

Historically, sovereigns have tended to use their monetary control as a source of revenue. Printing money is, of course, a revenue source. Today the USA makes vast profits out of printing $100 bills which are then used in Russia and other countries. This is possible because the US dollar is currently (since 1982) fairly stable. Given the choice, a ruble or dollar in their mattress, everyone would choose the dollar. The yen and the euro don't look very promising at the moment. We will shortly turn to the history of the dollar in recent years, but I would like to mention the risk the USA now runs. If it did inflate, these dollars would rush back, greatly magnifying the inflationary effect caused by domestic policy. In other words, the large profit now being made on paper and ink could become a disaster if the USA is not very successful in its monetary management.

There is further risk for the USA. If the new European currency is a success, then it would probably be more convenient for Russians who do not wish to hold their own currency to switch from dollars to the new currency. This again might lead to a sharp inflow of dollars to the USA, with potentially serious inflationary possibilities. Fortunately it does not seem to be imminent, but after a few years of success of the new currency the USA might face difficulties. As will be seen, I am not certain that there will be such a continuing success, but it is wrong to base the stability of the dollar on the instability of the euro.

Monetary management has not been very successful in the USA since J.P. Morgan was replaced by the Federal Reserve Board. The board financed World War I by printing money, which led to an inflation and then, when the War was over, they contracted the money supply and caused a very severe, but short, depression. Unfortunately the Federal Reserve Board, in 1929, apparently thought that the stock market was too high and took action to bring it down. Whether they might have set off the drop or whether it was on the verge of a correction anyway is uncertain.

It is, however, clear that between 1929 and 1933 the Federal Reserve

Board did absolutely nothing to cure the depression, indeed their policies made it worse. After 1933 they continued doing little or nothing about the disastrous situation. As a result Hitler gold flowed from Europe to the USA in the years 1933 to 1940 and the Federal Reserve Board did not permit this to lead to expansion of money supply and hence contribute toward curing the depression. The USA in fact had the slowest recovery from the depression of any major country. I do not of course blame this solely on the Federal Reserve Board, but they certainly did nothing to cure the depression, which was ended by the war.

World War II, like World War I, was financed largely by inflation. Whether this is a good way of financing wars is unclear, but, in any event, it is a very common method. Fortunately, after World War II the Federal Reserve Board (FRB) did not crack down and cause a depression. They did, however, permit one to happen just before the 1960 election. Nixon thought this cost him the election and made certain that in 1982 there would be no depression. His FRB created a mild inflation. This continued and accelerated under Ford.

Carter appointed Miller as chairman to the board, who accelerated the inflation. As a result he faced the 1980 election with a high rate of inflation, which would have been politically suicidal. He changed the chairman and his replacement began a radical deflation. This led to unemployment and a depression, but the bulk of the effects came after the election. Reagan kept the deflation going, which meant that he lost the 1982 congressional election. After that election, however, the USA began what can be called its longest continuous period of prosperity, if you ignore the minor dip of 1991.

Meanwhile Bush became president and Greenspan chairman. Bush asked Greenspan to eliminate the 1991 depression, but Greenspan didn't. Note that the depression was not caused by the FRB, but by the change in bank regulations, which forced a cutback in loans. The FRB could have offset this but did not do so in spite of requests from the president. This led to Bush losing the 1992 election and producing his one and only pun: 'I appointed Greenspan and he dis-appointed me.' Greenspan avoided major difficulties during the Clinton Administration and in fact took action to support the stock market at one point when it was in collapse. It's hard to say whether this shows brilliance or luck.

I've gone through this rather depressing history to indicate that central banks don't necessarily do a good job. The Bundesbank has done reasonably well. A monetary expert told me he would not give them an 'A', but thought a 'B' would be justified. It has generally avoided very much inflation, but at the time of unification it put some additional money in circulation and caused an inflation, albeit mild in Germany. At the same time it raised interest rates to minimize the inflation. This caused considerable difficulty for other European countries. Note that I do not criticize the Bundesbank since I also would have regarded unification as more important than currency stability. There were, however, other ways of financing unification. Still, this makes it clear that inflation is not the only mistake that a central bank can make.

All this has occurred with a continuing mild inflation. As far as I can see, the EMU intends to continue such a mild inflation. Whether it will follow the advice of Sinn and Reutter I do not know. A mild inflation, if it is relatively constant, is not much worse than stable money. The basic problem that it raises is one of bookkeeping. A stable money means that bookkeeping is easier and purchasing decisions can be based on last year's prices instead of being corrected by the rate of inflation.

These two tales about central banks do not mean that adopting a central bank which you hope will behave as well as the Bundesbank or the FRB Board is necessarily wrong. Surely both the Bundesbank and the FRB behaved much better than other central banks. Depending on a central bank as your major source of stability both in money supply and economic performance is risky. Even the best have done badly in the past.

Of course if the best have done badly, the worst have done much less in the way of sensible policy. France and Russia, just after the reform, and almost any of the minor countries selected at random did worse than the FRB. A major South American country hopes to reduce the rate of inflation next year to 10 percent. That is above average in efficiency.

There seems to be a general feeling that a central bank largely under control of its board and only subject to weak political influence is somehow an ideal. It may, of course, be the best we can do, but that does not mean that all problems are solved. If it does as well as the Bundesbank or the FRB it will still be far from ideal. We might hope that it would learn from history and do much better, but hope is different from certainty.

So far I have been focusing on the experience of other currency schemes. What do you want out of your monetary managers, whether they are a central bank or, as was true in the USA for much of the early nineteenth century, a private bank? There are three duties we would like the bank to perform. The first of these, which is minor, is to provide foreign exchange for people who want it. This can be easily done by the private market, but governments frequently prohibit it. I remember being somewhat inconvenienced by a Bank of France regulation which suddenly made it impossible for me to get dollars for my francs at the local bank.

The central bank will also be responsible for designing the new money and perhaps for printing it. So far I have not read any discussion of what it will look like. It would technically be possible to produce notes for each country with somewhat different appearances. For example, there would be a general Europe-wide design on one side and a local design on the other. This would, however, have various disadvantages since the French note would probably circulate in Germany. Arranging for banks to make the exchange would be possible but would not improve the situation much. Still, there does appear to be considerable sentiment in favor of the current appearance of the notes. Possibly the bank might decide to make concessions to that sentiment. The present arrangement in which different notes are used in each country is only mildly inconvenient, but why have any inconvenience, even mild? Printing new bills seems to be continuously far off, and now it is not planned for quite a while.

One clear-cut advantage of the current arrangement is that exchange is now easy inside Europe and the exchange for dollars is also easy. Still, it is necessary to exchange your money when you cross international boundaries. This inconvenience would be eliminated if the same currency were used throughout. With several current currencies all held at par, there would still be such problems in deciding whether a given price was a bargain if it were denominated in currency which you did not use on a day to day basis. It would appear that the internal exchange will gradually be replaced by a single currency, so we don't need to worry about that kind of currency regulation.

Most people assume that the regulations on new printing of currency by the nation states will be obeyed. So far as I know, this raises no questions, although I was rather surprised last time I visited Italy to be given brand-new large-denomination lira notes by the money machine at the airport. I presume this was just an accident and the Italian government was not going back to its traditional money printing.

The other two duties of a central bank are more difficult. They should both prevent inflation and depression. Most of the discussion that I have seen of the new regime is devoted to its unlikely creation of a new inflation. As mentioned above, nobody seems to be particularly disturbed by the continuing sizeable unemployment. That might change with the resulting pressure to create employment by Keynesian methods of inflation. Keynes is unfashionable at the moment, but that could change.

One can imagine financial difficulties that might lead to a printing of money to cover deficits, but the deficits would be national and the bank could presumably ignore them. If, however, the proto-government of Europe, which is apparently developing, began having financial difficulties I can imagine the bank being put under pressure to fund them. This is obviously not an immediate problem but I'm surprised that I don't seem to read much about future plans in this connection.

The opposite problem, what to do if there is a sharp downturn in the economy, also seems to be ignored. Perhaps it is thought that this will not happen. Except for the continuing unemployment, there hasn't been a serious depression recently in Europe. In other parts of the world, Brazil, for example, there have been. Further, the phenomenon of simultaneous inflation and depression which the USA suffered towards the end of the Carter regime does appear in other parts of the world. It may indicate that I should read more widely, but I have seen no discussion of what the central bank should do in such circumstances.

But more important, it would seem that the governments and banks of the nation-states would be in much the same situation with regard to the euro that they were in with regard to gold before World War I. Politicians are very apt to want to stimulate their own economy. They could take much the same stimulative actions as were taken in that earlier genuine gold standard period, that is, press the banks to expand credit, and we would anticipate much the same results. There would be a short-term business boom followed by a sharp contraction as the government and the banks found their supply of euros insufficient.

It is easy to argue, and indeed I will not dispute the matter, that these minor expansions and contractions were much less serious than the monetary problems we have had since World War I. But to say that they are less serious is not to say that they are trivial. In a way the old-fashioned gold standard was an unstable system but the instability was less than that experienced since World War II. Unfortunately that instability was great enough that reforms were demanded. These reforms in the USA took the form of the FRB, whose history I have recited above. I feel we would have been better off under the previous system, although that was far from ideal.

These problems do not seem to be discussed very much, and perhaps they will never become reality. But let us engage in a little speculation about possible future history. Suppose we did have a serious depression in Europe. There would be demands that something be done and pressure put upon the central bank to take action. Its organization might even be changed, as was the organization of the American banking system just before World War I and in the early years of the Great Depression. We might once again get into the American alternation of inflation and depression with the new mechanism. We might, but then again, we might not. Still, I think this is a serious problem that should be thought about carefully. Perhaps people have been thinking about it and my not knowing the solution they offered reflects my ignorance rather than the genuine lacuna in the discussion.

There are, however, reasons other than a depression which might put pressure on the government or the bank for drastic changes. The monetary history of Europe in recent years has been depressing. Thus it's hard to argue for the *status quo*. On the other hand, we should look very carefully at any proposed reform because it might turn out worse than the *status quo*. Less radically, it might turn out to be a little better than the *status quo* but not very much so.

I now offer a few scenarios of how things could go wrong. Before starting, I should point out that banks, like speculators, exhibit a certain amount of herd behavior. All banks may develop over-optimism as when most American banks became over-enthusiastic about South American investment opportunities. They loaned a lot of money, discovered it wasn't as safe as they thought and tried to get out again almost simultaneously. The American government came to their rescue. Sometime after their experience I was talking to a prominent banker and said that these loans were foolish. He looked indignant and said vigorously: 'Everyone thought they were good loans.' I don't doubt he was correct, but everyone was depending on the opinion of everyone else. In other words, it was a herd effect.

More recently loans to Southeast Asia, although smaller as a share of American bank capital, exhibited the same phenomenon. In this case rescue was mainly by international organizations. Once again the herd effect was visible. In both of these cases the banks faced a genuine risk in that a similar herd effect on the part of depositors might have bankrupted them. Contagious runs can occur when one bank is in trouble and depositors not only try to remove their deposits from that bank, but also from others. This is usually offered as one of the explanations for the Great Depression, although not all economists believe it. It was of course the reason for the Deposit Insurance Act.

Contagion can also apply to undue pessimism. As mentioned above, toward the end of President Bush's first term, the Federal Deposit Insurance Corporation and bank examiners sharply raised their standards and forced some apparently sound banks to close. This frightened the other banks and they cut back on their loans, thus causing the depression which in turn led to Bush's defeat. The FRB could have counterbalanced the shrinkage and hence prevented or cured the depression. They didn't.

What would the new central bank in Europe do in either of these contingencies? If there were a contagious spread of over-confidence in, let us say China, and Italian banks loaned too much money to China with a result of many of them facing bankruptcy, what would the central bank do? So far I've seen little discussion of this point.

On the other side, suppose something happens which leads a number of banks to worry about their solvency and they cut back. This could cause a depression. Would the central bank take action, and effective action, to offset this? Will it in essence guarantee banks against contagious failure?

The FRB from time to time changes the interest rate on overnight money.

This is actually not in itself a very important matter, but the investment community and newspapers assume that its behavior with respect to this variable is a sign of more important things that it may do. The reserve bank can easily increase the money supply by buying government bonds or shrink it by selling. If the banking community thinks it knows what it's going to do based on the varying overnight rate, it may take action which makes it unnecessary for the reserve bank to do anything else.

The central bank being established in Europe does not face a large body of bonds which represent the debt of Europe as a whole. There is of course no reason why it could not purchase or sell other bonds. This would have much the same effect. So far as I know this is not a major part of the planned operations of the bank and no precautions have been taken to make sure that its purchase of other bonds does not give it too much control of either subsidiary governments or companies. In any event, the American experience with this policy which is outlined above is hardly encouraging.

In closing, I should say that Simons, in that long-ago first course, suggested that the political arm exercise direct control over the money supply. This was of course during a depression which he tended to blame largely on FRB inaction. He may have been wrong, but in any event leaning on politics to correct the behavior of a central bank is surely leaning on a reed which is not only broken, but thoroughly disintegrated.

I titled this chapter 'A curmudgeon's view of EMU'. Readers will surely agree with the title 'curmudgeon.' I think we should all hope that I am wrong.

NOTE

1. Hans Werner and Michael Reutter, 'The Minimum Inflation for Euroland', CES IFO Working Paper No. 377.

COMMENT

Bernard Grofman

In the USA an apocryphal tale is told of a craggy Vermont shopkeeper who refused to accept either checks or credit cards at his store. When asked why, he supposedly said: 'In God we trust, all others pay cash.' While reading Tullock's chapter, I was struck for the first time by what was implicit in that Vermonter's response, to wit his apparently absolute confidence in the value of the US dollar.[1] Americans have, for at least a half-century, lived with the comforting notion that inflation levels in the USA will be sufficiently low that accepting the paper currency printed by the central bank is a completely reasonable thing to do. Even the post-oil-shock bouts with stagflation in the 1970s and 1980s didn't really affect that faith. In particular, it is still common in the USA among the cognoscenti to attribute near-mythical powers to the Chair of the Federal Reserve, at least when the occupant of that position is named Alan Greenspan. Similarly, in Europe, at least until reunification, the Bundesbank was often credited with a degree of control over the German economy that Adolf Hitler might have envied. Yet, as Gordon Tullock reminds us, when we look elsewhere in the world, we often find long periods of very high levels of inflation, and even bouts of hyperinflation, as well as many countries that appear reconciled to living with a permanent high (10 per cent plus) level of inflation. For example, looking today (early 2003) at what were, once upon a time, relatively strong economies, for example, Argentina or Venezuela, reminds us how far the mighty can fall.[2] Indeed, as Gordon Tullock also reminds us, the long-term record of performance of even the Federal Reserve and the Bundesbank should not be exaggerated.

A high degree of skepticism about the powers of even the best and most autonomous central banks to achieve some desired range of inflation/deflation is thus clearly called for. As my colleague A Wuffle (personal communication, 1 April 2002) puts it, 'No amount of monetary discipline can compensate for fiscal folly.' In fact, sometimes even 'necessities,' for example German reunification, can come with a very high price tag that disrupts the best-laid plans of politicians and bankers.

Still, we need to ask whether Gordon Tullock's apt and historically well-grounded deflation of the supposed anti-inflation abilities of central banks[3] bears directly on the narrower question of whether to the marriage of central banks (into one big bank) one ought to admit impediments, recognizing, of course, that such a question is now largely money over the bridge.[4] We already do have a European bank and a European currency – at least for most of Europe. (Prime Minister Tony Blair's views notwithstanding, for the moment, England is still 'in for the pound.') Why might a single European central bank be better than a congery of smaller central banks? Why might it be worse? Before we attempt to answer that question, we need to take a step back and ask ourselves: 'What, from a political economy standpoint, are the central tasks for a central bank?'

My answer to that last question is three-fold: (1) a central bank can print money that can be used as a directly acceptable medium of exchange throughout a wide geographic area (say within the bounds of a single nation-state, or even outside that state's boundaries), (2) a central bank can provide mechanisms – even if only reputation – that allow that currency to serve as a convertible medium of exchange throughout the world;[5] and (3) a central bank can regulate its nation's economy by using monetary policies (controlling the amount of currency in circulation, changing interest rates on federal securities, setting the prime rate) as levers to keep the value of the currency stable (or at least not fluctuating too wildly), and to affect levels of unemployment as well as (long-run) economic growth.

In addition to these central tasks there are many other roles that a central bank might play in its nation's political economy, some good, some bad. For example, it might (1) protect political incumbents by timing economic interventions so as to benefit them, with good news coming just before an election and bad news just after; (2) it might help finance wars (via 'controlled' inflation); and (3) it might regulate the banking system to protect against risky investments that might lead to insolvencies and collapse of consumer confidence. Now, we can turn to consider some of the more important of the positives and negatives of a single currency/single central bank.

On the plus side: (1) the larger the area of direct acceptance for a currency, the lower the transaction costs to users; moreover, if other currencies are forced out of existence, transaction costs are lowered still more; (2) a single central bank will be more resistant to political pressures, since it will be subject to more competing (national and other) pressures, and a single central bank will be able to use the strength of the strongest members to discipline the weaker members of the EMU and prevent them from engaging in inflationary ways. Thus we expect a single central bank to be better able to generate stable economic growth; and (3) a single currency is an important 'psychological' sign of a unified Europe and reinforces the stability of the EU.

On the minus side: (1) we already had easy convertibility of currencies within (Western) Europe; shifting to a single currency presumably does not gain us that much, especially since convertability is more and more being handled by credit card companies as an incidental cost of doing business. Mastercard and Visa, not the euro, or even the dollar, are increasingly the 'true' international media of exchange;[6] (2) if we have a single central bank and something goes wrong with its policies, the consequences will be severe, and there will no longer be separate systems operating under different rules that can step in to help repair and contain the damage; and, perhaps most importantly, (3) attitudes toward the relative costs of inflation and unemployment are fundamentally political and we cannot expect that identical values will be held by each of the national governments (since some countries might have center-right governments and others center-left, for example); thus a single central bank will inevitably make decisions about interest rates that some countries will wish to resist. Thus a single central bank can be a destabilizing force.

I do not really know how to balance off these pluses and minuses. Both sides of the argument can find support within the public choice literature. What can be said, with some confidence, however, is that the most extreme scare scenarios abut the euro haven't yet materialized. In particular, despite some (essentially unsubstantiated) claims that shopowners used the conversion from the local currency as an excuse to raise prices, throughout Europe the euro won immediate acceptance among the public as well as the business community as a medium of exchange.[7] While euro-denominated transactions are still often supplemented by values expressed in the older currency, that seems to me to be clearly a transitional phenomenon. Moreover, concerns that the euro would crash in value relative to the dollar also seem misguided. While the euro initially fell relative to the dollar, it later rebounded, and the currency range in which it is fluctuating seems no greater (and perhaps less) than the historical ranges of variation against the dollar of currencies such as the German, the British and the Japanese.

In any case, while you may wish to call me a 'cock-eyed optimist,' let me close this comment with a toast: 'Long live the euro – and the Europe for which she stands!'[8]

NOTES

1. Our hypothetical shopkeeper might have insisted on being paid via barter or in 'precious' minerals.
2. As a recent Latin American example also shows, even tying your currency to the dollar is no panacea.
3. I will not try to comment on his argument that a little inflation is not just a bad thing other than to note that, once you accept some inflation as desirable, it may become harder to keep it in check.
4. Here the pun, on the design of the euro, is indeed, intended.
5. Note that to achieve these first two ends, at minimum, the currency must be seen as (relatively) non-counterfeitable.
6. Here I might note that my colleague, A Wuffle (based on his experiences in Italy and France), has argued that the true international currency of Europe is Nutella.

7. In this context it is useful to recall the remarks of one of the Italian scholars at the conference – a member of the Italian Parliament – who expressed his fears about the possibility of ordinary Italians refusing to accept the euro.
8. Cognoscenti will recognize this as a paraphrase of language from the US 'pledge of allegiance' recited by schoolchildren.

PART III

Two issues at work: voting and contracting

8. Towards a more consistent design of parliamentary democracy and its consequences for the European Union

Charles B. Blankart and Dennis C. Mueller

1. TWO WAYS TO DEPART FROM DIRECT DEMOCRACY

During the last decade of the twentieth century, a large number of democratic states emerged out of the ashes of the Soviet empire. They all took the form of parliamentary democracies, that is, of governments mostly elected by parliaments re-sorting themselves from elections on a proportional basis, some with an elected president, some with a second chamber. Their relative merits have rarely been put into question. An often-mentioned exception is Barro (1997), who has asked whether more authoritarian or more pluralistic democracies are able to generate higher rates of economic growth. His intention was to find an optimal democracy with regard to growth. In our view, however, democracy is not so much an instrument to generate growth, but rather a mechanism to find out and to execute what voters want. The question we want to ask is: what is the form of democracy that most faithfully transforms the outcome of democratic voting into collective actions? A point of reference to this question is direct democracy of the town-hall type. For in a direct democracy, there is no need for an intermediating agent interpreting and transforming the outcome of voting into political action. Political decisions are rather simultaneously decided and put into action by the citizens themselves.

Direct democracy rests on the following three core principles:

1. Sovereignty is exercised directly by the citizens
2. The condition of one-man one-vote applies
3. The citizens engage directly in the deliberative process of opinion formation.[1]

Direct democracy, however, only applies in small communities. In practice, deviations from the pure principles of direct democracy are required. Principle (1), that of citizens' sovereignty, is obviously unlikely to be given up, for it would turn democracy into a farce of a dictatorship in the clothing of a democracy. Therefore, one may prefer to reduce either the number of active participants in the democracy (principle (2)) or one may simplify opinion formation by condensing the number of alternatives (principle (3)). In the first case, the 'pure form of representative democracy' (PRD), citizens vote for persons sharing their views and forming opinions similar to theirs in the parliament. They economize the time used for debates by reducing the number of participants. In the second case, the 'pure form of two-party democracy' (TPD), the voters are confronted by platforms of policy bundles between which they can choose in a similar way that they choose between single issues in a direct democracy. They decide themselves, but among a small set of alternatives.

In most parliamentary democracies, however, the second and the third principles are applied in combination. The citizens are supposed to give their parliamentary representatives a mandate, that is, to let them speak, discuss and decide for themselves, and they choose among the party programs in the election. We shall argue that the mixture of these two procedures leads to inconsistent results which are further away from the outcome of direct democracies than if only the one or the other principles is applied.

We proceed as follows. In sections 2 and 3, the properties of the PRD and TPD are presented. Section 4 explains the disadvantages of mixed forms of the two systems, and yet why they nevertheless are often found to exist. In section 5, we evaluate the combination of PRD or TPD with elements of a direct democracy such as a referendum or a popular initiative. A brief look at bicameral systems is presented in section 6, while section 7 discusses the proper role of the executive branch in each form of government. The results of our analysis have implications for the design of a constitution for the European Union (EU), which will be discussed in the concluding section 8.[2]

2. THE PURE FORM OF REPRESENTATIVE DEMOCRACY (PRD)

The pure form of representative democracy rests on the parliament which has to be elected so as to mirror as closely as possible the preferences found in the population at large. It simulates the town-hall meeting, but with fewer citizens. Such a procedure was described several years ago by Gordon Tullock (1967, ch. 10). Each citizen is allowed to transfer her vote to another citizen whom she trusts will vote in the assembly in the same way as she would vote were she to participate. Citizens are expected under this procedure to transfer their votes to those representative citizens whose preferences come closest to matching their own preferences. Each representative citizen taking a seat in the representative assembly would then possess as many votes as the number of citizens having the same preferences as her in the community at large. The representative assembly fulfills each of the three characteristics of direct democracy listed above, albeit with each citizen participating only indirectly by proxy through the person to whom the citizen assigned her vote (see principle (2) above).[3] Despite these attractive properties of the procedure, it has some potential disadvantages.

First, it still is possible, of course, that the number of individuals needed to represent all citizens' preferences faithfully is too large to allow effective deliberation in the representative assembly. This difficulty can be easily overcome, however, by limiting the number of representatives to some manageable number as, say, 100. If the first round of voting produces too many representatives, a second round is held with only the 100 persons who received the most votes in the first round being allowed to run in it. Votes in the assembly are then assigned to the 100 representatives in proportion to the number of votes that they receive in the second round of voting. This amendment to the procedure would continue to ensure that each person would be represented by someone to whom she had entrusted her vote. Assuming that the number of different sets of preferences in the community is not inordinately large, and 100 seems like a much larger number than would be needed, each citizen would be represented by someone whose preferences came very close to matching her own. Given this property, the procedure would again fulfill the requirement that the assembly constituted an accurate representation of all preferences in the community in terms of both their characteristics and their numbers. Even an assembly of only 100 would allow for the representation of a far wider spectrum of preferences than is represented in the parliamentary systems of the major developed democracies.

Second, the voters could be overwhelmed by having to compare too many candidates, and the candidates may be overwhelmed by the challenge of having to make their positions on issues known to all voters. However, in this situation intermediaries have an incentive to intervene to facilitate the dissemination of information on candidate positions. For example, interest groups on both the left- and right-hand sides of the political spectrum can be expected to make efforts to inform voters of the positions of candidates who favor the interest groups' positions. And, of course, they have an incentive to contribute funds to their favorite candidates, so that the candidates themselves can inform the voters. Alternatively, the distribution of state funds to candidates for the purpose of informing voters can also be justified on the grounds that this sort of information constitutes a pure public good.

Third, the citizen-voter is confronted with a principal–agent problem. She delivers her vote to someone who will, she hopes, vote it the way she would have had she been in the assembly, and not merely to serve his own interests. This principal–agent problem is present under all systems of representative democracy, however, and is if anything likely to be a smaller problem with this procedure than it is when citizens are represented by parties. The citizen can observe the voting record of her representative and has a wide spectrum of alternative candidates to choose among should her representative deviate from his promised positions. The citizen can also count on both other candidates and interest groups to inform her about any 'shirking' by her representative.

Voters will have the broadest possible spectrum of positions from which to choose, if the polity is treated as a single electoral district with citizens free to choose among all of the candidates rather than having the polity divided into geographic districts. Each set of preferences will then be represented in the assembly in direct proportion to their number across the entire polity, irrespective of the geographic location of the person holding a given set of preferences. Persons representing the preferences of citizens from a particular geographic area might also get elected, of course, but in general one expects representatives of narrow geographic interests to gather fewer votes in a national assembly than persons representing positions that appeal to citizens from all parts of the country.

Just as under direct democracy, the proposal, discussion and determination of policies under PRD takes place within the assembly. The only difference is that under PRD it is an assembly of faithful representatives of citizen preferences that discusses and decides issues, while under direct democracy it is the citizens themselves who determine 'the general will' of the community. Political theorists from Rousseau to Wicksell (1896) to Buchanan and Tullock (1962) have proposed that this general will should ideally be determined by demanding *unanimous* agreement among the members of the assembly. Although fulfilling such an ideal would be impractical, this does not imply that the best voting rule would be the simple majority rule. This rule is known to be prone to cycles. If one confines one's attention to the family of qualified majority rules (for example 2/3, 3/4), then some higher qualified majority is required.[4] But there is no reason to confine one's choice of a voting rule to this limited set. Public choice has developed several voting rules – like point voting and voting by veto – which do not produce cycles, and which give every member of parliament an impact on the outcome (see Mueller, 1996, ch. 11).

Once policy proposals have been put forward, discussed, perhaps amended and eventually ratified in the legislative assembly, the only remaining step is to implement the policies. This is the task of the executive branch under the PRD. The implementation of policies is logically a separate function from their determination, and should, therefore, be administratively separate from the legislative process. Such a separation between the legislative and executive functions of government is, of course, not characteristic of the parliamentary forms of government prevalent in Europe and in many other countries. We shall return to this point in section 7, but we turn now to a discussion of the pure two-party form of representative democracy.

3. THE PURE TWO-PARTY FORM OF REPRESENTATIVE DEMOCRACY (TPD)

The point of departure of TPD is direct democracy too. Citizen preferences should determine policy outcomes. But the process by which this determination takes place is quite different. Instead of the citizen choosing a person or party to represent her preferences in the legislative assembly where policies are decided, under TPD the citizen effectively gets to choose the final set of policies herself. TPD intends to overcome the large-number problem of direct democracy by economizing the number of alternatives presented to the citizens (principle (3) above). Each of the two parties competing in the election proposes a set of policies which they promise to implement if they obtain a majority of seats in the parliament and the citizen votes for the party promising the most attractive set of policies. The party receiving the most votes in the election is awarded a majority of the seats in the parliament and implements its promised platform. As under PRD, the entire nation should be treated as a single electoral district, with seats in the parliament awarded in proportion to the votes won across the entire nation. But if parties are free to enter the competition for votes, how can one be sure that the voters have only two parties from which to choose? To ensure that this is the case, or at least that the winning party has obtained a majority of the votes cast and seats in parliament, TPD requires that there be a second, run-off election between the two parties getting the most votes in the first election. Voters would then have to choose between only two parties if a run-off were needed, and in the long run such a run-off system should result in there being only two major parties competing for votes across the country (Cox, 1997).

At first glance the TPD resembles the so-called 'Westminster system' of government. In both systems one cannot presume that there will be only two parties competing for votes, but in the long run one expects this to be the case as the smaller parties drop out or merge with other parties to avoid always being in opposition. The TPD proposed here has, however, two important advantages over the Westminster model: (1) the convergence process should occur much faster, since in any election with a run-off the parties coming in third or lower in the first round would receive no seats in the parliament; (2) the Westminster system does not ensure either that a single party wins a majority of the seats in the parliament or that a party which does obtain a majority of the seats has won a majority of the votes. We return to this point in section 4.1.

Unlike in the PRD, the function of the legislative assembly under TPD is not to formulate, debate and determine policies. This takes place either during the election when the parties formulate their platforms or in caucuses held by the majority party outside of the assembly. To maintain the appearance of deliberative democracy, the opposition may be allowed to express its dissatisfaction with the majority party's program, and the majority party may defend the virtues of its program, but this is mostly show. The real policy choices are made outside of the legislative assembly by the majority party alone and by the voters who elected it.

Another important difference between PRD and TPD is that the logic of TPD demands that the majority party form the government, that is, select the prime minister and Cabinet. Under TPD the executive and legislative branches are combined. The election has expressed the 'will of the people' in so far as which party platform is most preferred. The winning party will be in the best position to implement its platform if it controls both the legislative and executive functions of government. Thus, it is possible to characterize PRD as 'parliamentary democracy without a government (cabinet),' and TPD as 'government without a parliament.'

While the simple majority rule is unlikely to be the optimal choice for the legislature under PRD, it is the appropriate voting rule under TPD. The electoral rule ensures that a party wins a majority of the votes and thereby obtains a majority of the seats in the parliament. The parliamentary voting rule should ensure that this party can implement its program. The simple majority rule achieves that goal. Unlike with PRD, however, under TPD cycling will not be a problem when the simple majority rule is used, since one party has a majority and it will simply choose its most preferred outcomes. Assuming that elections are fought over a multidimensional issue space, cycling could conceivably be a problem at the electoral stage. The probabilistic voting literature suggests, however, that equilibria in two-party elections will exist, and furthermore that they have the attractive property of maximizing some form of social welfare function. In this sense, the TPD also achieves the goal of matching policy outcomes from the democratic process to the preferences of the citizens.[5] Once one allows for campaign contributions and other interest-group activities, however, the individual utility functions, which appear in the social welfare function that is maximized through the competition for votes by the two parties, receive different weights, and the normative attractiveness of the TPD is somewhat reduced.[6]

4. PRD AND TPD IN COMBINATION?

We have seen that both PRD and TPD have attractive properties. PRD ensures that all citizens' preferences are faithfully represented in the legislative assembly that decides government policies. TPD allows the citizen to choose these policies and the government directly. Neither system in the pure form described here exists anywhere, however. Mixed systems are the rule. This fact raises two questions: what produces mixed systems? What are their properties in comparison with the ideal types described here? This section attempts to provide some answers to these questions.

4.1 The Emergence of Systems of Combined Representation?

Combined systems come about through a combination of provisions in the constitution that, for example, specify that the parliament should form the government, that is, the cabinet as under the TPD, and the use of an electoral rule that produces a multi-party parliament in which no party has a majority of the seats. Space precludes an exhaustive discussion of all of the electoral rules in use and their properties, so we shall content ourselves by describing only a few illustrative examples.[7]

First, the smallest deviation from the PRD comes about when a country elects its parliament using some form of party list system rather than the kind of vote-transfer system described under the PRD. In a national list system as employed in the Netherlands and Israel, voters in all parts of the country are presented with the same lists of candidates. Each citizen votes for one party and the parties are awarded seats in the parliament in proportion to the numbers of votes they receive. The seats are filled with the people whose names appeared on the lists. This system resembles PRD except that the citizen transfers her vote to a party instead of to a person. Instead of a representative who received 10 percent of the votes getting 10 percent of the votes in the assembly, as would occur under PRD, each representative gets one vote under a list system, but his party gets 10 percent of the votes in the parliament if it got 10 percent of the votes in the electorate. This system is inferior to PRD in that it greatly reduces the range of choice for the voters for any given-sized legislative assembly. Voters in Europe, for example, typically choose among five to ten parties even when there are hundreds of seats in the parliament, while under PRD a voter would choose from among 50 positions on issues with a parliament as small as 50. The range of choice facing voters is further restricted in many multi-party systems by denying parties any seats at all in the parliament, if they fail to reach a minimum threshold of votes, which can be as high as 5 percent, as in Germany and Austria. Such a rule guarantees that at most 20 different sets of preferences are represented in the parliament, and *de facto* that far fewer are. Minimum cut-offs such as these are defended on the grounds that they reduce the number of parties in the parliament and thereby make the task of coalition formation to form a government easier. They are an obvious compromise between trying to represent all citizens preferences fairly, as PRD would do, and producing responsible government, as TPD would do. Such systems produce large parties and hence make the emergence of fixed coalitions more likely.

Second, in most countries the country is divided into several voting districts and the citizens can only vote for candidates or parties with lists in their districts. When the districts are large and many representatives can be selected from each district, the outcomes of these systems approximate those of the national list systems. When only a few persons can be elected from each district, these systems further disadvantage small parties and those voters whose preferences do not appear in greater number across the country. These systems also have the disadvantage of giving representatives elected on a regional basis an incentive to introduce regional/local issues into the national legislative agenda. This tendency is readily apparent in the European Parliament, whose members are all elected from electoral districts corresponding to the boundaries of the member countries (see section 9).

Third, the polar case of a system of geographically defined electoral districts designed to disadvantage minority parties is the system of single-member-district representation practiced in the UK, the USA and many other Anglo-Saxon countries. The rationale behind these systems is generally not only to disadvantage small parties, but to produce a two-party form of government. Within a district they tend to achieve this goal, but there is no guarantee that they will produce two dominate parties across the entire country. Both Canada and India have single-member-district representation systems and neither of them comes close to having two dominant parties today, and even the UK – the arch-type of Westminster system – has had three major parties (and a half dozen or so minor ones) for many years now.

Fourth, perhaps the most mixed of the mixed systems of representation is the increasingly popular tendency to elect some representatives to parliament using single-member-district representation and the rest using some form of multi-member-district representation. Germany elects half the Bundestag from single-member districts and then fills the remaining seats applying a proportional representation formula to the votes across the entire nation. The result is a fairly close approximation to what one would get using a national-list, proportional representation (PR) formula, but with a local flavor. Italy has attempted to introduce a degree of stability into its system by implementing such a mixed system. So far it has produced neither stability nor two-party government.

4.2 How should Systems of Combined Representation be Evaluated?

Combined systems have several disadvantages with respect to the pure systems of PRD and TPD.

4.2.1 The confounding of the objectives of representation and responsibility

Although the proportional representation (PR) systems of continental Europe come closest to the PRD, they do not achieve its potential as a system for representing the preferences of all citizens. In a PRD system not only would all preferences be represented in the parliament; they would also have the potential to affect the outcomes. This influence would be felt through both discussion and debate and also through the use of a voting rule that allows all members of parliament the opportunity to affect the outcome. In contrast, by requiring that majority coalitions form to choose a cabinet, European PR systems ensure that the process of discussion and debate is limited to members of the parties forming the majority coalition. The other parties are left to criticize, but not to influence, the legislative outcomes. At the same time, European PR systems do not produce the kind of responsible government that would arise under the TPD. None of the parties in a coalition government can claim sole responsibility for the program implemented; neither can they promise with any conviction that they will be in a position to implement a particular program in the future, since in the best of circumstances they will only be in a position to bargain with other coalition partners over the characteristics of the government's program.

4.2.2 Voter alienation

The inability of parties to take responsibility for policies undertaken, and to make and keep credible promises during elections reflects back onto the attitudes of the voters to the parties. Often during an election, a member of the coalition that formed the government will try to dodge criticism of the government's program by blaming other members of the coalition for some of the outcomes. A voter who is unhappy with a government's achievements often does not know which party to punish, nor can she believe the promises of the parties in opposition, because they too are going to have to reach compromises with other parties should they be part of the next government. The difficulties voters have under existing PR systems in trying to decide whom to punish and whom to trust may help to explain the increasing alienation of voters to electoral politics in Europe in recent years.

4.2.3 Strategic voting

Should a citizen vote for the party that comes closest to her favored position on the issues, if she thinks that this party has a small chance of joining the government, or should she cast her ballot for a party with a better chance of joining the government? Many voters in Europe do not vote for their most preferred parties for this sort of strategic reason and thus an election outcome does not in fact constitute an accurate representation of the preferences of the electorate across the ideological spectrum.[8]

4.2.4 Instability

Any party that deviates from its promised program to become part of a coalition government stands to lose votes in the next election. Recognizing this, parties in the government often have an incentive to exit the coalition sufficiently far in advance of an election, so that they have time to stake out their position on the issues for the next election and to distance themselves from the programs of the present government. Such exits from the government can lead to its premature downfall and help explain why coalition governments tend to be shorter-lived than one-party governments. More generally, the multidimensionality of the issue space combined with the lack of a single party with a majority of the seats in the parliament makes PR systems prone to cycles, and thus to unstable governments.

4.2.5 Majority parties with minority support

When single-member-district representation does succeed in producing a single party with a majority of the seats in the parliament, as has generally been the case in the UK, the party winning a majority of the seats seldom wins the support of a majority of the voters. The Labour Party's landslide victory in the last election in terms of seats occurred despite its gaining the votes of only slightly more than 44 percent of the electorate – about what the losing candidate gets in a landslide presidential election in the USA. Not once during the last century did the party which 'won' the election in the UK also win a majority of the votes cast.[9]

5. SUPPLEMENTARY REFERENDA IN PRD AND TPD?

The pure systems of PRD and TPD, we have argued, would be superior to the combined forms of proportional representation and two-party systems that are observed in practice. We have also extolled the virtues of direct democracy, however. Are the properties of the PRD and the TPD as mechanisms for representing individuals' preferences so attractive that institutions of direct democracy are not needed? If this is not the case, what role would referenda play in an ideal PRD or TPD system? Should citizens be allowed to supplement the actions of their elected governments with proposals of their own approved in a referendum? Should the citizens be free to introduce initiatives in which an action of their government is reversed? As it turns, out the answers to these questions differ somewhat, depending on whether the PRD or the TPD has been chosen.

Under the PRD the preferences of all voters should be faithfully represented in the legislative assembly, and thus it might appear that there should be no need for additional referenda. They should simply reproduce what the legislature does or would decide. Further reflection suggests, however, that the option to call referenda might still have a beneficial role to play under PRD. The possibility of citizens calling referenda should increase the incentives that their representatives have to vote in accordance with their campaign promises. In addition, the possibility of calling referenda allows the citizens the opportunity to take actions that their representatives have failed to undertake, perhaps out of ignorance of what the citizens' preferences are on a particular issue. Thus the potential for calling referenda should be an important aid to overcoming the principal–agent problem between citizens and their representatives that would exist even under PRD.[10] In a well-functioning PRD system, one would not expect that the citizens would need to resort to referenda very often. In Switzerland, where referenda and citizen initiatives are firmly established, the actual outcomes from referenda and their preventive role of keeping representatives in check have both proven to be of considerable importance.[11]

The situation is quite different under TPD. In choosing a party to form the government, the citizens have effectively endorsed the platform of the party, which consists of positions on several issues. One citizen might vote for Party *A* despite its position on issue *X*, because she strongly supports its position on *Y*. If then *A* wins the election and implements *Y*, but *Y* is reversed in a referendum, the citizen will in some sense have wasted her vote for Party *A*. More generally, the role of elections as mechanisms for picking the best platform (package of issues) will be vitiated if citizens are able to reverse parts of the platform through referenda. To put it differently, citizens would have to make unduly difficult calculations to anticipate the outcomes of possible referenda before casting their votes.

Against this position there are naturally some counter-arguments that can be made. Because two-party elections revolve around large numbers of issues, it can happen that some issues receive little attention from either party during an election campaign and thus the winning party does not have a clear picture of the voters' preferences on this issue. New issues can also arise that were not even discussed during the previous election. Despite these possibilities, we find it somewhat problematic to couple the TPD with citizen initiatives that would reverse parts of the winning party's platform, given the normative justification for having the entire winning platform implemented.

An additional danger arises when governments themselves call referenda to induce the citizens to ratify decisions that the government has already made. Such plebiscites are almost always called to manipulate the voters into taking an action that strengthens the existing government. They thus serve no constructive purpose in an ideal form of representative government and should not be allowed. The only forms of referenda that are potentially capable of achieving the goal of having government policies advance citizens' interests are the ones that they themselves initiate.[12]

Referenda over constitutional questions are a quite different matter, on the other hand. In many countries, parliaments are able to change the constitution. Here the danger of significant principal–agent problems arising is very great, particularly when it comes to changes in electoral rules and the like, which have direct effects on the welfare of the elected representatives. To maintain citizen sovereignty over constitutional matters, we recommend that all changes in the constitution introduced by the parliament, however elected, be put before the citizens in a referendum.[13]

6. A SECOND LEGISLATIVE CHAMBER?

A further, possible variant on the PRD and TPD would be to introduce a second legislative chamber. Many countries have such second chambers with similar or slightly narrower jurisdiction than the first. In the USA, France and Italy the second house is called the Senate, in the UK the House of Lords, in Germany the Bundesrat, and in Switzerland the Ständerat. Historically these second houses came into being to represent the interests of a particular group or class. The Roman Senate was supposed to protect the rights of the patrician families of Rome; the House of Lords was to protect the interests of the British aristocracy. Der Reichsrat, the forerunner to the German Bundesrat, was supposed to protect the rights of the federal states of Germany. The British House of Lords was also the model for the USA's upper house in the minds of many of the drafters of the US Constitution. The Senate, not being popularly elected, was supposed to protect the interests of America's landed aristocracy. It was seen as both contributing to the overall structure of Checks and Balances in the Constitution, and more specifically to the protection of the privileged classes.[14] Today second chambers are not generally defended on the basis of protecting class interests, but rather that they somehow improve the process of representation of citizens' preferences. Such an argument is difficult to press, however, if the first chamber has been properly constituted as under our PRD and TPD systems.

Under the PRD all citizens' preferences are faithfully represented in the parliament. Collective decisions are made following discussions in which the views of all citizens can effectively be heard. The principle of one-man one-vote is satisfied and, if a voting rule has been selected that allows all voices represented to influence the outcomes of the collective choice process, all of the goals of PRD are fulfilled (see section 3). What purpose can a second chamber fulfill? If it is less representative of all citizens' preferences than the first, the legitimacy of the collective decisions will be reduced to the extent that they are influenced by the second chamber. If the second chamber is equally representative, it will merely reproduce the outcomes of the first. The latter result seems highly inefficient, and the first implies that for some reason the preferences represented in the second chamber should get more weight than those in the first. Given that the first chamber has been fairly constituted, it is not clear how such a reweighting can be defended. Alternatively, one might ask why, if a second chamber improves the outcomes of the collective choice process, would a third not improve the outcomes still more, or even a fourth?

Nor is it easy to defend the existence of a second chamber under the TPD. Each citizen votes for the party promising her the best platform of policies and the winning party's platform maximizes the welfare of the community. Why place a second chamber against the first and risk delaying or distorting 'the will of the people' as expressed in the election? How can the party ruling the lower house be held fully responsible for the government's policies, if it shares authority with members of an upper house chosen under some other principle? The entire *raison d'être* of two-party government – that it produces responsible and accountable governments – gets called into question, once responsibility for the outcomes of the governmental process is shared between two or more seats of authority. If the goal of representative government is to bring about a correspondence between these outcomes and the preferences of the citizens, then there is no place for a second chamber in a system of government in which the first chamber has been properly constituted under either the PRD or the TPD.

Anyone who shares this view regarding the merits of a second chamber must view with considerable skepticism the proposals of several authors to have two chambers in the EU, one in which the citizens are directly represented, and a second in which EU states are represented. It would be much better to set aside the current practice of electing representatives to the European Parliament from the individual states with a system in which voters from across the entire EU can transfer their votes to individuals, or choose parties under a party-list system. Either proposal would result in a representation of citizens' views on EU matters that was proportional to their appearance in the EU at large. The wrestling over the distribution of representatives across the national parties would disappear, and along with it the struggle among the delegates from each country over the geographic distribution of the EU budget. At the same time, responsibility for the budget could be shifted from the Council to the Parliament. With representation according to geography eliminated in the Parliament, and in charge of the budget, perhaps it would come to pass that less money gets allocated to geographically defined redistribution programs than the 80 percent that is now so allocated.

7. DESIGNING THE EXECUTIVE UNDER TPD AND PRD

In a TPD, the two parties present platforms to the voters, the voters choose the party/platform they prefer, and the party delivers the promised set of policies to the people. Combining the executive and legislative functions of government should facilitate this delivery. The logic of the TPD demands that the executive and legislative functions of government be combined. The leader of the party winning the election becomes the chief executive, the winning party chooses the cabinet and forms the government.

What should the relationship between the legislative and executive functions of government be under the PRD? In section 2 we described the PRD as a parliament without a government. The logic underlying the PRD demands that the parliament, in which the preferences of all citizens are represented, not choose the cabinet to avoid the parliament's having to form a stable coalition in which some representatives are excluded, and to avoid the possible instabilities that often accompany coalition governments. The logic underlying the PRD demands that the legislative and executive functions of government be separated. We describe two alternative models for accomplishing this goal.

7.1 An Executive Committee

At a minimum the PRD requires that there be some sort of executive committee separate from the parliament to propose issues and set the parliamentary agenda. This committee might be elected by the citizens or appointed by the parliament. The Swiss Bundesrat is an example of such a committee.

7.2 A President

Under the American-style presidential system there is a complete separation of the executive and legislative branches of government. The president is directly elected by the people, and appoints the cabinet ministers who are in charge of carrying out the programs passed in the legislature. Although the president might be assigned certain proposal and agenda-setting powers, it is important to avoid the kinds of political stalemates that have plagued Latin American countries and have become common in the USA, that the president not be given veto power over the decisions of the legislature. His duties should be confined literally to that of the chief executive of the government bureaucracy.[15]

In both of these models, the executive is separated from the legislature. The Swiss Bundesräte are dependent on the parliament in the sense that it appoints them, but the appointments are for fixed terms and thus the Bundesräte can carry out their tasks without fear of parliamentary interference. The American president's selection is totally independent from that of the legislature. Combining either variant of these two models with the PRD would leave the legislative assembly free to carry out its function of debating and deciding the legislative program of the country. This process would not be constrained by the need to form a stabile majority coalition. All representatives could be expected to participate in the collective decision process. If some sort of qualified majority rule were the parliamentary voting rule, then one would expect shifting coalitions to form to pass different pieces of legislation as occurs today in the Swiss Parliament and the US Congress under the simple majority rule.

8. SUFFICIENT CHECKS AND BALANCES?

A central characteristic of the American Constitution is checks and balances. The Founding Fathers of the USA were greatly concerned about the possibility of one branch of government overstepping its authority and undertaking actions that harmed the citizenry. This fear led them to introduce an elaborate set of checks and balances into the US system. Our proposals, in contrast, focus on the design of institutions that would better align the outcomes of the political process with citizen preferences. Many will object that our proposals contain insufficient checks against possible misuses of power by one or the other branch. It is impossible to design a political system which provides the state sufficient authority and legitimacy to carry out 'the will of the people' without at the same time granting it sufficient discretion to implement policies that harm the people. And it must also be recognized that failing to introduce good policies can harm citizens just as much as the introduction of bad policies.

It would be wrong to conclude, however, that our proposals contain no effective checks on the state. Under both PRD and TPD the parties in the parliament have an incentive to adopt policies that advance citizen interests, if they hope to win seats in the next election. This constraint is particularly salient under TPD, since a party can only fulfill the wishes of its supporters if it wins an absolute majority of the votes cast. Under PRD there is the additional constraint of the parliamentary voting rule which should, as we have stressed, ensure that a mere majority of the members of the parliament cannot continuously impose their preferences on the remainder. To these constraints we would add referenda called by the citizens, and a judiciary sufficiently powerful to block the implementation of policies that violate citizen rights as defined in the constitution. An additional possible constraint on the state, which we do not have space to elaborate upon, would be a strong federalist system.

9. CONCLUSIONS FOR A CONSTITUTION OF THE EUROPEAN UNION

In this chapter we have evaluated two forms of parliamentary democracy. Each has its merits. But we do not want to reconsider them in this conclusion. Rather we want to apply our findings to the questions: which of the two systems is more appropriate for the EU and what does that imply for the executive branch of the government and for citizens' participation in referenda?

We have seen that both systems reduce the costs of the democratic process compared to direct democracy. PRD economizes on the number of people participating in the political discussion and in opinion formation. TPD, in contrast, reduces the discussion, but allows all citizens to express their views directly by choosing a particular party program. Concerning the EU we have to ask: what is more important – political discussion and opinion formation or direct voting on particular programs? We believe that, for the EU, it is the former. The EU consists of a large number of rather different member states forming a confederation rather than a federation. Discussion is needed among the elected representatives in the European Parliament to detect what their citizens' preferences in the different member states are. Therefore, we would propose an election system for the European Parliament similar to that proposed by Tullock (see section 2) or alternatively a list system (see section 3). We recommend that the European Parliament be voted in one electoral district, for it grants minorities a higher chance of being represented in the Parliament than in the present system of multi-member districts.[16] In the case of the list system, the persons to be sent to the Parliament may be chosen by the parties according to the number of votes they received or they may be selected by the voters under the single-transferable-vote (STV) system[17] in which they designate not only the party they prefer but also their ranking of candidates within the party. The restriction to one electoral district moreover avoids quarrels about which member state should receive how many seats in the European Parliament (see section 6 above). The only way national governments can influence the number of their own representatives is by promoting a high voter turnout. But even then, it is not evident that the representatives will support the goals of the particular member state government. Voters may prefer to vote for cross-country candidates promising to promote Europe-wide instead of domestic public goods.

Hence, the ever-returning question of whether Europe already has its own *demos* and could therefore be regarded as a federation, or whether it is a confederation, because it consists of several peoples with different views and attitudes, cannot be resolved by introspection and collective decision; it results from the voting behavior, that is, from the extent to which citizens prefer cross-country candidates over own-country candidates under STV.

A European government that is formed according to the logic of PRD does not need a powerful government. It would suffice to have an executive board (see section 7 above), say the Commission, whose members may be elected for a fixed period of time by the European Parliament. Overlapping of the terms of office of the Commissioners may be desirable in order to suppress any tendency to establish a mixed system of PRD and TPD.

The Council has actually no role in our design of the EU. Indeed, it lacks democratic legitimacy and could only be considered as a form of a second chamber. But we have shown above that a second chamber cannot improve democratic decision making in the Union when the first chamber is representative in the sense defined. It would be superior and indeed to be recommended to require the European Parliament to decide by qualified majority rule or by an inclusive voting procedure such as voting by veto or point voting (see section 2 above). These voting rules would also put a brake on the actual tendencies to centralize national competences at the Union level.[18]

Collective decision making has to be checked by referenda and by the European Court of Justice. Optional referenda are designed for acts of legislation. They have to be held on request of, say, 5 percent of the citizens or of 10 percent of the member state governments. For changes in the constitution, however, a mandatory referendum is required. For political agents must be prevented from setting their own rules.[19]

We believe that our institutional design could serve as a starting-point for a new Constitution of the European Union, an alternative to that proposed by the European Convention. There is not enough space here to elaborate further issues such as the assignment of power, taxation, rights and citizenship and the subsidiarity principle. But our approach is enough to emphasize the need to start from citizens and their preferences and to postpone other issues such as supreme values, which are thought to be common (or imposed as common) for all citizens of Europe. We propose a bottom-up approach, whereas the constitutional process in the European Convention was rather one of top-down. It risks adding to alienation instead of consensus.

NOTES

1. An often-mentioned fourth principle, simple majority rule, is, however, deliberately excluded. For direct democracy can be practiced with different less-than-unanimity rules and obviously also with unanimity rules. We shall show below that more inclusive rules generate political outcomes which are more faithful to individual preferences.
2. The material of sections 2 to 6 is partially taken from Blankart and Mueller (2002) and Mueller (1996).
3. For further discussion of this procedure see Mueller et al. (1975).
4. Caplin und Nalebuff (1988) have demonstrated that the probability of a cycle declines as the required majority is increased, when voting is restricted to issues having the characteristics of pure public goods, and that this probability reaches zero at a majority of 64.
5. Kirchgässner (2000) has questioned the plausibility of the assumptions under which these results follow, and shown that cycles may appear when these assumptions are changed. Unfortunately, since no TPD systems exist, Kirchgässner's hypothesis cannot be tested. Mueller (2003, ch. 12) defends the plausibility of equilibria existing in an electoral competition involving only two parties.
6. See Coughlin et al. (1990).
7. Ibid.
8. In Germany the Free Democratic Party has often been the beneficiary and victim of this sort of strategic voting, see Cox (1997, pp. 197–8).
9. Although the British-style Westminster system can be said to result in stable government, it cannot be claimed that it results in some form of social welfare maximum, as can be demonstrated for the TPD. Because there are generally at least three parties winning votes in the UK, it can happen that a majority of the voters would actually have preferred one or both of the other parties to the one that wins a majority of the seats in Parliament. To avoid this sort of outcome and achieve the other possible advantages

from two-party government, the winning party should be selected using the kind of two-stage procedure described above as part of the TPD.

10. For a closer examination of the organization of referenda, see Blankart (2000).
11. See Blankart (1992).
12. See the examples and discussion in Butler and Austin (1978, pp. 5–16 and 221–37), and Mueller (1996; pp. 182–5).
13. From time to time questions arise that are of a quasi-constitutional nature, but do not technically require a constitutional amendment, as for example whether a country should adopt the euro or not. These sorts of issues are quasi-constitutional in the sense that once made they need to be taken off the normal political agenda, since a continual shifting back and forth of policy would have high costs. Allowing the citizens to decide these quasi-constitutional issues via referenda is an attractive option.
14. See Nedelsky (1990, ch. 2) and Sundquist (1986, pp. 22–3).
15. Although deadlocks in the USA to date have merely meant that neither the program of the president nor that of the Congress gets implemented, in Latin America political impasses have often been followed by military *coups* and dictatorship. For more on Latin America and references to the literature, see Mueller (1999).
16. A minimal number of some seats may be granted to the very small member states.
17. As used in Ireland and Northern Ireland.
18. The European Constitutional Group (1993) proposes a second chamber consisting of members of the national parliaments in order to safeguard the subsidiarity principle and to prevent centralization. We believe that inclusive voting rules represent a more efficient way to achieve this goal. This may be achieved more efficiently by a more inclusive voting rule; see above explanation.
19. As far as rights and citizenship are concerned, see Mueller (2004) and European Constitutional Group (1993).

REFERENCES

Barro, R.J. (1997), *Determinants of Economic Growth – A Cross Country Empirical Study*, Cambridge, MA: MIT Press.

Blankart, Ch.B. (1992), 'Bewirken Referendum und Volksinitiative einen Unterschied in der Politik?', *Staatswissenschaften und Staatspraxis*, **3**, 509–23.

Blankart, Ch.B. (2000), 'Wie sollen Abstimmungen auf Bundesebene organisiert werden? Lehren aus der Weimarer Verfassung,' *Wirtschaftsdienst*, **80**, 607–10.

Blankart, Ch.B. and D.C. Mueller (2002), 'Alternativen der parlamentarischen Demokratie', *Perspektiven der Writschaftspolitik*, **3**, 1–21.

Buchanan, J.M. and G. Tullock (1962), *The Calculus of Consent: Logical Foundations of Constitutional Democracy*, Ann Arbor: University of Michigan Press.

Butler, D. and R. Austin (1978), *Referendums*, Washington, DC: American Enterprise Institute.

Caplin, A. and B. Nalebuff (1988), 'On 64%-Majority Rule', *Econometrica*, **56**, 787–814.

Coughlin, P., D.C. Mueller and P. Murrell (1990), 'Electoral Politics, Interest Groups, and the Size of Government,' *Economic Inquiry*, **28**, 682–705.

Cox, G.W. (1997), *Making Votes Count*, Cambridge: Cambridge University Press.

European Constitutional Group (1993), *A Proposal for a European Constitution*, London: European Policy Forum.

Kirchgässner, G. (2000), 'Probabilistic voting and equilibrium: An impossibility result,' *Public Choice*, **103** (1–2), 35–48.

Mueller, D.C. (1989), *Public Choice II*, Cambridge: Cambridge University Press.
Mueller, D.C. (1996), *Constitutional Democracy*, New York, Oxford: Oxford University Press.
Mueller, D.C. (1999), 'Fundamental Issues in Constitutional Reform: With Special Reference to Latin America and the United States,' *Constitutional Political Economy*, **10** (June), 119–48.
Mueller, D.C. (2003), *Public Choice III*, Cambridge: Cambridge University Press.
Mueller, D.C. (2004), 'Rights and citizenship in the European Union,' in D.C. Mueller and Ch.B. Blankart (eds), *A Constitution for the European Union*, Cambridge, MA: MIT Press, forthcoming.
Mueller, D.C., R.D Tollision and Th.D. Willett (1975), 'Solving the intensity problem in a representative democracy,' in R.D. Leiter and K. Sirkin (eds), *Economics of Public Choice*, New York: Cyro Press, repr. in R. Amacher, R. Tollison and T. Willett (eds), *Political Economy and Public Choice*, Ithaca, NY: Cornell University Press, 1976, pp. 444–73.
Nedelsky, J.L. (1990), *Private Property and the Limits of American Constitutionalism*, Chicago: University of Chicago Press.
Sundquist, J.L. (1986), *Constitutional Reform and Effective Government*, Washington, DC: Brookings Institution.
Tullock, G. (1967), *Toward a Mathematics of Politics*, Ann Arbor: University of Michigan Press.
Wicksell, K. (1896), 'Ein neues Prinzip der gerechten Besteuerung', *Finanz theoretische Untersuchungen*, Jena, trans. as 'A New Principle of Just Taxation', 1958, repr. in R.A. Musgrave and A.T. Peacock (eds), *Classics in the Theory of Public Finance*, London: Macmillan, 1967, pp. 72–118.

COMMENT

Barbara Krug

What follows addresses a point not mentioned in the Blankart/Mueller contribution. The reason for this is, first, that the insights presented are thoughtful, straightforward and well argued. Any comment would be limited to some marginal remarks. Second, their appeal to go back to the basics of democratic institutional design invites another step back to the basics by questioning the effects of size and scope of electoral districts.

What is striking in the literature, and in particular in the literature that focuses on the necessary political reforms in the EU, is that the existing delineation of electoral districts is taken as a given. Yet we know that the delineation of such districts can function as a strong substitute for voting rules. If, for example, electoral districts were designed so that all voters shared the same political ideas and faced the same constraints, no voting rule would be necessary. The number of electoral districts each of which represented a different constellation of political preferences and constraints would then predetermine the overall outcome rather than the median voter in each district. On the other hand, if each electoral district reflects heterogeneity, giving full power to the median voter in each district, the outcome might still be undesirable on the ground that the aggregate election outcome does not reflect the result of votes cast, or that a meta-consensus claiming that electoral districts should follow predefined historical boundaries is violated.

To illustrate this last point (and the limits of democratic constituency building) the problem involved in the attempt to design a constitution for Northern Ireland might prove instructive. In Northern Ireland, that is, a country geographically divided into Catholic and Protestant parts, a constitution needs to obey a 'fairness' rule which states that there must be as many Protestant as Catholic constituencies. Otherwise the two rival groups will not consent to a political solution. In the countryside that is a rather simple, mechanical affair, as segregation of the two groups is neatly reflected in Catholic and Protestant villages. In the cities, for example Belfast, the delineation sometimes means cutting neighbourhoods if not streets in several constituencies, some of which might become so small that 'rotten boroughs' become (re-)established. In this way another fairness rule is violated if, for example, in one constituency only 30 votes are enough to carry a seat while in others 300 are needed.

Simplistic public choice would not see the problem, so long as it adheres to the assumption that there is 'voting by feet', meaning that on one side like-minded people congregrate, while those disenchanted by a political or economic environment will emigrate to a more promising place. If that were the case, then electoral districts of compatible size could be defined in Ireland, and internal migration would occur so that a median voter of a special nature – namely the one district the least inclined to vote according to religious inclination – would play a decisive role.

Yet such a scenario does not reckon with a people whose political preferences include the possession of an inherited, or otherwise claimed, territory. It can be argued that if possession of land becomes more important than the wellbeing of those inhabiting the land, then all democratic constitutions might fail. History and the recent wars in the Balkans prove the point. We would need to accept this, were it not for the fact that there is a whole literature on federalism in public choice and a literature on multi-layered government in the political sciences. On the empirical side, history also provides enough examples of countries where multi-ethnic (or multi-religious) groups have learnt to live together peacefully, and to base their vote not exclusively on territorial claims or ideological affiliation. As the historical examples suggest, decentralization or federalism plays as large a role as the design of constituencies, whether based on residency, religion or functions.

The difference in design and policy between a European Union where voters vote directly for one parliament, and one which is built on nation-states (and their inherited design of electoral districts) is not hard to imagine. A new design of electoral districts that might cross national boundaries might also lead to different outcomes in election results. This is not to take sides in the discussion. It is rather an appeal to the authors to go further: most people would agree that at the moment there are too many levels of government; thus a 'disaggregation of the state' is called for. If as a consequence the whole constitutional architecture for a future Europe is to be broadly discussed, then to include the topic of electoral districts seems appropriate.

COMMENT

Christoph A. Schaltegger

Political institutions matter – this insight is not new and has many forerunners (see for example Frey, 1990). However, the chapter by Charles B. Blankart and Dennis Mueller brings a novel and very interesting aspect into the discussion: the effect of combining specific political institutions in a democracy on representation and accountability.

Recent empirical literature in this field of research has focused on constitutional rules for elections and legislation, and has found that the specific design of these institutions affects the size of government (see, for example, Persson et al. 2000; Persson and Tabellini, 2001, 2002; Milesi-Ferretti, et al. 2002). What could be the reason that electoral and legislative institutions shape economic policy from a theoretical perspective? Political decisions are the result of the institutional framework in which voters, politicians, bureaucrats and pressure groups, all with particular interests, solve their conflicts. Rules for elections and legislation constitute the environment in which these conflicts can be solved. In an adequate institutional framework political conflicts can be solved efficiently. Thus constitutional rules for election and legislation are crucial for economic policy by defining the process of conflict resolution. According to the findings of Persson and Tabellini and others, two political institutions are crucial. First, electoral rules matter. Persson and Tabellini consider the different impact of proportional versus majoritarian representation. Under the majoritarian rule, politicians have to internalize the policy benefits of a larger share of population than under proportional elections, where the interests of a probably very small but decisive district are important. Furthermore, in a majoritarian system policy decisions can be personalized, making accountability easier than in a proportional system where parties have a stronger position. Second, according to this literature, the regime type is of importance. Here, empirical evidence shows that presidential regimes perform better than parliamentary regimes. This is because presidential regimes imply a separation of powers. The president is elected separately by parliament, thus constituting a system of checks and balances. All in all, this literature finds that presidential and majoritarian electoral rules are both associated with smaller governments than parliamentary and proportional systems.

Blankart and Mueller take a very similar approach in their chapter investigating the interaction between rules for election of the parliament and the electoral rules for the executive authority. However, in contrast to the above-mentioned literature they do not argue from a comparative political economy point of view and they do not empirically evaluate the effect of different electoral and legislative institutions on policy outcome. Blankart and Mueller's approach is one of a constitutional designer; that is, it is a strictly normative approach. The main message of the chapter is that if the pure representative democracy, no matter whether proportional or majoritarian, is combined with the two-party competition democracy, no matter whether parliamentary or presidential, inefficiencies will occur. Both forms of democratic rules have their advantages: the pure representative democracy best helps to represent voters' preferences, whereas the two-party competition democracy strengthens accountability. But in combination the advantages will dilute. On the one hand, representation is weakened when the parliament elects the executive authority since the winning coalition only represents a small portion of voters.[1] On the other hand, with combining the two rules of democracy, accountability is not granted since policy decisions cannot be traced back to a single decision maker. Thus the normative conclusion for a constitutional designer is to concentrate on one of the two systems.[2] According to Blankart and Mueller, the European Constitution, as an example, should concentrate on the aspect of representation since Europe does not need a powerful government but a system that is able to strengthen the sensibility for Europe's constituency.

From a comparative static point of view, Blankart's and Mueller's proposal for constitutional designers has an intuitive appeal even though it would imply a complete change in the institutional framework of presumably all democracies. If representation is the goal of democratic policy, the executive authority is not needed, only a parliament has to be elected. If, on the other hand, accountability is important, we do not need a parliament; only an elected executive authority is of importance. Moreover, according to Blankart and Mueller, policy decisions would be more consistent when relying solely on one of the two democratic powers.

However, from a dynamic perspective, Blankart's and Mueller's proposal poses some natural questions. Why do most democracies, if not all in some way, rely on a combination of representation and accountability, if this constitutional design is not efficient? Is it only because institutions are path dependent and costly to change? Or is there a further aspect which should be considered when evaluating democratic rules? Probably, the combination of representation and accountability by a parliament and an executive authority creates a system of checks and balances, which is not efficient in a comparative static perspective but efficient in a dynamic view. Probably the institutional combination of the two systems gives voters *ex ante* the confidence that governmental power is limited in the sense of additional veto points (see Tsebelis, 1999). In practice additional veto players imply that policy changes become less likely as there are many players with the ability to block changes. Thus it is possible that voters see that the combination of the two political institutions is costly but they are willing to bear this burden as a kind of insurance premium against unintended policy changes. They prefer the *status quo*. When the representative form of democracy is combined with an accountable executive authority, voters have confidence that different governmental powers will check each other – most suitable with a presidential regime and majoritarian election rules, according to Persson and Tabellini. Thus, with a system of checks and balances governmental power is limited so that agents are prevented from abusing their discretion.

Of course, it is very difficult to evaluate the relevance of all these considerations. Unfortunately, there are no field data available to check the isolated impact of the pure form of representative democracy or the two-party competition democracy. But it is interesting to note that voters often elect different majorities for the executive and the legislative authorities. Thus it seems that voters like to have a political system with checks and balances, at least from time to time.

What can be learned from the analysis by Blankart and Mueller? Most importantly, democratic institutions have to be analyzed in detail since different electoral institutions lead to different economic policy decisions. Democratic rules based on representation stand in conflict to democratic rules based on accountability. Thus the combination of a representative democracy with a separately elected executive authority weakens representation as well as accountability of policy decisions by a government. From a static point of view, a consistent constitutional design should therefore rely only on one of the two rules. In a dynamic perspective, however, the combination of both systems creates additional veto points restricting governmental discretion in the sense of checks and balances.

NOTES

1. Interestingly, Persson and Tabellini (2002) argue in a very similar way but, according to them, parliamentary democracy does not weaken representation but rather checks and balances are weakened when the executive authority is elected by the parliament.
2. Following Persson and Tabellini (2002), the problem of accountability arises in a proportional election system. Thus, according to them it is not necessary to concentrate on one of the two rules but to combine a presidential regime with majoritarian elections.

REFERENCES

Frey, B.S. (1990), 'Institutions Matter', *European Economic Review*, **34**, 443–9.

Milesi-Ferretti, G., R. Perotti and M. Rostagno (2002), 'Electoral Systems and Public Spending', *Quarterly Journal of Economics*, **117**, 609–57.

Persson, T. and G. Tabellini (2001), 'Political Institutions and Policy Outcome: What are the Stylized Facts?', CESifo Working Paper No. 459.

Persson, T. and G. Tabellini (2002), 'Do Constitutions Cause Large Governments? Quasi Experimental Evidence', *European Economic Review*, **46**, 908–18.

Persson, T., G. Roland, and G. Tabellini (2000), 'Comparative Politics and Public Finance', *Journal of Political Economy*, **108**, 1121–61.

Tsebelis, G. (1999), 'Veto Players and Law Production in Parliamentary Democracies: An Empirical Analysis', *American Political Science Review*, **93**, 591–608.

9. A small country in Europe's integration – generalizing the political economy of the Danish case

Martin Paldam*

1. INTRODUCTION: THE SMALL-COUNTRY PROBLEM

This chapter presents a simple model explaining the stylized facts about the behavior of small countries in big unions. It is done by considering the Edgeworth box for a voluntary agreement between a small country, 'Sland', and a big organization, 'org'. The model is fairly general, and it is illustrated by the case of Denmark in the EU. The subject of the chapter has been much discussed in all small EU countries, but few efforts have been made to make a formal theory.[1] The model has other uses, as will be briefly sketched in section 4.5.

The chapter proceeds as follows: section 2 deals with the set-up of the analysis. Section 3 considers the gap between the elite and the population, while section 4 puts the model together, and considers several possible cases. Section 5 discusses the long-run dynamics of the union, and the possibility that the resistance of the population of Sland to the organization will erode over time. Finally, section 6 concludes as regards the longer run.

1.1 Two Stylized Facts

The starting-points of the analyses are two facts about the European Union (EU):

(F1) EU is less popular the smaller the country.
(F2) EU is (much) more popular in the elite than in the population at large.[2]

Table 9.1 EU membership and country size

Countries and their sizes			Membership status		
No.	Country	Population	Original	Joined	Euro
1	Germany	82.7	Founder		
2	UK	59.5		1972	Outside
3	Italy	57.5	Founder		
4	France	55.1	Founder		
5	Spain	39.8		1986	
6	Netherlands	15.9	Founder		
7	Greece	10.6		1981	1 year late
8	Belgium	10.3	Founder		
9	Portugal	9.8		1986	
10	Sweden	8.9		1994	Outside
11	Austria	8.3		1994	
12	Switzerland	7.4		Not	–
13	Denmark	5.3		1972	Outside
14	Finland	5.2		1994	
15	Norway	4.4		Not	–
16	Ireland	3.7		1972	
17	Luxembourg	0.43	Founder		
18	Malta	0.38		Not yet	–
19	Iceland	0.28		Not	–

Note: Malta is now applying. Norway has applied, but the voters have rejected membership.

F1 is illustrated in Table 9.1. Western Europe has a total of 19 countries that could be members of the EU.[3] It appears that the probability of being outside/joining late is larger the smaller the country for the three dimensions of membership covered by the table.[4]

F2 will not be documented at present. The evidence for the countries I know is strong, but it has appeared in newspaper articles that do not allow a simple summary. In Denmark approximately 50 percent of the people but more than 80 percent of the members of Parliament are in favor of the EU. I know of no other similarly large and persistent gap between people and elite.

1.2 The Case of Denmark in the EU[5]

Denmark has a referenda institution, and six referenda have been held on different aspects of EU; see Table 9.2. The EU is therefore a permanently

Table 9.2 Danish referenda on EU themes

No.	Date	Theme	Yes	No	Part[a]
1	02/10/1972	For joining the EU	63.3	36.7	90.1
2	27/02/1986	EU integration package[b]	56.2	43.8	75.4
3	02/06/1992	For the Maastricht Treaty	49.3	50.3	83.1
4	18/05/1993	For the National Compromise[c]	56.7	43.3	86.5
5	28/05/1998	For the Amsterdam Treaty	55.1	44.9	76.2
6	28/11/2000	Joining the euro	46.9	53.1	87.5

Notes:
[a] Participation in percent of all eligible. The 'yes' and 'no' fractions sum to 100 percent.
[b] Advisory. The constitution allows advisory referenda, but governments obey referenda.
[c] When the Maastricht Treaty was rejected (item 3) the proponent and opponent parties agreed to a national compromise, which was a renegotiated treaty with a set of exceptions.

hot issue in the country. Consequently, EU is better known in Denmark than in the other membership countries.[6]

Figure 9.1 shows the popularity of the EU during the last 40 years, including the 29 years when Denmark was a member. As a rule of thumb barely 50 percent of the Danes are in favor of the EU, while almost 40 percent are against. The graph illuminates several popular conceptions and hypotheses. Two points are worth noting:

(P1) The referenda do not deviate much from the curves,[7] but the theme, the political situation and the propaganda/information during the campaign play a small role.

(P2) Many used to believe in an 'erosion hypothesis', in which resistance erodes as people get accustomed to membership.[8] The data do not support this notion, see section 5.

When popularity is disaggregated, a pattern appears which looks roughly as predicted by economic theory: human behavior goes by the book – that is the pocketbook. Groups for whom EU has favorable arrangements support the organization, for example Danish farmers. Groups having an especially favorable national arrangement – threatened by the joint policies – dislike the EU, for example Norwegian farmers.

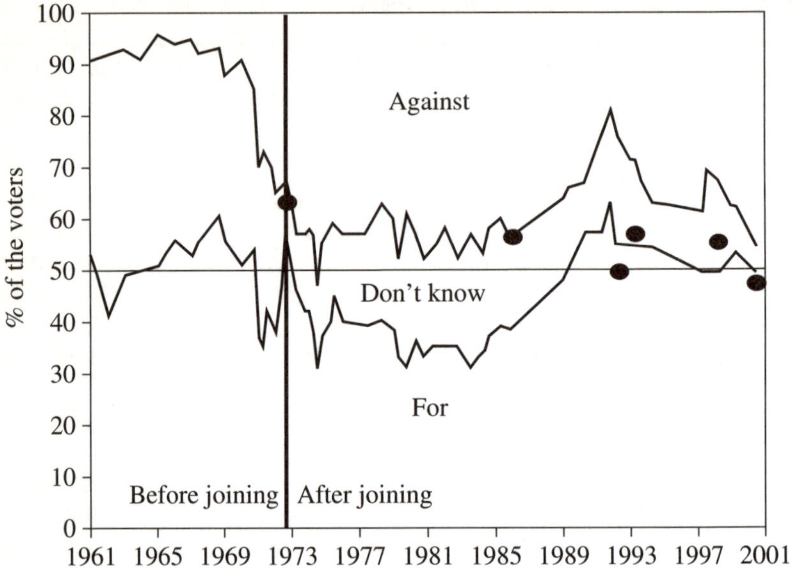

Note: The question is: 'What would you vote today, if you should decide about membership in the EU?' The 'for' percentage goes from 0 percent up to the lower of the two bold lines. The 'against' percentage goes from the upper of the two bold lines up to the 100 percent. The 'don't know' percentage lies between the two lines. The six referenda on EU themes are shown as dots. Data from Gallup.

Figure 9.1 The EEC/EU's popularity in Denmark

2. THE SET-UP: FIVE VARIABLES AND SOME STYLIZED FACTS

This section defines the set-up. It: (1) discusses the key reason to join an international organization, 'org': the big-country advantage; (2) looks at the sovereignty exchange in org, notable the EU; (3) considers the rent destruction and generation of the EU; and finally (4) presents the contract between the country and org.

2.1 The Big-country Advantage, *F*

The last 50 years have seen two reverse trends:

(T1) The big empires have dissolved – mostly voluntarily. Most colonies have simply been set free, as explained in section 4.5.
(T2) Increasingly countries are joining a growing number of interna-

tional organizations. Several explanations of this proliferation will be considered; see also Frey (1997).

The most straightforward explanation is economic advantage. Many statistical studies have tried to explain the wealth and growth of countries. Here the size of the country, *S*, normally contributes positively.[9] Crudely, a variable for log *S* gives a coefficient of 1 percent. A country of 50 million inhabitants tends to grow 1 percent faster than a country of 5 million. A country of 500 million may even grow 2 percent faster. The small-country disadvantage is mainly observed in less-developed countries (LDCs) with autarchic development strategies. Such strategies may work for large countries, but they fail – often spectacularly – in small countries, such as socialist Albania.

The main reasons for the big-country advantage are: (a) economics of scale, and (b) in closed economies rent-seeking tends to be pervasive. The evidence suggests that (b) is far stronger than (a). A major part of *F* is thus caused by a reduction of domestic rent-seeking. Most small rich countries are therefore keen members of many international organizations, to counteract the small-country disadvantage. However, the problem is sovereignty.

A country joins org(*i*), as it pays to coordinate a group of decisions. These decisions constitute a fraction $\beta_i \in [0,1]$ of all decisions made by the country. All members thus give up the sovereignty β_i to org(*i*), but gain an influence over the joint decisions, $\beta_{\text{Org},(i)}$, made by org. The members of org typically give up the same β to a given org, that is, $\beta_i = \beta_{\text{Org}(i)}$ for all *i*. Most orgs have small, stable and well-defined βs. A country that is a member of *N* organizations has given up the sovereignty:

$$\beta = \Sigma_{i=1,\,N}\,\beta_i \qquad (9.1)$$

The country thus obtains two advantages, F_i and $\beta_{\text{Org}(i)}$, from joining org(*i*), but loses, β_i. If all possible organizations existed, and the country consistently optimized *F*, an *F*-curve, $F = F(\beta)$, as depicted in Figure 9.2 would appear. For the optimal portfolio of organizations, β*, the country obtains the maximum, *F**. For a small country *F** may be 10 percent or even 20 percent of GDP for the first decade – if the alternative is to be fully independent.

In the figure, β* is placed in the middle of the interval [0, 1]. For a small country it is perhaps optimal to be half-independent. For a big country β* will be (much) smaller. It is likely that some of the organizations in an optimal portfolio have many members while others are small; see Frey (1998). In practice the choice of organizations is limited, but most small countries join many soft organizations (with low βs), as GATT (General

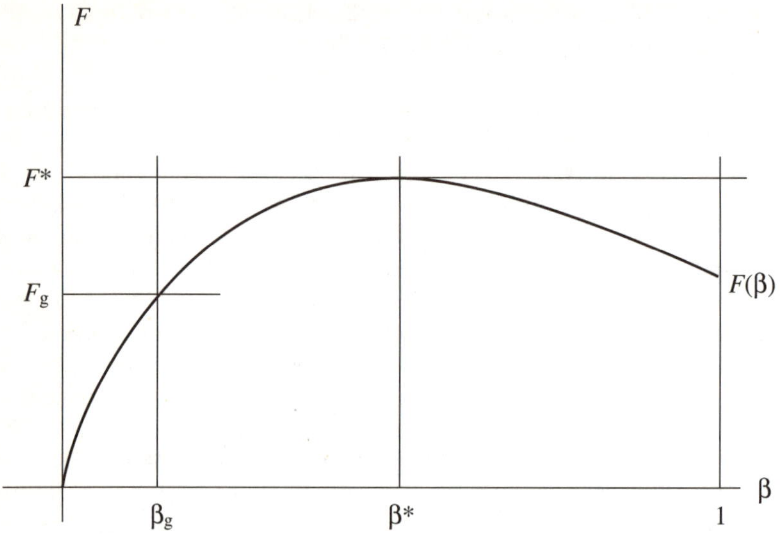

Figure 9.2 The advantage F *as a function of the degree of integration β*

Agreement on Tariffs and Trade)/WTO (World Trade Organization), OECD (Organization for Economic Cooperation and Development), the UN system, BIS (Bank for International Settlements), The International Postal Union, and so on. Sland is thus at point $g = (\beta_g, F_g)$, where it has already harvested $F_g < F^*$.

Now an additional organization, the EU, is considered. It has two characteristics: (i) β is unusually high, though still well below β*. The additional *F* to be gained is perhaps 5 percent (of GDP) for the first decade; (ii) the EU contract is dynamic, so that β is scheduled to grow. Thereby *F* grows, but the marginal productivity $\partial F/\partial\beta$ is falling.

F includes the political risk reduction. EU is often seen as a peacemaker, as it has tied Germany, France and England and other old enemies together with many subtle strings. Maybe the risk of war in Western Europe is reduced by 50 percent, that is, from 2 percent per decade to 1 percent or even less.[10] This political advantage is hardly affected by the inclusion of Sland. The small country obtains most of the political advantage when the big countries cooperate. In fact, this also applies to the economic advantage, as long as Sland is close to the big-country block and has a set of agreements (partly through other organizations) with the members of org. So for Sland some – perhaps most – of *F* appears as a positive externality, F_e.

$$F = F_m + F_e, \qquad (9.2)$$

where F_m is the net gain due to membership. F is hard to calculate, as it is a cumulative and dynamic sum of many small effects. It is even more difficult to sort out F into F_m and F_e. Below, F and F_m are not distinguished.

2.2 Country Size and the Two Power Variables: γ, β

From now only one organization is considered. Also, all other members of org are aggregated as one unit org makes the joint decisions, β. Sland thus gives up sovereignty β_{Sland}. To distinguish as clearly as possible β_{Sland} is termed γ.

γ is thus the decisions org makes in Sland, or the power of org in Sland. The graphs assume that the two variables are one-dimensional, $\gamma, \beta \in [0,1]$. If they are 0, the country is fully independent. If they are 1, it is fully integrated. Member states in a federation, as the USA or Germany, have large βs (and γs), but they are well below 1. All federations experience political fights between those who want to increase β and those who want to reduce γ.

When Sland joins org, it loses sovereignty, γ, and gains a share, α, of the power over the joint decisions, β. In principle, α should be proportional to the size of the country.

$$\alpha \approx \pi = S(\text{Sland})/S(\text{org}) \qquad (9.3)$$

If strict proportionality applies, Sland receives as much power in org as it loses domestically:

$$\text{Strict proportionality: } \alpha = \pi \Leftrightarrow \alpha\beta = \gamma \Leftrightarrow S(\text{org})\gamma = S(\text{Sland})\beta \qquad (9.4a)$$
$$\text{Power gain: } \alpha > \pi \Leftrightarrow \alpha\beta > \gamma \Leftrightarrow S(\text{org})\gamma < S(\text{Sland})\beta \qquad (9.4b)$$

We assume that Sland is a small country, where $S(\text{Sland}) \ll S(\text{org})$. The term 'small country' is used in the following precise sense:

Sland is a small country if people consider $\alpha = 0$, so that $\alpha\beta = 0$.[11] (9.5)

A small country is thus one in which people feel that they give up sovereignty without getting a corresponding power in org in exchange. In a big country people feel that they get power αβ in org in exchange for the power, γ, it gives up; see section 4.5.

A careful review of the data normally shows that small countries get a power gain, as defined in (9.4b). If Sland has to be represented in committees and boards and they must be of a manageable size, Sland must become overrepresented. Also, Sland's representatives will surely become pivotal in some cases. Thus Sland gets a power gain by joining an org. This has no reality for people in Sland, but is well understood by the elite, which has to provide relatively large numbers of representatives to committees and boards. In fact, the smaller the country, the larger is the fraction of the elite that gets (extra) jobs.

2.3 The Remaining Two Parameters: *T* and *R*

The net transfer, *T*, from org to Sland, is a tangible variable that can be found in the budgets. Apart from administrative costs, *T* is a zero-sum game within org. The second variable is much less tangible. It is the rents, *R*, that are generated by org.

In addition to the necessary administrative costs, a rent, *R*, appears in every org. The decision process in all international organizations is separated by one step from the normal democratic controls, and the potential recipients of the rents have a relatively large influence upon their sizes. Three points are relevant:

- (R1) The rent is likely to grow with the number of organizations. This is a second explanation for the proliferation of international organizations.[12]
- (R2) Most of Sland's share, *R*, of the total rents accrues to the elite.
- (R3) The rent revenue, *R*, is difficult to measure. It is conceptually difficult, and those participating in the feast do not try to make measurement easy.

R is the sum of new rents produced by org. When org creates an international arrangement in a field that used to have large domestic rents, they are normally reduced, but then new rents are created by the arrangement. The whole idea of the EU (and several other orgs) is to replace domestic regulations with international ones. Thus the process of rent-seeking becomes more cumbersome. It does not, of course, become impossible to obtain rents, and a swarm of lobbyists has descended upon Brussels. The net drop in old rents is included in *F*, while the new rents are termed *R*. While *F* is hard for people to see some of *R* is highly visible to them.[13]

The agricultural policy, CAP, of the EU illustrates the relation between *F* and *R*. The CAP surely creates very visible surpluses and payments to farmers, and the EU agricultural bureaucracy was set up without a corresponding reduction of the old national ones. It is much more difficult to assess *F*. A comparison of the CAP with the agricultural policies of the West European countries outside the EU – Iceland, Norway and Switzerland – points to a very large *F*. However, this assessment has a self-selection bias, that is, the three countries may have declined to enter the EU precisely because they like high farm subsidies.

2.4 The Contract between Sland and org

The contract has three explicit parameters: $A = (\gamma, \beta, T)$. Sland trades some γ to obtain some β and T. In addition, Sland hopes to obtain a large positive F, and finally there is R. Both F and R are hard-to-calculate side-effects, which are implicit parts of the contract. The EU differs from other orgs in two relevant ways:

(E1) The contract, A_t, is dynamic. Integration is small in the beginning, but it is scheduled to grow in the treaty; see section 4.4.
(E2) Something is known about the likely orders of magnitudes for R.

The EU budget is around 1.16 per cent of the EU GDP. The budget does not contain all rents generated and most of the budget is not rent. A small fraction of the budget goes to wages, where some rents are known to be included. Assume that (1) the EU wage level is 20 percent too high,[14] (2) that this is typical for the R margin, and (3) that the budget contains half the R generated. These assumptions lead to the guess that $R \approx \frac{1}{2}$ percent of the EU GDP. This is surely a wild guess, but it gives an indication of the orders of magnitudes.

The elite knows F and R better than the people do, but the question is if the assessment of the two parts can be systematically different. The hypothesis that people's assessment of F and R is an unbiased estimate of one of the elite is our *RE* hypothesis.

Up to now the four stylized facts of Table 9.3 have been reached. The logic of facts 2 and 4 relies on the well-known $1/N$-complex – even if there is a small deviation from strict rationality it is in a field where such deviations are common.[15]

Table 9.3 Summary of four stylized facts

Fact 1	In practice small countries get a net power gain as members of an org: $\alpha > \pi$.
Fact 2	People in the small country feel that $\alpha\beta$ is zero, so that the gain is of no consequence.
Fact 3	In addition to net reduction in old rents included in the big-country advantage, F, org produces new rents R. It is mainly due to the relatively large wages and fringe benefits in org.
Fact 4	All of β and most of R accrues to the elite of Sland, while R is paid by people.

3. TWO POINTS: THE PROFITS OF ORGANIZATIONS AND THE GAP

Before the contract is discussed, two perspectives are considered: one treats the organization as a producer of $(F+T)$. The second explains the gap between people and elite.

3.1 The Rent, *R*, as a Cost in the Production of $F+T$

R can be understood as a cost in the production of *F*. To produce *F* a bureaucracy is necessary, and it generates a rent, *R* (of ½ percent of GDP). The rent is larger than the usual bureaucratic rent as the international bureaucracy is by necessity removed by one step from the normal decision process and the democratic controls. The profit, Π, which org gives people in Sland is the excess gains:

$$\Pi = (F+T) - R \tag{9.6}$$

Thus formulated, *R* becomes a cost to be minimized, but the problem is that many of those who have to minimize *R* are also consumers of *R*. However, an even more important problem is the risk that the competition to obtain the rent ends up expending all of *R*. The competitive forces on this rent market may even compete the profit, Π, down to zero.[16]

If $F \approx 5$ percent of GDP, Sland obtains a handsome profit if *R* is ½ percent of GDP. That is, the EU does have a large *R*, but it is a small price to pay for a much bigger *F*. In other orgs – including some of the organizations in the UN family – it appears that Π has been competed down to zero. From the argument in section 2.1 follows that it is a problem for Sland to put together an optimal portfolio of many soft orgs. With many orgs the control problem becomes impossible – the result is likely to be a much bigger aggregate *R*.

3.2 The Gap between Elite and People – Two Models

It appears that two theories can be constructed to explain the big gap between people and elite. The first is a typical 'dinner conversation theory', which is quite popular in the elite:

The mob model

The mob model sees people as a mob, an irrational and chauvinistic crowd, who just do not understand. However, the elite understands. This model is supported by polls of people's knowledge about the EU. They do not know much. On the other hand, they do have strong opinions which they vent in their crude way. There is no end to the low motives the elite ascribes to the primitive mob. And, in fact, when one listens to the kind of statements people regularly voice at anti-EU rallies one has to pinch oneself to determine if it is not a nightmare.[17] Fortunately, the wise and tolerant elite has undertaken to lead the prejudiced and ignorant mob, so that things do not fall apart.

This model is not sound economic theory as it builds upon a big irrationality. The alternative theory is impeccable economics.

The rational model

Here the gap is due to the different interests as regards β and R. β is power obtained by the elite. It enters their utility function, while people do not care, so it does not enter their utility function.[18] R is a levy the elite extracts from people, so it has the reverse sign in the utility of people and the elite.

The story as regards F is more complex. However, the gain people get as citizens of a member state in org does come in all kinds of unrecognizable ways. It is taken for granted. This point will be taken up in section 5 discussing myopia and the grievance asymmetry.

4. THE MODEL: A UNION BETWEEN A LARGE ORGANIZATION AND A SMALL COUNTRY

A voluntary agreement $A=(\gamma,\beta,T)$ between org and Sland must be better, for both parties, than no agreement: $0=(0,0,0)$. This situation lends itself to an Edgeworth-box presentation. Between org and Sland a non-empty lens, K, must exist, which is better than 0, in the case where the two parties look like the EU and Denmark. The lens must be empty in the similar case, where the two parties look like Norway and the EU.

4.1 The Bound for Sland's Indifference Curves, I_{Sp} and I_{Se}

Consider first how Sland's people see the contract $A=(\gamma, \beta, T)$. They get utility from T and F, disregard β, and get disutility from γ. Their indifference curves, I_{Sp}, hence look like those in Figure 9.3. People want a low value of γ and a high value of $T(+F)$. The arrows show the direction for increasing utility. The curves bend upward as people in all small countries know that international cooperation is necessary (that is, that $F>0$). To give up a bit of sovereignty to get $T+F>0$ is thus acceptable, but if γ becomes significant, people react.

T is explicit in the contract, but F is not and neither is R. The RE hypothesis argues that people come to know both F and R, but also that they do

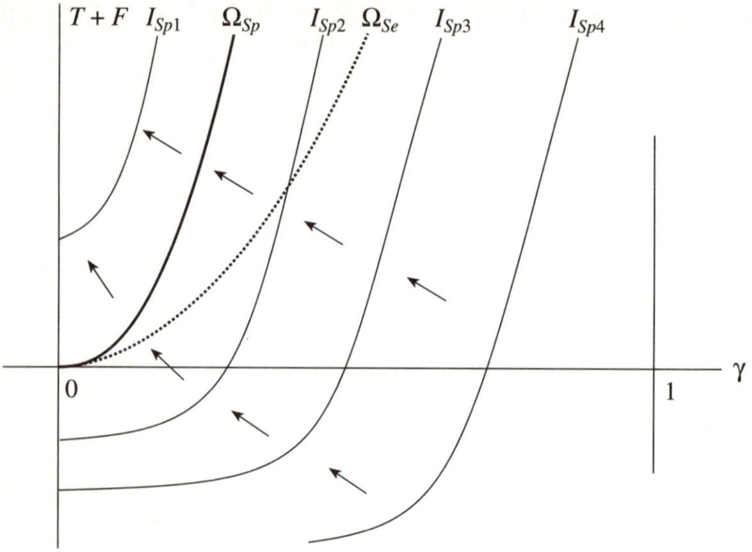

Figure 9.3 Sland's indifference curves

not follow these variables closely. So, in the short run they are predetermined: F, R=**F**, **R**. If F grows, the curves move upward and become steeper. The situation is the reverse for R. If R grows, the curves move down and become flatter. Therefore, $I_{Sp}(F, R, \beta, \gamma, T) \approx I_{Sp}(\mathbf{F} + T, \gamma, \mathbf{R})$, as drawn.

One indifference curve, Ω_{Sp}, is singled out as it goes through (0,0). It is the outer bound of the lens, which divides the plane into two parts: to the left of the bold Ω_{Sp} line people in Sland will voluntarily accept contracts, while they will not do so to the right of the curve.

In the indifference curves for the elite, I_{Se}, β and R enter differently, as discussed. R shifts the elite curves to the right, and the curves become flatter compared to people's curves. As γ and β are roughly proportional, the new elite curves, $I_{Se,}$ are x times the people curves, I_{Sp}, where $x>1$ is a factor of proportionality. The bold dotted line, Ω_{Se}, is the bound for the lens of the elites. Ω_{Se} also starts in (0,0) and then proceeds at a flatter path relative to Ω_{Sp}. Other indifference curves for the elite have been omitted so as not to clutter the graph.

4.2 The Bound for org's Indifference Curves, I_O

Figure 9.4 shows the indifference curves, $I_O(F+T, R, \gamma)$, of org regarding the contract. One γ_N shows how a 'naive and legalistic' country fulfills the

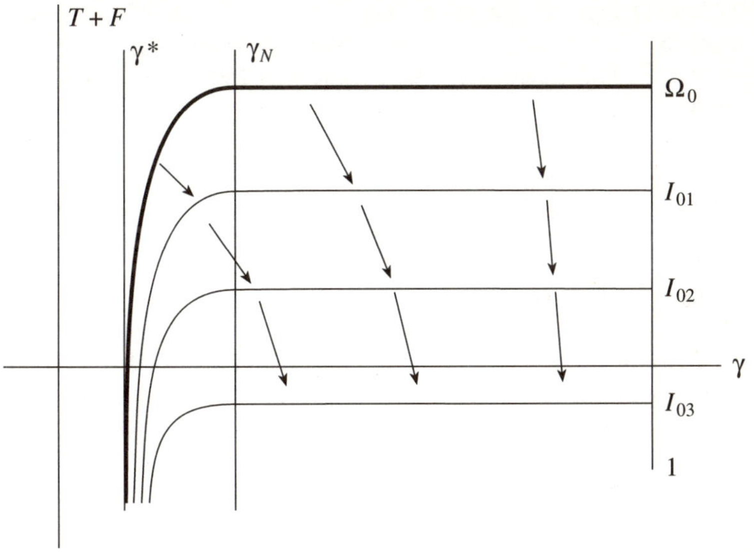

Figure 9.4 The indifference curves of org

contract. However, everybody tries to do some free-riding, but it has a limit, γ^*, which org does not allow any country to cross, so $\gamma^* < \gamma < \gamma_N$. The interval from γ^* to γ_N appears to be large in the EU. Greece and the UK do much as they please and stay members.[19] Also Denmark has been allowed a γ, well below γ_{id}.

The other variable shown is $T + F$ (where F is semi-fixed as before). If org were free to choose, it would surely give Sland as small a T as possible. The indifference curves are flat to the right of γ_{id}, but they must bend downwards to converge toward γ^*, and org has a higher utility for a curve with a lower T than with a higher T at the flat part. However, rules exist giving Sland a 'right' to a certain T_g, at the time of entry. The rules change over time as new members join, but new members get an offer from org when they negotiate about the treaty.

Note that without a positive F only countries with a positive T would join org. F is probably seen as reasonably large by everybody. However, T is the more variable and visible part of the gain drawn on the vertical axis. In the EU case two factors determine the T offered: (a) agricultural exports and (b) relative poverty. When Denmark negotiated, it had a large agricultural export and received a high T offer. When Norway negotiated, it was both rich and without agricultural exports, so it got an offer with a low T. The reason why $T + F$ differ from one country to the next is thus mainly that T differs.

The bold Ω_o curve that starts as a tangent γ^*, and goes up to the maximal T acceptable by org is thus specific to Sland. The set of curves drawn in Figure 9.4 is thus for a country like Denmark or Ireland, who had an offer of a high T.

As before, the curves depend upon F, R, and β. F shows how much the F of org changes if Sland becomes a member, R how much the R of the org changes and so on. It is likely that $I_O(T+F, R, \beta, \gamma, T) \approx I_O(T+\mathbf{F}, \gamma, \mathbf{R})$, much as before.

4.3 The Small and the Large Lens between Sland and org

Figures 9.3 and 9.4 are easy to superimpose on an Edgeworth box. To make the resulting graph easy to read only the bound curves – that is, the Ωs – are included. Note that the drawing includes one small trick: the vertical axis of Figure 9.4 is shifted so that the two $(F+T)$s – of Sland and of org, when Sland joins org – are the same. Since the curves become virtually vertical at the lower end, this does not change the way the curves look.

Figure 9.5 shows how things look in the case termed the 'Danish' one, where org offers a substantial T. Here a small lens exists, where voluntary contacts can be made. It also appears that a much greater lens exists for the elite and org. The bound curve for the elite is situated in the direction generating a larger lens, and hence gives a larger addition to the lens.

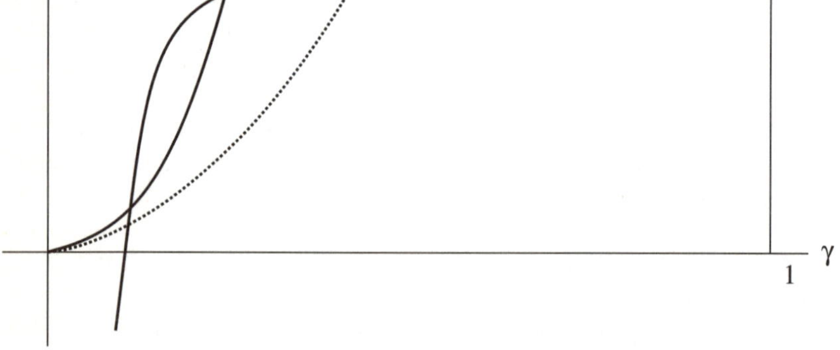

Figure 9.5 The two lenses between Sland and org – the 'Danish' case

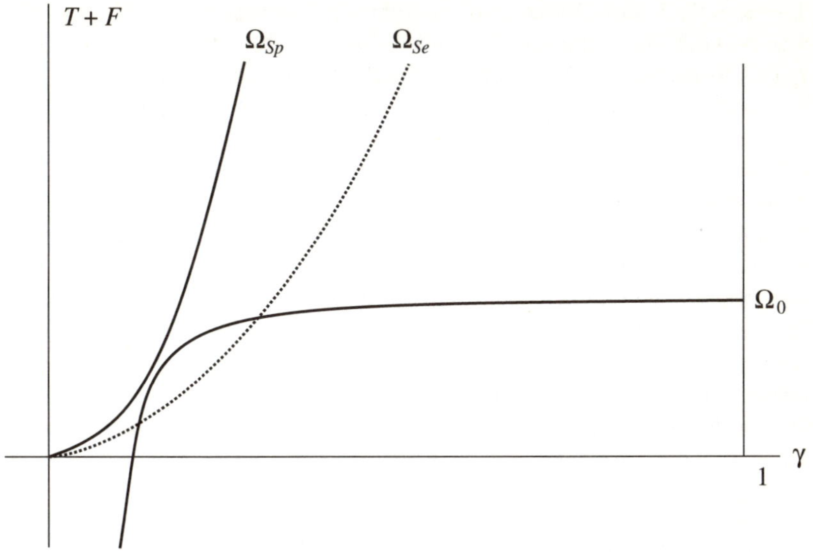

Figure 9.6 The one lens between Sland and org – the 'Norwegian' case

Figure 9.6 is the 'Norwegian' case, where hardly any T is offered even when F is still positive. Here no lens appears between people and org. However, the elite and org has a lens, so from time to time the elite negotiates a treaty and puts it to a referendum, where it promptly fails.

In a broader perspective our analysis has an interesting implication. It shows why it is difficult for a small country to join an organization with a large β and γ. If people disregard β, they must have something else to compensate for the loss of sovereignty, γ. A normal F is not enough. Small countries get either a big T (as Denmark, Greece, Ireland or The Netherlands), some special political advantage (as Finland) or a particularly large F (as Belgium).[20] Both Iceland and Switzerland know that they would get a negative T if they joined – they have not even tried to negotiate – also, they know that they get F_e anyhow.

4.4 The EU as a Dynamic org: Growing out of the Lens

The EU is an org with the explicit aim that β (and hereby γ) is growing over time. The treaty itself contains promises looking as equation (9.7). The promises are vague and have to be interpreted, but the goal is to reach considerable integration.

$$\gamma_t = \beta_t \rightarrow \beta_M \text{ for } t \rightarrow 100 \tag{9.7}$$

The goal β_M is not full integration, but rather to become a federation that is somewhat looser than the USA or Germany, which have β_Ms well below 1. The hope is probably to hit the optimal β^* (see Figure 9.2) for the average country. The countries have to reach the same $\beta_M = \beta^*$. However, the optimal β^* is larger in small than in large countries; maybe a compromise will be reached, where the large countries become too integrated, and the small countries become too little integrated.

Hence the dynamics promised by the treaty mean that β (and hence γ) has to grow a great deal in the future. The latest step was the implementation of the euro and the upgrading of the ECB (European Central Bank) to a real central bank.[21] If this is depicted in Figure 9.5, it means that the contract $A = (\gamma, \beta, T)$ will move to the right. The next step is the increase in membership within Eastern and Central Europe.

In addition, T is dynamic. The big positive Ts that several small members obtained when they entered EU are likely to fall – as has already happened. In particular the big net contributor, Germany, is unlikely to continue paying as much in the future as it did in the past.[22] Also the more different the new members become, the more difficult it is to have rules that generate large payments in extreme cases. However, there is a counteracting force. When β grows, so does F, though F grows less and less as β approaches β^*, as discussed in section 2.1. The dynamics of the three variables are thus:

(D1) β and – hence γ – will increase.
(D2) The increase of F will decrease, until ΔF reaches zero.
(D3) T will decrease for most old members.

From (D2) and (D3) it follows that the sum $T+F$ has already or must soon start to fall. Both the increase in γ and the (eventual) fall in $T+F$ makes it less likely that the contract can remain voluntary. The lens shrinks as $T+F$ falls, and γ's growth pushes the contract out of the lens to the right. From the whole argument so far – and Figure 9.1 – it is obvious that the lens was always small. The analysis thus predicts that the dynamics of the contract inevitably threatens Sland's EU membership.[23] While the movement of the contract will push it out of people's small lens, it will still remain inside the elite's large lens.

4.5 Generalizing the Model

This model is easy to generalize, but only two generalizations will be sketched: (G1) to big countries and (G2) to the colonial liberalization process.

(G1) The big-country case

The main reason to treat the case of a small country as a particular one is the assumption that people care about γ and not about β. In a big country it is different. Here people are accustomed to be far away from the government, and they take it for granted that their country plays a grand role in the world – think of the French. Therefore the assessment of the two power variables is much less asymmetric than in the small countries. The asymmetry might even be the other way, causing the indifference curves to have a negative slope around (0, 0). The asymmetry as regards R is inevitable, but the indifference curves are likely to look quite different. Hence large countries do not need to be compensated to be members of an org.

The reader will see that a theory has been constructed that produces the same result as Olson and Zeckhauser (1966) – that is, the small countries get the best deal in the organization. However, it is more due to a self-selection bias than free-riding.

(G2) The colonial liberalization process

The colonial 'contract' was based upon the use of force, though in the beginning little force was actually needed.[24] However, the twentieth century saw two trends: (a) the idea of self-determination spread, so more power became necessary to control colonies; (b) the use of power became less acceptable for the peoples of the colonial powers. Both developments caused a movement toward a voluntary contract. Since it included some domination, for example $\gamma > 0$, it became more and more necessary for the colonial country to pay a subsidy, T, compensating the colony for the disutility of γ. The lens of the contract moved upward and to the left.

This gradually made large colonies impossibly expensive. Even the Soviet empire became expensive in the end. Hence most colonies were given freedom, sometimes after some violence, but mostly voluntarily and with relief. Only a number of small countries have remained as voluntary member countries of a union, and they have become more and more expensive. Paldam (1996) shows, by the same model as above, how such a limiting case occurs for the union between the large country Denmark and two small ones, the Faeroes (\$3000) and Greenland (\$10 000), where the amounts in parentheses are the annual subsidies per capita. In addition, the old 'mother' country has accepted very low γs. The last of the colonies have turned into very expensive voluntary parts of a union.[25]

5. WILL RESISTANCE TO THE EU ERODE OVER TIME?

The model thus gives a growing problem, where the small country, Sland, finds it increasingly difficult to stay in org, the organization. Sland will thus leave org if Sland's people do not become accustomed to org, and their resistance erodes.[26] Figure 9.1 shows the EUs popularity over 40 years in Denmark. No erosion is apparent in the series, but the variables $F+T$ and γ (and β) have changed, so maybe the popularity should have changed.

5.1 How does the Popularity Function of EU Look in Sland?

The model for the popularity of the EU emerging from the previous pages looks a great deal like the one for I_{Sp}. That is, people's indifference curve for the EU is:

$$\text{Pop}_t = \text{Pop}(\gamma, T, F, R, t) \approx \text{Pop}((T+F)_t, \gamma_t), \qquad (9.8)$$

where t is time.

Table 9.4 sketches two hypotheses about the dynamics of the resistance to the EU.

Table 9.4 Two hypotheses on the resistance erosion

H1	The rate of erosion is constant	People get accustomed to the *status quo* with a constant underlying rate. $\partial\text{Pop}_t/\partial t > 0$. If γ and T keep constant, $\text{Pop}_t \rightarrow 1$.
H2	Pop_t has a natural level, Pop*	Pop* depends upon underlying factors. When γ changes, Pop jumps in the reverse direction; but it later returns to Pop*, as people adjust to the new γ.

(H1) If the graph for Pop_t shown in Figure 9.1 is taken to be trendless, it follows that the erosion in the resistance to the EU corresponds roughly to the growth of γ. Unfortunately, no attempt to measure γ has been made, and it appears a difficult variable to quantify. My hunch is that γ has grown, but not much.[27] So the erosion process is slow if hypothesis 1 is true. This is possible, but it seems that nothing supports such a notion.

(H2) Figure 9.1 shows a couple of sudden movements in Pop_t, which roughly corresponds to known movements in γ. If that is the case, the long-run constancy must indicate that Pop_t returns to the old level. In other words, Pop_t has a natural level.

Unfortunately, the polls are few and are taken at irregular intervals, and no data are available for γ, so it is hard to make a formal empirical analysis to determine if (H1) or (H2) is true. The only way to choose between the two hypotheses is to look into the findings on related phenomena, that is, the popularity of other political agents.

5.2 Is the Vote and Popularity (VP)-Function Literature Relevant?

A large literature analyzes the popularity of governments at elections and polls; see Nannestad and Paldam (1994). Only a few papers deal with the popularity of the EU; see Anderson and Gelleny (2000) and Anderson and Kaltenthaler (2001). The pattern found is much like a weak version of the standard pattern.

The VP-function literature mainly deals with the changes in the popularity of the government, while it says little about the levels. However, an old theory exists in political science about people's long-run attachment to parties – often known as their party identification. It gives long-run stability to the party system. (H2) is a hypothesis of the same type. It says that people obtain a pro-EU identification or an anti-EU identification. What is important is the possible changes in the identifications.

The theoretical basis of the VP-function literature is the responsibility hypothesis: people hold the government responsible for changes in the economy. But what do they hold the EU responsible for? Maybe there is a connection between the popularity of the EU and of the government. This will be discussed in section 5.3.

Two robust results in the literature deal with adjustment over time. First, Voters' myopia says that voters adjust quickly. If a change occurs in either a political or an economic variable causing a change in the popularity of the government, then the effect goes away within a year. This result may be taken to be contrary to (H1) but to support (H2). If Pop_t returns to Pop*, the return should be quick. Second, the cost-of-ruling result says that the popularity of the average government has a downward-sloping trend (amounting to 0.5 percent per annum).[28] The cost-of-ruling result is powerful, as it causes parties to change in power, and thus creates long-run stabilities of the parties – just like Hotelling's median-voter result and the party-id theory. But in the EU the power does not change between parties, so the relevance of this result is dubious.

This all provides a very weak basis for understanding the popularity of the EU. (H1) appears to find no support, while only weak support was found for (H2). If (H2) is true, one can continue with an integration process, if it is done slowly.

5.3 The Governments and the EU's Popularity

Imagine that a connection exists between the popularity of the national government and that of the EU. The closest parallel in the literature is probably to the French case, with both a president and a government between whom to split the blame. The US case is a bit similar, with the Congress and the president being independently elected. In these models one often sees a complex trade-off of popularity between the two levels – often in the form of 'coat-tail' effects, where the popularity of the most visible agent rubs off on the less visible one. Once again it is doubtful if this is relevant. But perhaps two connections do exist:

(C1) Maybe there is a coat-tail effect: $\partial Pop/\partial VP > 0$. The voters may want to punish/reward a government by sending it signals at a EU referendum or poll. Perhaps such a connection is likely, but it is not supported by the data.

(C2) The EU is less popular among left-of-center voters than among right-of-center voters (at least in Denmark). This is often said to imply that a left-of-center government is more likely to be able to carry through a EU referendum.

(C2) relies on a can and a will claim: only a left-of-center government can convince left-of-center voters to vote yes. Also, it is likely that a left-of-center opposition will only make small efforts to persuade their voters to vote for the theme the right-of-center government has proposed for the referenda. The right-of-center voters are likely to vote yes in any case.

6. CONCLUDING REMARKS

When the Danes voted no to the Maastricht Treaty in 1992, the *Economist* printed a front page with a longboat full of fierce-looking and fairly dirty Vikings. They were surely against. The picture gave a clear impression that the elite of the country had good reasons to fear the great unwashed, and Danish politicians do indeed fear anything pertaining to the EU.

The theory presented explains how a steadily ongoing process of integration inevitably runs into trouble, leading to a break between the small country and the international organization. The only possible escape from that predicament is if a process of erosion undermines the resistance. Little evidence and only weak theoretical reasons exist why such erosion should occur, but perhaps there is a long-run level to which the popularity of the EU returns each time an upward change in the integration causes the popularity to drop. If this hypothesis is true, it is possible to go on with an integration process provided it is slow.

However, a corresponding problem is the existence of alternatives. The small rich Northwest European countries are not faced with a choice of all the possibilities they may want. If they were, most Danes (and Norwegians, Swedes, and so on) would probably choose a different organization from that of the EU, provided it consisted of approximately the same members.

Maybe the best solution for the small Northwest European countries is to move toward some sort of semi-membership, as indeed several of them seem to be doing.

NOTES

* A version in Danish was presented at a Bank of Norway EMU conference in Oslo in October 1997 (see Paldam, 1998). The English version was presented at the EEA98 meeting in Berlin, and at the ECSPC/CIDEI meeting in Rome. I am grateful to the discussants and to Jens Thomsen, Louise Andersen, Niels Thygesen, Gunnar Thorlund Jepsen, Jan Rose Skaksen and my students.

1. My efforts suffer from the problems of pioneering efforts. I hope readers will forgive a few loose ends and the fact that I mostly manage to formalize and join up well-known insights. I deal with large issues and make heroic guesses, giving orders of magnitudes where serious estimates do not exist. Such guesses are illustrations presented with no references. On the political economy of the EU, see Vaubel (1994).
2. The word 'elite' covers the most powerful 0.1 percent of the population, that is, 25 percent of the group is politicians and perhaps twice as many civil servants, while the rest work in organizations, business and the media. The model predicts that the gap between the elite and people is larger, the smaller the country.
3. The countries of the former Soviet bloc are only now relevant as possible members and have been disregarded. Micro states are not included as they have special possibilities for semi-membership.
4. It is easy to show that the difference is highly significant by dividing the countries in two groups by size and running binomial tests, or by giving countries a membership score and correlating.
5. Few foreigners seem to understand the Danish relation to the EU. The key to understanding is that Denmark has a long tradition of free trade, and wants the EU to be a free trade organization – also for agricultural products – not a European Union. Danes thus want to be members of an unavailable organization.
6. Nannestad and Paldam (2000) show that elections give a large increase in the level of knowledge; see, however, note 15.
7. The vote hence reflects the general popularity of the EU as such. The referenda themes are complex, dealing with decisions reached by compromises, and codified in an impenetrable bureaucratic language.
8. The alternative – but much shorter – series from Eurobarometer shows a similar pattern. EU membership is a salient issue for most Danes.
9. S is measured in million inhabitants or another reasonable measure. The effect of S has already been found in 'the pattern of growth' literature, see, for example, Syrquin (1988).
10. The data for the last couple of centuries give at least ten times higher risk estimates, but the argument of Fukuyama (1992) suggests that risk has dramatically decreased.
11. The assumption that $\alpha \approx 0$, so that $\alpha\beta < \gamma$, is crucial for our analysis. It is my strong impression that this assumption is realistic, and not only in Denmark.

12. Imagine that the same aggregate β is produced by ten small organizations or one large one. The aggregate R is likely to be less controllable – and hence larger – in the first case. This is an illusion result, like the complexity of tax structure results in the fiscal illusion literature; see Holsey and Borcherding (1997).
13. R is a newsworthy variable. Many stories circulate via the media and among people about the great salaries and wining and dining in Brussels. Also, certain aspects of the CAP – the mountains of grain and butter and the lakes of wine – greatly appeal to the public imagination and wit. People understand and greatly disapprove of R.
14. Those who have tried making the concrete choice know how complex the calculations are. The advantage is not as large as it seems. Much depends upon job possibilities of the spouse, choice of car, house and so on.
15. Decisions where the expected utility or costs are multiplied with a small or very small probability – such as $1/N$, where N is the population; see Aldrich (1997). Here ignorance becomes rational. The $1/N$ problem affects the effort people make to be well informed when they vote at EU referenda. It also matters when assessing the weight (α) people assume Sland has in org.
16. The models of rent-seeking competitions often converge to the zero-profit result – see the surveys by Nitzan (1994) and Tollison (1997). If this occurs, the elite has managed to consume all of F while people get nothing. However, one may argue that it is the elite that produces F, and that people only lose if R becomes larger than F.
17. The combination of the EU membership and the inmigration of 6–7 percent immigrants (from outside the EU) into the hitherto very liberal and tolerant Northwest European countries has revealed ugly parts of the 'souls' of our peoples.
18. In Figure 9.3 the two groups both need a γ axis. In principle, a β axis is also needed for the elite, but as β and γ are roughly proportional, the β axis can be suppressed.
19. Some countries have national exceptions from EU rules. Others are slow to use the legal machinery to pursue their citizens when they cheat the EU. All countries have experienced that the EU court has declared one law or another to be against the treaty. Everybody wants special exceptions, so all γs are well below γ_{id}.
20. Belgium receives most of the activity effect generated by the EU administration and the lobbies in Brussels.
21. The European central banks hold a group of the elite who were keen proponents of the EU. However, the euro has changed the situation. It is better to be a central banker than a bureaucrat in the local office of a European Central Bank system.
22. The main reasons why Germany accepted a large negative T are: (1) Germany was politically weak due to the German horrors, but they fade with each new generation; (2) the key national aim of Germany was a reunification, which is now achieved; (3) the reunification has proved a great financial burden.
23. Therefore, Danish politicians need time for the resistance to the EU to erode; see section 5. Thus they want to slow the speed of integration in three ways: (i) reduce γ relative to β; (ii) fight against the individual steps of integration; and (iii) add as many new members as possible. These policies have costs: (i) and (ii) cost influence in the EU, and (iii) is a threat against T.
24. The small sizes of colonial armies dominating large areas illustrate this point. At first, the new 'white masters' were seen as relatively benign in many colonies, compared to the previous local masters.
25. The extreme story of Greenland is told in Paldam (1997).
26. The erosion hypothesis was widespread among both opponents and proponents in 1972. The proponents assured the voters that the EU was basically a question of getting more money for the agricultural exports, and that all these promises in the treaty about future integration were typical Latin hype – big words they did not need to worry about. In particular all these ideas – whatever they meant – about a union were baloney. Today the belief in the erosion hypothesis has weakened.
27. Joint policies are often announced, but frequently a pathetic gap appears between words and deeds. Think, for example, about the declarations on joint EU foreign policy.
28. Several explanations exist for the cost of ruling; see Nannestad and Paldam (1997).

REFERENCES

Aldrich, J.H. (1997), 'When is it rational to vote?', in Mueller (1997), Ch. 17.

Anderson, C.J. and R.D. Gelleny (2000), 'The Economy, Accountability, and Support for the President of the European Commission,' *European Union Politics*, **1**, 173–200.

Anderson, C.J. and K.C. Kaltenthaler (2001), 'Europeans and Their Money: Explaining Public Support for the Common Currency,' *European Journal of Political Research*, **40**, 139–70.

Frey, B.S. (1997), 'The public choice of international organizations,' in Mueller (1997), Ch. 5.

Frey, B.S. (1998), 'Developing democracy in developing countries', in S. Borner and M. Paldam (eds), *The Political Dimension of Economic Growth*, an IEA conference volume, Basingstoke: Macmillan, Ch. 17.

Fukuyama, F. (1992), *The End of History and the Last Man*, London: Hamish Hamilton.

Holsey, C.M. and T.E. Borcherding (1997), 'Why does government's share of national income grow? An assessment of the recent literature on the U.S.,' in Mueller (1997), Ch. 25.

Mueller, D.C., (ed.) (1997), *Perspectives on Public Choice. A Handbook*, Cambridge, UK and New York: Cambridge University Press.

Nannestad, P. and M. Paldam (1994), 'The VP-Function. A Survey of the Literature on Vote and Popularity Functions after 25 Years,' *Public Choice*, **79**, 213–45.

Nannestad, P. and M. Paldam (1997), 'The Grievance Asymmetry Revisited. A Micro Study of Economic Voting in Denmark, 1986–92,' *European Journal of Political Economy*, **13**, 81–99.

Nannestad, P. and M. Paldam (2000), 'What Do the Voters Know About the Economy? A Study of Danish Data, 1990–1993,' *Electoral Studies*, **19**, 363–92.

Nitzan, S. (1994), 'Modelling Rent-seeking Contests,' *European Journal of Political Economy*, **10**, 41–60.

Olson, M. and R. Zeckhauser (1966), 'An Economic Theory of Alliances,' *Review of Economics and Statistics*, **48**, 266–79.

Paldam, M. (1996), 'Købe venner, købe frænder,' in P.N.D. Buch and P. Skott (eds), *Markeder i Opbrud*, Aarhus: Aarhus University Press, pp. 201–19.

Paldam, M. (1997), 'Dutch Disease and Rent Seeking: The Greenland Model,' *European Journal of Political Economy*, **13**, 591–614.

Paldam, M. (1998), 'Den politiske økonomi for EUs integration. Et forsøg på at generalisere de danske erfaringer,' in H. Skånland and J.F. Qvigstad (eds), *ØMU og Pengepolitikken i Norden*, Oslo: Norges Banks Skriftserie nr 26.

Tollison, R.D. (1997), 'Rent seeking,' in Mueller (1997), Ch. 23.

Syrquin, M. (1988), 'Pattern of structural change,' in H. Chenery and T.N. Srinivasan (eds), *Handbook of Development Economics Vol I*, Amsterdam: North-Holland, Ch. 7.

Vaubel, R. (1994), 'The Public Choice Analysis of European Integration: A Survey,' *European Journal of Political Economy*, **10**, 227–49.

COMMENT

Sergio Ginebri

The declared aim of the chapter is to explain the limited popularity of the European Union (EU) in a small member country such as Denmark. A brief initial reference is given to the distribution of popularity among different groups of citizens. However, the attention is focused on a very restricted group: the elite. The popularity of the EU in the elite is next to 100 per cent.

The issue at the centre of the chapter then becomes: how to explain such different preferences between the elite and the rest of the country? The topic is tackled in an interesting analytical framework. A contract has to be determined between two entities: on one hand a small country, on the other hand an international organization, typically the EU. In the contract, there are two basic variables on which the bargaining is focused: the power the small country has to give in to the organization and the net transfers the small country is going to receive. Here the power is measured by the number of decisions which the small country is enabled to make freely.

Both the small country and the organization have preferences on those variables. An agreement among them is viable only if it is Pareto efficient. That is, an agreement will be struck and the small country will enter the organization only if the agreement improves the welfare function of both of them.

The preferences of the two entities are quite clear: the small country wants to give in as little power as possible and wants to receive net transfers in order to be compensated; the organization wants to receive an optimal level of power and uses net transfers in order to convince the small country.

Here two questions arise. First, could not the small country be compensated by the very participation to the decisions of the organization? The small country would lose national power, but it would share an international, bigger power. Here the assumption is: the size of the country is so small that the participation to the international decision process does not imply any perceived increase in the welfare of the small country. Second, if the net transfer were the unique advantage in joining the organization, the very existence of the organization would be unlikely. In the end, the sum of the transfers has to be zero; so, some countries would never receive advantages from participation. Here another variable comes in: the agreement gives rise to the 'big-country advantage'. That advantage stems from two sources: economies of scale and reduction of rent-seeking in the small country. The big-country advantage does not enter in the bargaining process. However, its presence allows the negotiated net transfer to be even negative in some cases.

Once the preferences of both the small country and the organization have been defined, the game is over. A small country will participate if the net transfer offered by the organization is enough to persuade the reluctant new potential member. In the case of Denmark the net transfer was big, given the presence of a large agricultural sector. In the case of Norway the net transfer would be negative, since the country is rich and does not have a big agricultural sector.

But the aim of the chapter is to explain why the elite has different preferences. Here the role of another variable emerges: the rents originated by the participation in the new international organization. Namely, any international organization creates its own bureaucracy, without reducing the national bureaucracy. The job positions available in the organization represent the rent the elite is aiming at. The new variable is not also negotiated. However, it affects the preferences of the elites and makes them more keen on giving up national power. Therefore, the different preferences between the elite and the rest of the country are simply explained by the presence of a rent which the elite wish to seize.

The main thesis of the chapter is clearly specified and the analytical framework is well developed and presented. However, a couple of questions can be raised. First, can the preferences of the elite in favour of the EU be simply explained by the perspective of larger rents for the elites? Second, can the participation to an international organization be conceived as a sort of constitutional choice? If this is the case, then both elite and the rest of the population should maximize a long-run objective function. That is, the elite members should consider the possibility of being out of power in the future. On the contrary, ordinary members of the population should allow for the possibility of being members of the elite in the future. In such a new framework, the rent-seeking explanation of elite's preferences could be much weaker.

Index